Perennials

Perennials

Carolyn Jones

Whitecap Books Ltd.
Vancouver/Toronto

Copyright © 1990 by Carolyn Jones
Whitecap Books
Vancouver/Toronto

Edited by Elaine Jones
Cover photograph and interior photographs by David Jones
Cover design by Carolyn Deby

The cover photograph is of German bearded irises (*Iris × germanica*), taken in the author's garden.

Typeset at The Vancouver Desktop Publishing Centre Ltd.

Printed and bound in Canada by Friesen Printers, Altona, Manitoba

Canadian Cataloguing in Publication Data

Jones, Carolyn, 1950–
Perennials
(Pacific gardening series)

ISBN 0-921061-50-1
1. Perennials – Northwest, Pacific. I. Title.   II. Series.
SB434.J66 1990   635-9′32′709795   C90-091167-0

Contents

Preface

Not so long ago, writing this book would have been much easier: the selection of perennials—even in the best garden centers—was meager. I started out in horticulture working in a tree and shrub nursery, so when I made the switch to a retail garden centre, I thought it would be a wonderful opportunity to learn more about perennials. I spent most of my nonworking time reading books about wonderful English gardens, full of old-fashioned roses, exuberant perennials and wonderful shrubs all tossed together. Victoria Sackville-West and Gertrude Jekyll were an inspiration. The garden center where I first worked had superb bedding plants, a wide selection of shrubs and trees and excellent fruit trees. But the perennials section . . . .

My visions of an English country garden vanished when I realized that the plants just weren't available here. It's probably just as well that my formal perennial borders got nipped in the bud, because I didn't realize that the required full-time gardener didn't come included with the delphiniums.

In the past few years, however, great changes have taken place in the perennials market. I was not alone in my yearning for more perennials, and the demand by gardeners all over the Pacific coastal region spurred growers on. Rather than concentrating only on perennials that could be grown from seed, more nurseries have imported special named perennial plants from Holland, Germany and England. Many such perennials must be sold in larger pots than those grown from seed, for financial and cultural reasons, so "one-gallon (20-cm pot) perennials" were introduced. Luckily, gardeners realized it was worthwhile spending more to get these outstanding plants, and they are commonplace today.

An exciting and quite new development is the use of ornamental grasses in gardens. We have two horticulturists to thank for this trend: the German Karl Foerster (1874–1970) and the American Kurt Bluemel. Karl Foerster promoted the use of ornamental grasses in Germany, where they are widely used in public and private gardens, and Kurt Bluemel has done much to introduce North Americans to their beauty. Availability is increasing as many Pacific coastal region nurseries grow or import ornamental grasses. Many species can also be grown from seed.

With such a wide field of plant material on the market and to be seen in public gardens, choosing the plants to be included in this book was very difficult. Tiny alpine perennials that need special care are not included, but more vigorous "rockery" plants, suitable for flowing over rocks and retaining walls, are described. I have included two ferns, just so that you will think of this excellent group of plants when you are planning. Needless to say, there are dozens of others suitable for our Pacific coast gardens. Three genera of grasses are listed as an introduction to this exciting group of plants. You may find that some of the perennials presented here are difficult to obtain. The extra effort of ordering by mail or a bit of pestering at your favorite garden center may be called for, but think of perennials as an investment. It is worth seeking out the best—you'll have them for many years to come. That is the beauty of perennials.

Acknowledgments

I like to think of my role as a sort of horticultural reporter—gathering information and sorting it in a way that I hope will be of value to the reader. Over the years, I have learned about gardening, of course, by working in my own garden, but also through the patience and generosity of many people—other writers, coworkers, gardening friends, employers and customers. In working on this project in particular, there are many people whose help I wish to acknowledge.

The following people own commercial nurseries and I would like to thank them for their generosity in showing me around their establishments and answering my questions: Guenther Bock, Bock Nurseries; Herbert and Christiana Fischer, Alpenflora Nurseries; Elke and Ken Knechtel, Rainforest Gardens; John Schroeder and John Valleau, Valleybrook Gardens; Geoff and Mary Schwinn, Westham Island Nursery; and Ken Wilson, Hopestead Gardens.

Bodil Leamy kindly gave me a tour of the perennial borders for which she is responsible at the UBC Botanical Gardens. Gerald Straley, research botanist at the Gardens, answered many questions on taxonomy and nomenclature. Sarah Scheffield, Agriculture Canada, gave me information on Canadian perennial breeders, and Susane Weber, from the perennial nursery Gräfin von Zeppelin in Germany, responded to my enquiries about German perennial breeders.

For technical information, I thank David Jack, Ferncliff Gardens; Carol Thompson, Safers Ltd.; Brian Tregunno, Ball-Superior Seed Company; and Nicola Luttropp, Lamb Nurseries, Spokane. Mark Stephens, Westgro Sales, was a great help with details about pests and diseases and Sue Olsen, Foliage Gardens, explained how to grow ferns from spores.

For information on various aspects of growing perennials, thanks go to Pam Frost, Daphne Guernsey, Pat Logie, Doris Page, Gordon U'Ren and Audrey Williams. Special thanks also to Margaret Charlton and Francisca Darts—gardeners extraordinaire.

Special thanks are also due to Frederick McGourty, Connecticut; and Alan Bloom, Bressingham, England, for answering still more questions about some of the thornier issues involving perennials.

I would like to thank Elaine Jones, whose editing skills have, at times, brought order from chaos and whose kind words have been most appreciated. Thanks also to my publisher, Colleen MacMillan, and all of the staff at Whitecap Books.

Douglas Justice had the unenviable role of reading for technical information. Characteristically, he undertook the job with dedication and humor. For that I am very grateful.

One of the most enjoyable tasks associated with the preparation of this book was visiting gardens to take photographs and see how other gardeners use perennials. Butchart Gardens, Minter Gardens, the University of British Columbia Botanical Gardens and VanDusen Botanical Gardens were generous in their support. We also had the pleasure of visiting the home gardens of Ed and Francisca Darts, Elke and Ken Knechtel, Elizabeth and John Moore, Ada Prior, Geoff and Mary Schwinn, Josephine Slater, and Ann and Tom Widdowson.

My deepest appreciation goes to my husband, David, for encouraging me to consider writing gardening books. With his kind offer to act as photographer and his patience and support, he has made that possibility into a reality.

Perennials for the Pacific Coastal Region

Perennials are like old friends—year after year, without a fuss, come rain or shine, they offer constancy and companionship. There is something so reassuring about looking out the window into the garden on a cold, rainy, March day and realizing that spring will arrive in the garden—with or without you. Dusky purple Lenten rose, yellow primroses and vivid blue lungwort offer cheer against the dismal weather. The fat buds of hostas, peonies and autumn sedum wait just at the soil line for the temperature to rise, with promises of color for the summer ahead.

What are perennials?

Technically speaking, a **perennial** is a plant that lives for three or more seasons. This definition excludes **annuals**—plants that sprout from a seed, grow, bloom, produce new seeds and die, all in one year. It also excludes plants that are **biennial**. A biennial usually has a two-year life cycle. The first year after sprouting, it makes vegetative growth. This usually consists of a basal rosette—an arrangement of leaves radiating from the crown or center of the plant, usually at or close to the ground. During the second year of its life cycle, the plant throws up a flower stalk and then usually produces seed after blooming. Some biennials form extra rosettes that go on to bloom the third year, becoming somewhat perennial in nature.

Correctly, then, because trees and shrubs live for three or more years, they are defined as perennials. To further identify the group of plants this book focuses on, the term **herbaceous** is added. Herbaceous means that the plants do not form woody tissue as trees and shrubs do; the term herbaceous perennials leaves us with a group of plants that live for three years or more but do not form a permanent above-ground structure of trunk or branches. The definition herbaceous perennials technically includes plants that overwinter from underground storage organs such as bulbs, corms and tubers—daffodils, tulips and gladioli, for instance.

Most gardeners drop the adjective herbaceous and simply use the term perennials, and it is commonly understood that they are referring not to shrubs and trees, nor to bulbous, cormous and tuberous plants—but to popular flowers such as irises, peonies, delphiniums, chrysanthemums and the like: the subject of this book.

Some gardeners confuse the term herbaceous with the term **deciduous.** Deciduous, when applied to perennials, means that the above-ground parts of the plant die to the ground in the fall. This is not true of all herbaceous perennials; some are **evergreen**—they retain their leaves (sometimes quite weather-beaten) all winter. The term evergreen is used loosely, for many perennials have silvery foliage that remains all winter.

A few perennials that are discussed in this book are actually **sub-shrubs**. That is, they form woody tissue only at the base of the plant. Examples include candytuft (*Iberis sempervirens*) and Cape fuchsia (*Phygelius capensis*).

Hardiness

Another term used when describing perennials is hardy, a relative term. Hardy means that a plant will survive the winter, but obviously this depends on the geographical area in question.

In North America, there are two similar systems in use to rate hardiness, one developed by the United States Department of Agriculture and one developed by Agriculture Canada. Both systems define hardiness zones according to ranges of average annual minimum temperatures, but the USDA system uses 10° intervals in the fahrenheit scale and the Canadian system uses 5° intervals n the centigrade scale. (See chart below.) In both systems, the higher the zone number, the warmer the winter temperatures. Both systems also designate a warmer subzone (a) and a colder subzone (b).

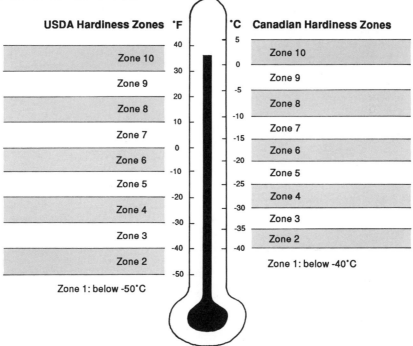

USDA Hardiness Zones	°F	°C	Canadian Hardiness Zones
Zone 10	40	5	Zone 10
Zone 9	30	0	Zone 9
Zone 8	20	-5	Zone 8
Zone 7	10	-10	Zone 7
Zone 6	0	-15	Zone 6
Zone 5	-10	-20	Zone 5
Zone 4	-20	-25	Zone 4
Zone 3	-30	-30	Zone 3
Zone 2	-40	-35	Zone 2
Zone 1: below -50°C	-50	-40	Zone 1: below -40°C

The Pacific coastal region includes zones 7, 8 and 9a—according to both systems. As you can see from the chart, the differences between the systems are a matter of a few degrees in the warmer zones, so the two systems are used somewhat interchangeably in our area. However, as you get into the colder zones, the systems can no longer be interchanged— confusing for gardeners in the colder parts of Canada.

Because hardiness ratings for perennials are generally only available according to the USDA system, those are the ones used in this book. Again, to Pacific coastal gardeners, this makes little difference.

In order to establish hardiness ratings, plants are grown in test grounds in each zone. Observations are made as to the coldest zone in which a

Plant Hardiness Zones of the Pacific Coastal Region

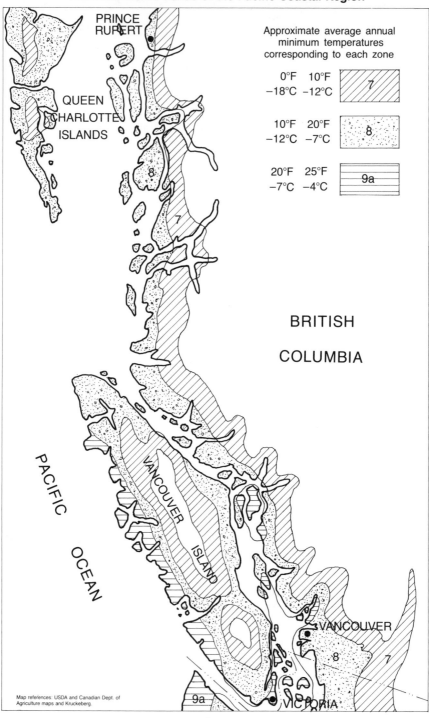

Approximate average annual
minimum temperatures
corresponding to each zone

| 0°F | 10°F | 7 |
| −18°C | −12°C | |

| 10°F | 20°F | 8 |
| −12°C | −7°C | |

| 20°F | 25°F | 9a |
| −7°C | −4°C | |

PRINCE RUPERT

QUEEN CHARLOTTE ISLANDS

BRITISH

COLUMBIA

PACIFIC

OCEAN

VANCOUVER ISLAND

VANCOUVER

VICTORIA

Map references: USDA and Canadian Dept. of
Agriculture maps and Kruckeberg.

4

Plant Hardiness Zones of the Pacific Coastal Region

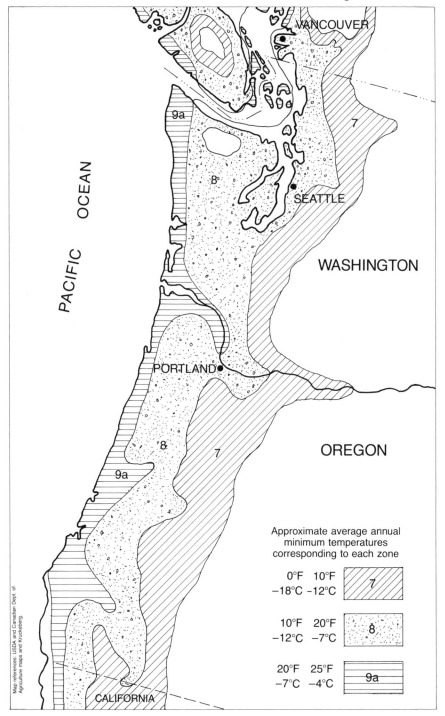

Approximate average annual minimum temperatures corresponding to each zone

0°F 10°F −18°C −12°C		7
10°F 20°F −12°C −7°C		8
20°F 25°F −7°C −4°C		9a

Map references: USDA and Canadian Dept. of Agriculture maps and Kruckeberg plant will grow and thrive, and the plant is then said to be hardy to that zone. **Note:** If a plant is hardy to zone 5, for example, it is also hardy in all warmer zones—6, 7, 8, 9 and 10, in this example.

Within each zone, there are microclimates with varying conditions. Watch where the snow melts first and last in your garden—this will indicate the warm and cool microclimates.

Plant hardiness is affected by many factors. A severe frost in November will do more damage than the same frost in January, because plants have not become fully dormant. Drying winds combined with frost will increase damage. Conversely, snow cover will insulate plants against damage in case of a severe frost. If the soil is very dry before a frost, cold air can more easily penetrate to the roots and damage them. A plant that was newly planted in the late fall may be more susceptible than one that has been established in the garden for some time.

The soil temperature in a planter box will drop to a lower level than that of the ground because the low ratio of soil volume to surface area results in rapid heat loss from the soil. Therefore, plants grown in containers should be at least two zones hardier than required for garden planting within the same zone.

Most of the perennials described in this book are hardy to zone 3 or 4. In Pacific coastal region nurseries, plants such as hosta and bearded iris (both hardy to zone 3) are left outdoors in their one-gallon (20-cm) pots all winter, without damage even in the most severe winters. About a dozen of the plants described are hardy to zone 5, still two zones hardier than the coldest Pacific coast zone. A handful are hardy to zones 6 or 7 and one, purple fountain grass, is hardy only to zone 8. It is therefore of borderline hardiness in the Pacific coastal region.

Rainfall and humidity

Hardiness zones alone don't give the full picture of climate in the Pacific coastal region. Rainfall and humidity influence the success of perennials in our gardens. In much of the region, the average rainfall is 60–80 inches (150–200 cm) per year. Some areas, such as the Olympic Peninsula, the north coast of B.C. and southeastern Alaska, receive over 150 inches (375 cm) of rainfall each year. The mountains of Vancouver Island and the Olympic Peninsula cause a rainshadow area on the Gulf Islands, the San Juan Islands and the southeast coast of Vancouver

Island. In these areas the rainfall is less, averaging 30 inches (75 cm) per year.

Whereas on the east coast of North America the bulk of the precipitation falls in the summer, and in the middle of the continent it is distributed more or less evenly throughout the year, in the Pacific coastal region we get the bulk of our precipitation in the winter, and in the form of rain rather than snow. Although not a problem for most of the perennials presented in this book, wet winters spell death for many perennials from alpine and Mediterranean climate regions. They are best grown in an alpine greenhouse, where there is no additional heat, but where the glass protects the plants from winter rains.

Summers in the Pacific coastal region are unpredictable. Some summers are hot—by our standards—and dry during July and August; some are marked by frequent rain. But even the hottest summers do not have the high humidity and hot nights experienced farther east. This allows Pacific coast gardeners to grow plants with fuzzy, silvery leaves such as lamb's ears, which would rot in a more humid climate. Cool Pacific coastal region nights result in a longer blooming period for many perennials and plants do not burn out as they do in hotter areas. It's hard not to feel blessed if you garden in the Pacific coastal region.

Historical notes and origins of perennials

Over the past 60 million years, the temperature of the earth has fluctuated greatly. Flowering plants, a recent development in the plant world in evolutionary terms, have a number of characteristics that enable them to adapt to climatic variations. These include the structure of their flowers and roots and the fact that they reproduce with seeds. Of great evolutionary significance is the fact that flowering plants and insects have evolved hand-in-hand, with interdependent life cycles. Bright colors, flowers clustered together into an inflorescence to attract more insects—the extremely successful daisy family is an example—and elaborately shaped flowers are all the result of this interaction between plant and animal. Beautiful floral colors, shapes and fragrance are what attracts humans to many flowers as well.

Gradually, flowering plants have outcompeted ferns, tree ferns, horsetails, mosses, and other ancient plant families, so that most plants on our planet are flowering plants. (In the Pacific coastal region, it sometimes looks like horsetails are trying hard to make a comeback!)

Surprisingly, considering their simple structure, grasses are very highly evolved. They have abandoned colorful flower parts and insect pollination, depending on the wind to pollinate their flowers. Although of major importance in feeding humans since ancient times—wheat, rye, corn, rice, for example—and used widely in landscaping for lawns, they have only recently become popular subjects for ornamental gardening.

After the ice ages, plants and animals gradually began the process of pushing away from the warm tropical areas and developing tactics for growing in new regions of the earth. Among the adaptations that resulted were mechanisms for surviving frost in winter, yet plant physiologists still do not fully understand how plants manage this feat. Naturally, therefore, plants that will survive frost in our gardens are usually native to parts of the world with frost in winter.

Over half the species discussed in this book are native to Europe. Virtually all of these have been in cultivation for over three hundred years, and many were cultivated in very ancient times. The emphasis in horticulture in ancient times was on plants with some medicinal or culinary uses. The species name *officinalis* is a remnant of a time when herbs were more widely used for healing than they are today; it indicates that a plant had commercial value—usually of importance to an apothecary. But their decorative value was not overlooked. In monasteries in the Middle Ages, it is known that the monk in charge of the sanctuary grew flowers for decoration, especially for holy days. Brewing was a big industry in those monasteries, and numerous herbs were grown to flavor the wine or beer.

During the end of the European Renaissance, social stability and prosperity resulted in the creation of purely ornamental gardens. In 1596, John Gerard published a catalogue of over nine hundred kinds of plants that he was growing in his London garden—plants of both ornamental and practical value.

Thirty years later, John Parkinson published a book entitled *Paradisi in Sole, Paradisus Terrestris*. (The title is a pun in Latin on his name; *Paradisi in Sole* means Park-in-Sun.) It was the first illustrated book in the English language devoted primarily to ornamental plants. It is interesting to note that by the time Parkinson wrote, double and bicolor flowers were in cultivation.

From the late 1600s and through the 1700s, plant explorers were also bringing plants back from all over the world. Expeditions were made to South Africa, eastern North America, Australia and New Zealand. It was the great age of gardening in Europe—a time which saw the creation of binomial nomenclature (the system of botanical names we use today) and the establishment of large botanical gardens, such as Kew.

Almost half of the perennials described in this book are from Asia, especially Japan, China and the Himalayas. From the late 1600s until the late 1800s, few westerners were allowed to travel far beyond the major ports in China and Japan. The plants introduced to the west from Asia during that period were generally those in cultivation, available in the ports. Chrysanthemums, peonies and irises are great favorites with the Chinese and Japanese, and they had developed hundreds of cultivars as early as the ninth century.

When greater access was allowed into Asia, plant hunters from Europe and North America undertook expeditions, often covering thousands of miles on foot to search out unusual plants. Such plant hunting still goes on today, with new plants being evaluated for garden use by botanical gardens and arboreta around the world. Our search for the unusual must, however, always be tempered with consideration for the conservation of plants in their native habitats.

The origin of cultivars

In addition to those species of garden plants that have been, and are still being, introduced from the wild, many garden plants exist only in cultivation. These cultivated varieties—**cultivars**—result from human intervention; techniques of plant breeding include selection and hybridization.

The process of **selection** results from the natural human fascination with the unique. Whether it be a flower of slightly larger size or deeper hue, leaves of an interesting shape or shade, plants with a more compact habit of growth or a longer period of bloom—plant lovers are always on the lookout for something different. A cultivar can be an outstanding plant selected from a natural plant population and subsequently maintained in cultivation.

In addition to selecting naturally occurring plants, plant breeders—both professional and amateur—use a number of techniques to increase the variability of plant populations. Plants can be treated with the chemical colchicine or with radiation to produce mutations (called "sports") such as double or striped flowers.

Plants can also be **hybridized,** that is, a cross can be made of two different species. The pollen from one species is used to pollinate the flower of another, so that if the cross is successful, the seedlings will have acquired chromosomes from both species. Hybridizers hope that this reshuffling of genetic information will result in something special. Complex breeding programs may involve many different species and dozens of generations of crosses. Astilbes, delphiniums, chrysanthemums and daylilies are examples of complex hybrids.

For plants that will be customarily grown from seed—annual flowers, vegetables and some perennials—once a unique cultivar is created (whether as a selection from a species or a hybrid) the plant breeder strives to reduce diversity of future generations. In a group of seed-grown plants, there should be as little variability in the desirable characteristics—height, ripening time of fruit, flower color or length of bloom—as possible. Breeders achieve this consistency by carefully controlling seed production, crossing and recrossing the same plants to reduce genetic variability. Seeds producing very similar plants that are distinct from their species are called a **seed strain.** 'Sugardaddy' petunia, 'Early Girl' tomato and 'Guinevere' delphinium are examples.

To sum up, cultivars can be selected from a species, they can be hybrids or they can be seed strains. If a plant breeder wishes to name a cultivar, it must be registered with Taxon, the international organization governing such matters. Cultivar names are always set off by single quotation marks. For more information on the propagation and naming of cultivars, hybrids and seed strains, see Propagation, page 33, and Encyclopedia, page 52.

Many of the best-known names in perennial breeding are from outside the Pacific coastal region: Foerster, Arends, and Walther (German); Blackmore and Langdon, the Allwood brothers, Bees, and Bloom (English); and Reinhelt and Cummings (American) have all made notable contributions to the perennial garden. With the current rise in popularity of perennials, let's hope that more and more of these interesting plants find their way to our small corner of the continent.

Using Perennials in the Garden

For some gardeners, thinking about gardening is at least as enjoyable as actually doing it. A stack of gardening books with gorgeous photographs of gardens around the world, mail-order catalogs for seeds and plants, a pencil and paper nearby and a cup of something warm to drink will pass many a dreary winter's day. Time spent exploring varying garden styles and options for your own garden is always well spent.

All-perennial borders

A glance at any book on English gardens will show you magnificent herbaceous perennial borders. The photographs are generally taken at the height of summer, with masses of color and interesting contrast of plant shape. Such borders, usually part of huge estate gardens, were designed to be enjoyed mainly during the summer months and were immensely popular during the late 1800s and early 1900s. The use of herbaceous perennials was promoted by Irish gardener and writer William Robinson (1838–1935). His friend Gertrude Jekyll (1843–1932), artist, garden designer and writer, refined the use of color in herbaceous borders. She designed borders for many of the most famous gardens of the time and explained her theories in her books.

Such design styles are rarely used in home gardens today because few have the space to devote to paired perennial borders up to 12 feet (3.6 m) deep. Few have the dark green yew hedges to set them off effectively; and few gardeners have the time to devote to staking, deadheading and dividing.

Island beds are a variation of the traditional formal perennial borders that have been promoted extensively by the English horticulturist Alan Bloom. They are set in the middle of a lawn, with the plants grading in height from the edges into the center. Photographs of the island beds at Bloom's gardens in Bressingham, England, are shown in his book *Perennials for your Garden*. This style of perennial bed is undeniably attractive in Bloom's garden, set off by the undulating grassy slopes and large trees. In the average home garden, however, island beds can create awkward design problems.

An excellent example of an all-perennial border in the Pacific coastal region is at the University of British Columbia Botanical Garden. This section of the garden was designed by Bodil Leamy to be a no-staking border, to incorporate as many native or unusual plants as possible, and to be at its peak in summer and fall. It avoids two common weaknesses of a perennial border. By using grasses and plants with attractive bronze or silver foliage—*Heuchera* 'Palace Purple' and *Artemisia* 'Powis Castle', for example—interest and solidity are added to the border. The color combinations in the border are well thought out, and although some of the plants are not readily available to the home gardener, the basics of design may be followed anywhere. This border is well worth a visit in summer or early fall.

Mixed borders

The biggest mark against all-perennial borders is that for about half the year—from late November to late April—they are exceedingly dull. Because gardens today are generally smaller and because the climate of the Pacific coastal region allows us to grow a marvelous range of plants, keen gardeners in this area strive to create gardens that provide beauty and interest in all seasons. A perennial border can be planned so that there is bloom almost all year, but the overall picture is enhanced by adding well-chosen bulbs, shrubs, trees and bedding plants—a mixed border.

Imagine a long, formal, all-perennial border in early spring. Most of the plants are dormant, their roots waiting underground for the temperature to rise, signaling another season of growth. The Lenten rose (*Helleborus orientalis*) is in bloom, but it looks a bit lonely in the middle of this somnolent border. Picture instead the same plant tucked in at the base of a small flowering tree. On one side of it is a rainbow leucothoe, whose richly variegated foliage has been attractive all winter. To the other side are the glossy leaves and fat buds of a rhododendron. In front of it are snowdrops and crocuses, which will be overplanted in May with impatiens, to provide color for the rest of the summer. This association sets off the purple cups and large, handsome leaves of the Lenten rose and provides an attractive scene throughout the year. Other perennials such as hostas, hardy geraniums and ferns could be added to complement the scene.

In autumn, grouping perennials with shrubs pays benefits in terms of rich fall color. A dwarf purple hardy aster (*Aster amellus* 'Violet Queen') and a beautiful dwarf hybrid goldenrod (× *Solidaster* 'Lemore') complement the autumn tints of *Fothergilla monticola*, the lacecap hydrangea 'Blue Bird' and *Rhododendron* 'P.J.M.'. This particular rhododendron keeps its leaves all winter, but they turn a burnished bronze in cool weather. Adding winter heathers to the grouping will provide color year-round.

A current design trend is toward more naturalistic gardens, freeing the gardener from pruning, spraying, frequent deadheading and replanting large areas of bedding plants each spring. Mixed borders, with generous use of perennials for summer color and foliage texture, are well suited to this style. In general, perennial flowers have softer colors and more natural forms than those of bedding plants—many of which are native to hot tropical climates. The addition of ferns and grasses complement the natural garden beautifully. Comments are made in the encyclopedia section regarding the amount of care required by each type of perennial. Plants of very formal style, such as delphiniums, are noted.

Planning the border. A border that can only be viewed from one side is generally easier to plan. Aim to make it as wide as possible, while keeping it in scale with the rest of the garden. If the border can be 8 to 10 feet (2.5 to 3 m) deep, several layers of plant material can be planted, and medium-sized shrubs, spreading up to 6 feet (1.8 m) across, can be included. If not as much depth is possible, consider shrubs with a somewhat upright habit of growth. Depending on the length of the border, including one or more small trees will add height. Taller plants should be placed at the back of the bed, with height grading toward the front. By placing a tall plant, such as a tree or a tall grass, more forward in one or two spots, the plan will avoid predictability.

If your border is to be viewed from all sides, even more care and planning is required to balance the plants. Give the most attention to siting trees and deciduous shrubs; as a rule, they are the most difficult to transplant. Members of the rhododendron family, ERICACEAE (also including azaleas, lily-of-the-valley shrub, heathers and many more), are an exception to this rule-of-thumb; their shallow roots make them relatively easy to move. No garden is ever static, though, and many gardeners play "musical plants" in the fall.

An excellent book with suggestions for planning the mixed border is *The Flower Arranger's Garden*, by Rosemary Verey. Although the emphasis of the book is on creating a garden with material to cut all through the year, there are fine color illustrations of several borders shown in each of the four seasons. If you have difficulty imagining what your border will look like through the year, this lovely book will help. You can easily substitute your favorite plants for suggested ones, keeping to the same height and color scheme.

Deciduous shrubs and trees. When choosing deciduous shrubs and trees for a mixed border, give preference to those that have an attractive shape and those that will add interest when the bulk of perennials are not doing so. For example, Chinese witch hazel (*Hamamelis mollis*), winter hazel (*Corylopsis*) and winter-flowering jasmine (*Jasminum nudiflorum*) bloom in winter when most perennials are dormant. Cutleaf Japanese maple (*Acer palmatum* 'Dissectum'), burning bush (*Euonymus alata*) and *Enkianthus* have outstanding fall color. Superb small trees for the home garden include Japanese snowbell (*Styrax japonicus*), Japanese maple (*Acer palmatum*) and sourwood (*Oxydendrum arboreum*), all of which offer attractive shape, beautiful flowers and brilliant fall color. Many deciduous shrubs have brightly colored fruit, extending interest into the winter.

Broadleaf evergreens. Mild winters in the Pacific coastal region permit us to grow hundreds of broadleaf (flowering) evergreen shrubs. Rhododendrons, camellias, lily-of-the-valley shrub (*Pieris*), rainbow leucothoe, Japanese azaleas and heathers (*Erica*, *Calluna* and *Daboecia*) are but a few. Including broadleaf evergreens in the mixed border adds form in the winter, and most broadleaf evergreens bloom in spring, getting the border off to an early start.

Vines. If there is not space to develop a border of more than four or five feet (1.2 or 1.5 m) in depth, plant vines or train shrubs vertically at the back of the border, on a fence, wall or trellises, to create another layer. Akebia is evergreen in mild winters, and climbing hydrangea has lacy white flowers in June and shows off its handsome bark in winter.

Bulbs. Spring-flowering bulbs such as snowdrops (*Galanthus nivalis*), crocuses, daffodils (*Narcissus*), winter aconites (*Eranthis*) and windflowers (*Anemone blanda*) add color to the garden when many perennials are just beginning to emerge. Summer-blooming bulbs such as lilies (*Lilium*) and ornamental onions (*Allium*) combine well with perennials.

Rock gardens are a specialized type of mixed border. Strictly defined, a true rock garden has very fast-draining soil and is finished with a layer of crushed rock, to keep water from accumulating around the crowns of the plants in winter. Species of plants native to mountainous regions are grown in a proper rock garden.

In this book, rock garden is used loosely to describe a sloping garden— perhaps with stone, brick or timber retaining walls or large rocks— planted with spreading perennials and dwarf shrubs. There are dozens of perennials included in this book for just such a setting, but many are too vigorous for the true rock garden. Refer to the "under 1 foot" column in the Quick Reference Chart for more suggestions.

Conifers (needle- or scale-leaf evergreens) can easily be damaged if the plants growing near them become too large and touch their foliage. Once light and air are cut off, a conifer's leaves may turn yellow or brown and fall off. Often such damage is permanent. For this reason, conifers are not easily incorporated into most mixed borders.

A rock garden, on the other hand, is the perfect place for conifers, particularly the many interesting low-growing conifers available. Sargent's weeping hemlock (*Tsuga canadensis* 'Pendula'), dwarf mugo pine (*Pinus mugho* var. *pumilo*) and spreading yew (*Taxus baccata* 'Repandens') are examples.

15

Woodland gardens are another variation of a mixed border—their dominant element is large trees. Although some gardeners view a shady garden with dismay, there are many wonderful plants that flourish in light shade. Rhododendrons, Japanese azaleas, camellias, leucothoe and Oregon grape (*Mahonia aquifolium*) are excellent broad-leaf evergreens for shady areas. Deciduous shrubs such as *Fothergilla* and *Corylopsis* add fall and winter beauty. Needle-leaf evergreens such as yew (*Taxus*) and hemlock (*Tsuga*) thrive in some shade. And there are dozens—hundreds if you count their cultivars—of interesting perennials for shady places. Ferns (*Adiantum pedatum*, *Polystichum munitum* and others), hostas, hardy geraniums, bugbanes (*Cimicifuga*), primulas, Solomon's seal (*Polygonatum*) and bleeding heart (*Dicentra*) are the life of the woodland garden. Refer also to the Quick Reference Chart for other shade-tolerant perennials.

Using perennials in containers. Perennials are not generally the first choice for container gardens because most do not bloom all summer. If you are looking for something to make a change in your container plantings, consider perennials with attractive foliage, such as *Artemisia stellerana* 'Silver Brocade', or those with a long bloomtime, such as *Geranium endressii* 'A.T. Johnson'. If you have a terra cotta strawberry planter, fill each of the pockets with a different sedum or sempervivum. They will tolerate irregular watering.

Plotting and planning

No matter how you have decided to incorporate perennials into your garden, some planning makes the job easier and the outcome more pleasing. In many ways gardening is like cooking. There isn't one correct way to cook eggs and there isn't one correct way to make a garden.

You can approach your garden from the "ingredients" point-of-view, deciding what plants you would like to grow and then working out an arrangement that will look attractive and meet each plant's individual needs in terms of sun and soil. Or you can start with the finished product—perhaps a garden you have visited and admired, one seen in a book or one imagined—and work backwards, searching for the plants to complete the picture.

Color combinations are a matter of personal taste. For every rule about combining colors, you can usually find an example of where the rule has been broken with good results. Having said that, some popular color combinations are:

- Pastels: blue, light yellow, white, soft pink and silver foliage
- Primary colors: bright red, deep blue, gold, white and silver
- Contrasts: purple, blue, red and lime green
- Sunset colors: rusty red, gold and orange

Think of the contrast of foliage to add interest to the border also. The spiky leaves of iris and daylily, the bold leaves of hosta and bergenia and the feathery leaves of maidenhair fern and meadow rue can be used to create striking combinations.

It helps to make a list of the plants you will be using. Include bloomtime, flower color, height and spread so you can get an overall idea of what you are working with. The Quick Reference Chart at the back of this book will help. The next step is to measure the garden area you will be planting. An outline of this area, with existing plant material accounted for, can then be drawn to scale on a large sheet of paper. To really allow yourself room to work, buy a 2-foot by 3-foot sheet of paper, marked in 1/4-inch squares, at a drafting supply store (60-cm by 90-cm sheets are marked in 1-cm squares). Using a scale of 1 inch=1 foot (or 1 cm=10 cm), you will be able to draw a bed up to 24 feet by 36 feet (6 m by 9 m).

The next step is to sketch circles on the paper to represent each plant. If a plant has a spread of 3 feet (90 cm), draw a circle 3 inches (7.5 cm) across. It is easiest to start with the taller plants and fit in the shorter ones (which are easier to juggle) around them. Perennials take about two years to reach the size indicated in the encyclopedia section, but it is best to allow them space to grow and have patience the first season. Shrubs, on the other hand, take years to mature. You can plant perennials a bit closer to shrubs and move them away later. (Some perennials, such as bleeding heart [*Dicentra*] and baby's breath [*Gypsophila paniculata*], resent disturbance; don't choose these for fillers.) An alternative for filling in gaps is to use bedding plants like cosmos and marguerite daisies.

Many gardening books recommend planting three to five of each type of perennial in a group. This is a good idea for small perennials, such as Lady's mantle (*Alchemilla mollis*), columbine (*Aquilegia*), coralbells (*Heuchera*) and London pride (*Saxifraga* × *urbium*), or very tall, formal plants like delphiniums. But for the average small garden, more than one plant of medium-sized perennials—ones that spread more than 1 foot (30 cm), for example—would just take up too much room. It also depends on whether your interest is more in creating a picture in the garden, or whether you like to grow as many different kinds of plants as possible.

A border that is visible from all sides, like an island bed, can be especially tricky to plan. If you find you are using your eraser too much, cut circles of paper to scale, write the plant's name, height and flower color on them, and shuffle these around instead of writing right on your plan. If you enjoy this sort of thing, try coloring in the circles with the flower color, or cut them out of colored construction paper—it helps to visualize the color combinations. Tape them down when you find an arrangement you like.

If you don't have patience for a pencil and paper—or even as an extra step to help visualize the real space outdoors—there is another technique that works well. If you have purchased some or all of your plants already, set the pots on the ground where you have tentatively planned to plant them. Then use a stick or a sprinkling of lime to draw a circle around each one with the appropriate spread. Stand back and try to imagine the plants in summer—not the easiest thing on a fall or spring day! Imagine the shapes of leaves and flowers, the colors and heights. Even if you don't have any pots of plants to play with yet, you can still consider various arrangements by drawing on the soil in this way.

This may sound highly organized, but the truth is that even if you go through all of this, your garden won't quite turn out as you had imagined. Some combinations won't work as well as you had hoped and some unexpected surprises will delight you. Keep a notebook on hand to record your observations during the season. The growing season is the time to cut sample flowers or foliage and wander around the garden with them to see if the plants might combine well with something else in bloom at the same time. Fall or early spring is the time for moving plants. (Be cautious about moving shrubs and trees—with the exception of members of the family ERICACEAE—unless they are only a year or two old; they may not survive the transplant).

Most importantly, relax and enjoy your garden. Don't be afraid to try new combinations. Try not to get frustrated if things don't work out just as you had planned. A garden is a living, changing, dynamic creation and gardening offers a chance to learn patience and persistence. One sunny fall afternoon I was visiting Dartshill, the three-acre (1.2-hectare) private garden of Ed and Francisca Darts. Dartshill is the home of over three thousand unusual shrubs, trees and perennials; it represents the work of two lifetimes. Francisca Darts was giving me a tour of the garden when a man suddenly appeared from one of the paths. A stranger who had seen all the trees and shrubs from the road, he had decided to drop in for some garden advice. After patiently answering his questions, she said, "The best advice I can give you is not to listen to anyone else, but make your garden the way *you* want it. Then it will make you happy."

From the Plant's Point of View

A basic understanding of a plant's biological requirements can often make the mysterious seem straightforward. The light a plant needs in order to produce its own food through photosynthesis and the soil in which it will secure its roots and take up water and nutrients are the two most important factors in its environment. Gardening is a combination of putting a plant in the right spot and at the same time modifying its environment through watering, fertilizing and improving the soil. As you work, keep a mental checklist of plant needs, and you will find that your skill and appreciation increases enormously.

Light

Because light is the most difficult aspect of plant culture to control in the garden, it is the factor limiting which plants you will be able to use in each specific setting.

The amount of sun a location receives is usually defined in terms of full sun, part (or half) shade and shade. Full sun is defined as at least four hours of sun during the middle of the day, between about 10 a.m. and 4 p.m. Part shade is sun during the early morning or late afternoon, or the light received under trees with small leaves, such as birch. Shade cast all day by a building or trees with large leaves is full shade.

However, other factors should be taken into consideration. Reflected light bouncing off a white wall, for example, will brighten an otherwise shady area or turn a sunny location into a baking hot spot, and plants that normally prefer some shade will tolerate more light if the soil is not overly dry or if the area is protected from drying winds.

As with many situations in gardening, often you won't know until you try. If the light factor is not right, your plants will soon let you know. Lack of light will cause the plant to become stretched, possibly floppy. The leaves may become thin and the plant will not bloom well. If a plant gets too much sun, the leaves will look bleached, dry or burned-looking. If you observe these symptoms, make a note in your gardening notebook and move the plant to a better location in fall or spring.

When planting under trees, remember that even though the light factor may be right for a shade-tolerant plant, the roots of a tree tend to steal all the moisture and nutrients from the soil. This is especially true of coniferous trees. Before planting under large trees, add generous amounts of well-rotted manure or compost and sprinkle 6-8-6 fertilizer over the area. Ferns, hostas, and hardy geraniums will grow very well in such a setting; replenish the fertilizer each spring and water regularly through the growing season.

To sum up, the first consideration when choosing the plants for any location is light. If you are planning your garden in winter or early spring, be sure to consider the light factor when the sun is higher in the sky and there are leaves on the trees.

Soil

Even a very difficult soil situation can be modified to become a successful growing medium. With a little work (or sometimes, to be quite honest, a lot of work), any soil can be improved. The most difficult soil to deal with is one that is poorly drained. Drainage tiles should be laid to improve drainage, but this is very expensive. There are some alternatives to drain tiles on the market, but there is no way to avoid the digging. An easier solution for the home gardener is to construct raised beds or planters. Landscape ties or timbers make this an easy and relatively inexpensive job.

Soils have both a mineral and an organic component. The mineral component is derived from weathered rock. The size of mineral particles contributes to soil texture: many very fine particles result in a clay soil; as particle size increases the soil becomes sandy. This texture determines the rate of flow of water, with water moving slowly through a clay soil. That means it takes a lot of watering to thoroughly wet a clay soil, and it doesn't dry out quickly. A sandy soil needs less water to be wet to the same depth, but it dries out very quickly. To get an idea of which type of soil you have, squeeze a damp handful of soil, then gently press on the ball. If it stays as a firm, hard ball, you probably have clay soil; if it crumbles easily, your soil is probably sandy.

Clay and sandy soil differ in their ability to retain plant nutrients. Fertilizer molecules, particularly those of nitrogen and potassium, are easily washed out of sandy soils, but are held in clay soils more firmly, remaining available to plants. If you have a sandy soil, you will use more fertilizer to keep your plants healthy than if you have a clay soil.

The organic component of soil is derived from living material. In a woodland, for example, decomposing leaves contribute to the organic matter. In our gardens, we add organic matter in the form of well-rotted manure, compost, peat moss or wood chips. Organic matter improves soil immensely, making clay soil drain more quickly and keeping sandy soil from drying out as quickly. Because it is 60 percent carbon, decomposed organic matter—humus—darkens the soil, causing it to absorb heat and warm faster in the spring.

If adding wood chips or sawdust to soil, it is necessary to add extra nitrogen to the soil to compensate for that taken up by the microorganisms breaking down the wood. Add 1 ounce (30 g) of nitrogen per 5 pounds (2.2 kg) of wood chips. It is best to use a form of nitrogen that releases slowly—bloodmeal or a lawn food with sulfur-coated urea (S.C.U), for instance. Depending on its formulation, the actual amount of fertilizer you use will vary. The number of ounces (grams) of fertilizer you use multiplied by the nitrogen number on the box or bag (the first number of the three) should be close to one hundred (three thousand). For example:

- Use 8 ounces (240 g) of 12-0-0 bloodmeal (8 × 12 = 96 or 240 × 12 = 2880)
- Use 5 ounces (150 g) of 20-3-4 lawnfood with 50 percent S.C.U. (5 × 20 = 100 or 150 × 20 = 3000)

A spongy soil with plenty of organic matter makes it easier for plant roots to penetrate, allowing plants to grow faster. In addition, organic matter has the ability to retain fertilizer molecules, of particular benefit in sandy soils.

Soil pH

The pH is a measure of the acidity of a solution and is always expressed as a number from 0 to 14; 7 is a neutral pH. The lower the pH, the more acidic the solution; the higher the pH, the more alkaline. For example, lemon juice has a pH of 2; vinegar, pH 3; beer, pH 4. Milk has a pH of nearly 7; sea water, pH 8; and milk of magnesia, pH 10. Soil pH is determined by mixing the soil with water and measuring the pH of the resulting solution. Gardeners often refer to acidic soils as being sour and to neutral or slightly alkaline soils as being sweet. Depending on the pH of the soil, certain nutrients may exist in unavailable forms or may be present in toxic amounts.

In the Pacific coast region, the high rainfall causes naturally acid soils. At pH of about 5.5 or 5.0, such soils are ideal for acid-loving plants, such as azaleas and rhododendrons. A slightly sweeter soil, about pH 6–7, is better for most of the perennials discussed in this book. At pH 6.5, there is the greatest availability of all soil nutrients. For perennials that like sweet soil, a note is made in the encyclopedia to add extra dolomite lime.

Ideally, you should test the pH of your soil each year. There are test kits available in shops, garden centers often have soil-testing clinics, or you can go to a private soil-testing laboratory. Testing results from a laboratory include nutrient levels, pH, salinity and soil texture as well as recommendations for improving soil. For a soil-testing lab near you, refer to the yellow pages under laboratories–testing. Samples may also be sent to most labs through the mail, if you live out of town. Fees are surprisingly reasonable.

To make your soil sweeter, it is necessary to add lime. There are three liming materials available to the home gardener. Hydrated lime (calcium hydroxide) is fast-acting and should only be used in preparing new beds before planting, never around existing plant material. Ground limestone (calcium carbonate) is sold as home and garden lime or agricultural lime. It takes from one to three months to act, depending on the particle size of the lime. Dolomite lime (calcium-magnesium carbonate) is ground from limestone high in magnesium, an important plant nutrient and one often deficient in Pacific coast soils, making dolomite the lime of choice. Like calcium carbonate lime, it takes one to three months to act. Wood ashes also make the soil sweeter.

In general, adding 5 pounds of lime per 100 square feet (2.2 kg per 9m²) of soil will raise the pH one point. Do not use more lime than this in one application. If a greater change than one point is necessary, apply twice a year. For faster results, use hydrated lime at 3¹/₂ pounds per 100 square feet (1.6 kg per 9m²), in new beds only, never near plants. Do not add lime and fertilizer to the soil at the same time; allow at least a week between the two.

Plant nutrients: N, P and K

The three major plant nutrients are nitrogen, phosphorus and potassium. N is the chemical symbol for nitrogen, P is for phosphorus and K is for potassium. The three numbers which must appear on all fertilizers represent the percentage of N, P and K in a standardized reference form. For example, 20-20-20 has the equivalent of 20 percent nitrogen, 20 percent phosphorus and 20 percent potassium.

Nitrogen (N) is important for overall plant health, but especially for the leaves. As explained in the section on soil, some forms of nitrogen are readily washed out of some soils. A deficiency of nitrogen causes the older leaves to turn yellow and the new leaves to become quite small. Too much nitrogen results in dark green leaves, lots of soft leafy growth and few flowers. Excess nitrogen will also depress the amounts of phosphorus and potassium taken up.

Phosphorus (P) is particularly important in root development. Like nitrogen, the available phosphorus washes easily out of some soils. Too little phosphorus will show up as dark green leaves and retarded growth. Leaves may be purplish and drop early. This symptom is seen in a cold, wet spring, but more commonly in warm-weather vegetables and bedding plants, such as tomatoes and geraniums, than in perennials. Adding

24

phosphorus to the soil will help the plant cope with cool soil. Too much phosphorus is not usually a problem.

Potassium (K) encourages general plant vigor and maturity. It increases a plant's resistance to disease and cold weather. A deficiency shows up as mottled lower leaves, yellowing beginning at the margin. Serious root injury may result from excessive amounts of potassium.

Minor nutrients

Plants need other nutrients in smaller quantities. Calcium, magnesium, sulfur, iron, manganese, zinc, copper, boron, chlorine and molybdenum all play a role, but, with the exception of magnesium and iron, are unlikely to be deficient in most garden soils. If using soilless potting mixes in containers, however, it is worth adding "fritted trace elements" (FTE). This fertilizer has trace elements (all those listed above except calcium, magnesium, sulfur and chlorine) with finely ground glass (frit) as a carrier.

In terms of liming materials, calcium is present in lime and magnesium in dolomite lime.

Fertilizer application types

There are basically two application types of fertilizer—dry and wet. **Granular fertilizers** are mixtures of dry fertilizers. They are sprinkled on the soil surface, mixed into the top few inches (5–10 cm) and watered in well. They are easy to use and ideal for making up a flower bed. Adding a formula such as 6-8-6 or 4-10-10 will get plants off to a good start and last for about four to six weeks. The application could be repeated in late June and late July if plants seem to need additional fertilizer—not generally the case with perennials.

Soluble fertilizers are liquid or dry concentrates that must be diluted or dissolved in water. They are especially suitable for watering young transplants and container gardens, and take up less storage space than bulky granular fertilizers. Soluble fertilizers are fast-acting and give the gardener an opportunity to respond immediately to a plant's needs. At transplant time, use a fertilizer with plenty of phosphorus, such as 10-52-17, to promote root growth. If a plant has too much leafy growth and not enough bloom, use a fertilizer with less nitrogen, such as 15-30-15. If foliage is pale, use more nitrogen, for example, 20-20-20. (Check for spider mites first; they also cause pale foliage.)

Controlled-release fertilizers such as Osmocote or Nutricote are the deluxe way to go. Nutrients are released according to the soil temperature, so plants get food when they are growing the fastest. The beauty of controlled-release fertilizers is that they last from three months to one year, depending on the formulation. Most widely available to the home gardener is the three-month 14-14-14 formulation; applied in late May, it will feed plants through the summer.

Organic fertilizer

Some gardeners prefer to use natural products to provide plant nutrients. The following recipe is a general-purpose organic fertilizer. It may be used for vegetable and other garden plants. Omit lime if fertilizing acid-loving plants, such as azaleas and rhododendrons. Mix together:

- four parts by volume seed meal or fish meal
- one part by volume rock phosphate or 1/2 part bonemeal
- one part by volume dolomite lime
- one part by volume kelp meal

While organic fertilizers are a bit more expensive, they are much longer lasting in the soil than chemical fertilizers. As summer arrives and the activity of soil microorganisms increases, more and more nutrients are released. If used each year, the soil will improve continually.

Fertilizing perennials

If the soil is well prepared before planting and plants are top-dressed with manure or compost every few years, most established perennials do not need as much fertilizer as annuals. Annuals make a burst of growth all in one season, and the lack of fertilizer can have disastrous results. Perennials, on the other hand, make slow, steady growth, and benefit most from good soil and small amounts of fertilizer.

If you are growing perennials from seed, be sure to fertilize young plants carefully until they are established. Watch leaves for signs of any nutrient deficiencies and adjust your fertilizing regime accordingly.

Planting
and
Care of
Perennials

Some of the most unusual and hard-to-acquire perennials whose photographs appear in this book were found not in botanical or display gardens—as one might expect—but in home gardens. In many cases, the exact origin of the plant was long forgotten. Perhaps it was planted by the previous owner; perhaps it was a gift from another gardener. This ability of most perennials to flourish for many years makes them a delight for gardeners. A few pointers for the general care of perennials are outlined in this chapter.

When to plant

Gardeners always debate the pros and cons of spring versus fall planting. There are several factors to take into consideration. In general, plants make rapid root growth in the fall because the soil is warm, making fall the ideal planting time. However, there are a few exceptions. Fall-blooming perennials, such as florists' chrysanthemums, are best planted in the spring so that they will be well-established, bushy plants before blooming. For perennials that are borderline hardy in your area, spring planting is preferable to give the plant a season to become established before facing the frost. Plants with gray foliage are susceptible to rotting during very wet winters and should also be planted in spring if possible. This is especially true if you are planning to divide these perennials before planting.

One of the key factors determining planting time is, of course, availability. Some perennials are sold bare-root (without soil or pots) in the early spring. They are often packaged in boxes or plastic bags with some peat around their roots and a photo on the package. But most perennials sold in shops are in pots, often with picture labels giving you an idea of what they will look like. There is no doubt that plants in bloom sell fastest, so retailers tend to stock perennials when they are in bloom. Bear this in mind, and shop for perennials in their season. If you are buying spring-blooming perennials in the fall, for example, make sure the plants are in good condition. A 4-inch (10-cm) pot of aubrietia that has been in the nursery since spring may not be at the peak of perfection.

When shopping for perennials by mail-order, it is possible to get most of the plants you want in the season of your choice. Mail-order nurseries are geared to gardeners who know what they want, rather than impulse buyers. Their catalogues may not even have photographs, but if you do your homework, photos are not important. In addition, mail-order shopping saves you time and gas, going from shop to shop.

Preparing the ground

It is of paramount importance when preparing a bed for perennials that the area be weed-free, particularly of perennial weeds. These weeds have roots that persist in the soil and each tiny piece can produce a new plant. Morning glory, horsetail and couch grass are particularly obnoxious and difficult to eradicate. If you have these weeds, dig the soil thoroughly and remove all traces of root. Delay planting any perennials or shrubs for one growing season, until the perennial weeds are eradicated. Plant bedding plants or cover the soil with black plastic. You can check throughout the summer to see if you have missed any pieces of root, and then clean the bed up again in the fall.

Most plants appreciate plenty of organic matter added to the soil. Spread 4 inches (10 cm) of organic matter over the soil surface with the flat side of a leveling rake. Broadcast a general fertilizer such as 6-8-6 or 4-10-10 or an organic mixture over the surface at 2 pounds per 100 square feet (1 kg per 9m²). Turn soil surface to a depth of about 1 foot (30 cm) with a short-handled fork or spade to incorporate the soil amendments. As you dig, avoid walking on the freshly dug areas. Throw a board over the soil surface to walk on.

At this point it is wise to test the soil—at least for pH. If it is necessary to add lime and you have just added fertilizer or manure, wait a week before liming. Turn the lime into the top surface of the soil. After all digging is completed, level the soil with the flat side of a leveling rake and allow the soil to settle for a few days. If you are impatient to plant, gently tamp down the soil with the tines of your leveling rake. (A leveling rake has rigid tines at a 90° angle to the handle, as opposed to a leaf rake, whose tines extend in a fan from the handle.)

When planting wide-spreading perennials (or shrubs and trees) an alterative technique known as pocket planting can be used. For plants that spread about 2 feet (60 cm) or more, add organic matter and fertilizer to each planting hole, rather than broadcasting it over the surface.

On the whole, perennials do not need as much fertilizer as bedding plants and vegetables, and many gardeners use only ample organic matter instead of fertilizer.

Planting

Avoid planting on a hot day. During hot weather, plant in early morning or, better yet, evening. The size of the planting hole depends on whether you have dug the whole bed or whether you will do pocket plantings. If you have dug the whole bed, you only need to make the hole big enough to accommodate the roots when spread out. If you are pocket planting, make a hole several inches (10 cm) to a foot (30 cm) larger than the plant's rootball. When planting bare-root perennials, spread the roots out well in the hole. Look closely at the stem to see where the roots join the top and replant at the same level.

When planting container-grown perennials, turn the pot upside-down to get the plant out rather than tugging on the stem. When planting, loosen the root ball a bit, but it is not necessary to spread the roots out. If the roots look like they are growing around and around inside the pot, make three vertical slits along the outside of the rootball to encourage the roots to branch out. Position the plant at the same depth in the soil as it was in the pot.

Cover the roots with soil, firm gently and water well.

Staking

Some tall perennials require staking, and it works best to stake them before they get tall. Get four stakes of about the height that the plant will eventually reach. Green bamboo stakes are ideal. Insert them into the soil around the plant in a square shape, angling outward. Tie twine around the stakes in a square about 1 foot (30 cm) above ground level, looping it around each stake so that it won't slip down. Then make an X in the middle, connecting the corner stakes. The twine will make this shape:

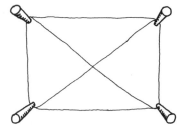

The many stems of the plant will grow up through the four sections the twine makes; they can move in the wind—making them stronger—but cannot collapse in heavy wind or rain. When the plants have grown taller, add another tier of twine. This method of staking produces more attractive results than bunching the stems together and tying them to a single stake.

For shorter perennials that are inclined to be floppy, simply insert small twigs into the soil around the base of the stems for them to grow through. These will offer the needed support.

Caring for perennials through the season

Deadheading (removing faded flowers) encourages length of bloom for some perennials. These will be noted in the encyclopedia section.

Deadheading is also necessary for some perennials, such as gayfeather (*Liatris*), whose blooms become messy looking once they have faded. Other perennials have attractive seed heads, which can be left on the plants.

In late fall, tidy up foliage of all perennials that have shown any sign of disease during the season. During wet weather, raindrops can disperse fungal spores, encouraging disease.

If plants are healthy, you need not take as much care in your fall tidy-up. In fact, some perennials such as chrysanthemums are best left untouched until spring. Leaving a few stems of most perennials standing will remind you where your perennials are if you plan to do any planting during the winter.

If you are interested in fostering beneficial wildlife, do not keep your garden meticulously tidy. Rake fallen leaves off your lawn and pile them under shrubs and trees. (But do not pile them thickly where perennials or bulbs will emerge in spring.) As they decompose, they will provide a soil-improving mulch, and a layer of leaves will encourage worms and other food for wild birds. Many useful insects, such as ladybird beetles, hibernate in dead vegetation—a good reason not to cut down herbaceous stems until spring. Seed heads also provide food for birds and the old stalks will protect the plant's crown from frost. Keeping your garden pesticide-free ensures the health of wild birds and insects.

Books written for eastern gardeners warn about the hazards of frost heaving the plants due to alternate freezing and thawing. This is rarely a problem in the Pacific coastal region. Nevertheless, it is not a bad idea to mulch borderline-hardy perennials with leaves in the fall. Do not mulch or allow blowing leaves to cover perennials that have gray or succulent foliage, which are particularly susceptible to decay when air circulation is decreased.

If you are new to gardening, you will find that perennials will give you tremendous satisfaction for the amount of care they entail. If you are already dedicated to growing them, you will know the pleasure that watching this fascinating group of plants grow and bloom over the years can bring.

P**ropagate**, prop′agat, *v.t.*, [L. *propagare, propagatus*, to peg down, to propagate.] To breed, continue or multiply by asexual or sexual reproduction; to cause to reproduce (itself), as applied to animals or plants . . . (*The Living Webster*).

Propagation is any method by which one increases the number of plants on hand. The root of the word is from the Latin word to peg down—a method of plant propagation still used today, usually called layering. There are basically two methods of propagation, as the above definition mentions: sexual and asexual.

Propagation in theory

Sexual propagation. It was not until the late 1600s that botanists realized that plants reproduce sexually. That is, they have male and female reproductive structures. The process of sexual reproduction (male pollen fertilizing female ovules) results in recombination of genetic material, the end product of which is seed—each with a slightly different set of chromosomes. Each seed will grow into a plant that is slightly different from its "siblings." Growing plants from seed, therefore, will result in a diversity of seedlings, and some plant species naturally show greater variation than others. An advantage of growing plants from seed is that seed can be obtained from all over the world at small expense, giving one the opportunity of growing some very exotic plants. For many types of plants, growing from seed is also the least costly method of propagation.

Seed propagation is ideal for seed strains and species, especially those of annuals, biennials and many perennials; growing shrubs and trees from seed often requires more patience.

Vegetative propagation. Division, cuttings, grafting or budding, layering and tissue culture are techniques of vegetative propagation. Each plant created by these techniques is genetically identical to the original plant—it is a **clone.** Because two parents are not involved and the sexual process of genetic recombination does not occur, vegetative propagation is asexual. Vegetative propagation is suitable for almost any plant, although some techniques are easier on some types of plants. Vegetative propagation is rarely used for annuals or biennials; because they have such a short life span, it is hardly worth the effort. For shrubs, trees and many perennials, on the other hand, vegetative propagation produces a larger plant in a shorter time than seed propagation. Some hybrids do not produce seed, so vegetative propagation is mandatory.

Propagating named cultivars. As explained on page 9, named cultivars are cultivated varieties of plants (rather than naturally occurring plants) that are distinct enough horticulturally to warrant a name. They can be selected from a species, they can be hybrids or they can be seed strains. The question of the best way to propagate named cultivars—from seed or vegetative techniques—has no simple answer and often leads to heated discussions among all who are interested in the subject. Two points are clear. First, if a named cultivar has been developed as a seed strain—as many annual flowers and vegetables have been—seed propagation is the way to go. Secondly, if a plant is propagated vegetatively, you know exactly what you will end up with—a clone of the original plant. But what happens if a named cultivar is not a seed strain and you try to grow it from seed? This is where things become confusing—more confusing with perennials than other types of plants.

33

With bedding plants, everyone knows which plants one would expect to grow from seed—marigolds, petunias, zinnias, for example—and which plants one would expect to grow from cuttings—fancy-leaf geraniums, fuchsias, marguerites are a few. In terms of vegetables, annuals such as carrots, tomatoes and cauliflower are started fresh each year from seed, whereas rhubarb, asparagus and horseradish (perennials) are divided.

Virtually all named cultivars of trees and shrubs are propagated by vegetative means; roses and fruit and ornamental trees are budded and most shrubs are propagated from cuttings or by tissue culture. These are all clones.

Regarding perennials, however, things are not so simple. When a new named cultivar is registered, the breeder does not specify whether it is a seed strain or not. Some named cultivars are presumed to be seed strains—many columbines and delphiniums, for example, are developed to be grown from seed. With most named cultivars, however, it is presumed that they will be propagated vegetatively as clones: named hostas, daylilies and exhibition chrysanthemums are examples. In fact, some named cultivars, particularly if they are hybrids or if the flowers are fully double, do not even form seed and must be propagated vegetatively.

Inevitably, after a new clone is introduced, if it sets seed, someone will plant it and see what comes up. If the seedlings are very similar to the parent, the named cultivar is said to "come true from seed," even though plants are not identical to their parents genetically. The seedlings or the seed may be offered for sale under the name of the original cultivar. All such plants, although under one name, are no longer clones.

In some cases, only a certain percentage of the seedlings will come true from seed; this is not always made clear in seed catalogues. It is necessary, therefore, to raise a dozen or so plants and to select for the characteristic you desire. For example, the double-flowered columbine (*Aquilegia*) 'Nora Barlow' comes about 90 percent true from seed. Once plants have flowered, you must select those with the double flowers and discard the others. Another example is coralbells (*Heuchera*) 'Palace Purple', grown for its purple leaves. When grown from seed, leaf color includes green, purplish green and the dark purplish red most gardeners desire. Again, a selection process must take place. What sometimes happens, however, it that a grower will not be aware of this problem and will label young plants as the named cultivar, when in fact not all of those seedlings will fit the description of the original named cultivar.

In the encyclopedia section, under propagation, you will see "propagate from seed (except named cultivars that are not true from seed) or by division." Unfortunately it is impossible to state exactly how true each named cultivar will come from seed. You can assume that if seed is offered by a reputable seed firm, seedlings will probably be very close to the original named cultivar. But remember to grow as many plants as possible and select the best ones for your garden.

Growing perennials from seed

As explained above, species and seed strains are the ideal candidates for seed propagation. While most of the named cultivars described in this book will not come true from seed, you may still wish to experiment with seed you have collected from your own plants.

In some ways, growing perennials from seed is easier than growing bedding plants from seed. Because perennials are native to the temperate rather than tropical regions of the world, extra heat (a heating cable) is not required for germination. Because perennials will be in your garden for many years, there is not the same time pressure to have a seedling at just the right stage to go into the garden by May. In fact, most perennials do not bloom until at least their second year from seed. You can wait until all the must-do garden chores are finished and then take time to sow perennials.

On the other hand, patience is required when growing some perennials from seed. While most germinate within one month of sowing, some, such as hellebores, can take up to a year and a half to sprout. For this reason, many gardeners prefer buying perennial plants to growing them from seeds. Perennials that are commonly grown from seed include pasqueflower (*Anemone pulsatilla*), columbine (*Aquilegia*), rock cress (*Arabis*), aubrietia, basket-of-gold (*Aurinia saxatilis*), thrift (*Armeria*), alpine asters, bellflowers (*Campanula*), cupid's dart (*Catananche*), coreopsis, delphinium, pinks (*Dianthus*), foxglove (*Digitalis*), gaillardia, coralbells (*Heuchera*), perennial lobelia, bee balm (*Monarda*), lupines, Jacob's ladder (*Polemonium*), primulas, black-eyed susan (*Rudbeckia*) and soapwort (*Saponaria*).

Breaking dormancy. In the normal life cycle of many perennials, the seed drops to the ground in summer or fall when it is ripe and germinates either in the summer or the following spring; young plants will usually bloom their second year. The seeds of some perennials, if they are not allowed to germinate immediately after they become ripe, become dormant and will not germinate without a cold treatment to break dormancy. This is a survival mechanism to delay germination until spring. Commercial seed companies generally give instructions on breaking dormancy on the package, but, in general, the procedure is as follows. Mix the seeds with a tablespoon (15 ml) of moist peat and place in a plastic bag in the refrigerator or freezer for one to six weeks. The following genera need a cold treatment: monkshood (*Aconitum*), columbine (*Aquilegia*), masterwort (*Astrantia*), delphinium, pinks (*Dianthus*), bleeding heart (*Dicentra*), burning bush (*Dictamnus*), Christmas and Lenten roses (*Helleborus*) and lupines.

Some seeds may be reluctant to germinate because of a hard seed coat or a chemical in the seed coat that inhibits germination. Soaking for twenty-four hours in tepid water will speed up germination. Thrift (*Armeria*), irises, lupines and primulas all benefit from soaking.

If you are buying seed from a garden club or society (for example the Alpine Garden Club of B.C. or the Royal Horticultural Society in Great Britain, both of which operate excellent seed exchanges), specific instructions will not accompany the seeds. In that case, sow them as described below, and let the natural weathering take its course.

Sowing seeds of perennials. Seed you have collected yourself should be sown as soon as possible, generally in summer or fall. Packaged seed can be sown almost anytime in the spring or summer. Some perennials, such as cupid's dart (*Catananche*), gaillardia and some types of Shasta daisy (*Chyrsanthemum* × *superbum*) and foxglove (*Digitalis*), will bloom the first year if sown in March, but most will not bloom until at least the second year.

Perennials can be sown in containers or directly into the garden. The advantage of sowing in containers of sterilized potting mix is that there will be no weed seeds present. Sow in a good-quality potting mix or make your own, as follows. Add 27 quarts (27 L) peat moss; 9 quarts (9 L) sterilized sand, vermiculite or perlite; 4 ounces (120 g) by weight dolomite lime; 3 ounces (90 g) by weight fritted trace elements and several handfuls of bonemeal. Mix well, soak in warm water to moisten the peat and let drain well. For sedums and sempervivums, use a smaller proportion of peat and increase the sand/perlite/vermiculite accordingly.

Put this mixture in clean pots. If you have used the pots before, soak them in a solution of hot soapy water with 10 percent chlorine bleach added. Pots approximately 4 inches (10 cm) across are a good size. Sow seed on the top of the soil and cover if indicated on the seed package. Where seeds need light to germinate, a note is made in the encyclopedia section. A general rule is that seeds should be planted at a depth of three times their size. Pots can then be placed in a nursery area of the garden, ideally close to a tap so they will get regular watering during dry spells. Remember that some perennials take up to eighteen months to germinate, so have patience. Seeds may need the chill of one winter to break dormancy.

When seedlings get large enough to handle, transplant them to individual pots or to a specially prepared nursery bed. A corner of the vegetable garden is ideal for this purpose. Turn over the top few inches (5–10 cm) of soil and remove stones and weeds.

Alternatively, sow perennials directly into the nursery bed. Because weed growth is most fierce in May and June, July is a good month to sow perennials in the ground.

Techniques of vegetative propagation

Vegetative propagation, as opposed to propagation from seed, results in a plant that is genetically identical to the original. The techniques of vegetative propagation that are used most often with perennials are root division, stem cuttings, root cuttings, layering, grafting and tissue culture. The catch, of course, is that you must have the plant on hand to begin with. Or perhaps you can convince a friend whose plant you covet to give you a division or cutting.

Root division is an easy technique that not only will give you more plants, but will restrain rambunctious perennials and renew declining perennials. All that is required is to lift the clump, cut the roots apart with a sharp spade and replant a smaller section with a bucketful of compost and a handful of bonemeal. Some plants have very tough roots, and you may wish to keep an old knife or even a small saw on hand to divide these. In general, spring-blooming perennials should be divided after blooming, summer-bloomers in the fall and fall-bloomers in the spring. If possible, divide plants with fuzzy, silver leaves in the spring. Such plants are adapted to dry climates and are less able to withstand diseases associated with wet weather; damage during the process of division may allow entry of disease organisms through the winter.

Large clumps can also be divided by merely cutting a pie-shaped section out of the rootball without disturbing the original plant. This works well for genera such as *Hosta* that build up into handsome clumps and do not normally need division due to declining vigor. You can remove a section for a friend without harming your own plant.

Stem cuttings are made of many types of perennials, especially by commercial nurseries. Rock cress (*Arabis*), *Artemisia* 'Powis Castle' and 'Silver Brocade', asters, aubrietia, florist's chyrsanthemum, candytuft (*Iberis*), pinks (*Dianthus*), sundrops (*Oenothera*) and sedums are often grown from stem cuttings. Each gardener or nurseryman has his or her own technique for making cuttings, but they are usually taken in July or August.

Suitable media for rooting cuttings include coarse builders' sand or a 50/50 mixture of peat with either perlite, coarse sand or vermiculite. Some growers fill rectangular flats with the rooting medium; some place cuttings individually in 3-inch (8 cm) square pots. The advantage of square pots (if you can get them) is that they fit tightly together, moderating fluctuations of temperature and humidity and taking less room. If you do not have square pots, consider setting your round pots in a flat and filling in the spaces with sand. Set the containers of rooting medium in warm water until the surface is moist and then allow them to drain.

The length of the cutting depends on the plant, but as a general rule cut below the fourth or fifth pair of leaves from the growing tip, using a clean razor blade to prevent infection. Remove the bottom two pairs of leaves and insert these two leafless joints into the rooting medium. They can first be dipped in #2-strength rooting compound if desired. Make a hole in the medium with a dibble or pencil, rather than using the end of the cutting to make the hole.

As noted in the encyclopedia section, some cuttings are taken from the base of the stems near the crown of the plant, sometimes with a bit of the crown attached. These are called basal cuttings.

Keep the containers of cuttings in a shaded place and water regularly. The rooting medium should not be soaking wet all the time, nor should it dry out.

If you have heating cable, this will speed up rooting, but is not necessary if cuttings are made during warm summer months. Cuttings will root very quickly at soil temperatures of up to 80°F (27°C) and air temperatures of up to 120°F (50°C) as long as the humidity is high and the plants are shaded. If you have a greenhouse, you might want to experiment with warmer temperatures for rooting cuttings.

Root cuttings can be made of plants with thick fleshy roots. Root cuttings are commonly made of Japanese anemone, cupid's dart (*Catananche*), red valerian (*Centranthus*), bleeding heart (*Dicentra*), purple coneflower (*Echinacea*), gaillardia, Oriental poppy (*Papaver orientale*), border phlox and pasqueflower (*Anemone pulsatilla*). Make root cuttings in the fall if you have a cold frame, in February or March if you do not. Gently remove soil around the base of the original plant and cut off pencil-thick sections of stem, about 2 inches (5 cm) long. Lay these sections of stem horizontally on the surface of a flat or pot of potting mix. Cover them with 1/2 inch (1.3 cm) of potting mix. These small root segments will sprout new roots and shoots in the spring.

If the roots are more than 1/2 inch (1.3 cm) thick, it is best to pot them individually into 6-inch (15-cm) pots. Make the root cuttings 3–4 inches (8–10 cm) long and insert them vertically into the potting soil, with the top of the root cutting about 1/2 inch (1.3 cm) below the soil surface. Be sure that you insert the cutting the right way up: the part of the cutting that was closest to the crown of the plant should be up, the part of the cutting that was closest to the outer tip of the root should be near the bottom of the pot. (As an aid to keeping track of which end is which, cut the end nearest the crown straight across and cut the outer end on an angle.)

Layering occurs naturally with many plants that creep along the surface of the soil: where the stems are in contact with the soil, they often root at their leaf nodes. This segment of stem can be removed and planted on its own. Layering can be encouraged many ways—a portion of stem can be covered with a bit of soil or it can be pressed into firm contact with the soil with a small rock or wooden peg. The growing end of the stem should still be exposed to air and sunlight. Rooting is slow, but can be speeded up with the application of rooting compound and regular watering. Suitable subjects for layering include rock cress (*Arabis*), aubrietia, pinks (*Dianthus*), creeping baby's breath (*Gypsophila repens*), moss phlox, soapwort (*Saponaria*) and campions (*Silene*).

Grafting, a technique used widely in growing fruit and ornamental trees, involves the joining of the roots of one plant with the stem of another, indirectly through stem-to-stem contact. In the realm of perennials, grafting has been used for years to propagate named cultivars of baby's breath (*Gypsophila paniculata*).

Tissue culture is a relatively new technique (since the 1920s) that is beyond the average home gardener because it is conducted in sterile laboratory conditions. Tissue culture is a method of cloning that takes advantage of the fact that newly dividing cells have the genetic information to produce another complete (and identical) organism.

At the very tip of growing shoots and roots is a rapidly growing and dividing group of new cells called the apical meristem. Cells from the apical meristem are carefully removed and placed on a nutrient gel in a sterile test tube. It is important that no fungal, viral or bacterial organisms are allowed to grow in the test tube and harm the plant's cells. Later these cells are separated and each is induced to grow roots and shoots. Each of these plantlets will eventually mature enough to survive beyond the sterile conditions of the lab—they are potted and make their way into nurseries. Tissue culture was first used primarily in the propagation of orchids, but now it is used widely for baby's breath (*Gypsophila paniculata*), hostas and daylilies (*Hemerocallis*).

Growing ferns from spores

Ferns are not flowering plants, so they do not produce seeds. They reproduce by spores and it is possible to grow new ferns from spores. Sow the spores on a sterilized potting mixture (1/2 oak leaf mold and 1/2 earthworm castings, for example) in clear plastic boxes under grow lights. These spores produce the alternate generation of the fern's life-cycle, the prothallium, a tiny plant one cell-layer thick and about 1/4 inch (.6 cm) wide. This tiny prothallium carries out the sexual phase of the fern's life cycle. It produces female organs (archegonia), each containing one egg, and male organs (antheridia), containing many sperm. When water moistens the prothallium, the sperm can swim to the eggs and fertilize them. The fertilized eggs then develop into the second stage of the life cycle, the plant we recognize as a fern. It grows on the prothallium to draw moisture and nourishment, but gradually the prothallium shrivels and disappears. Once the tiny ferns reach about 1 inch

(2.5cm) in height (about five months to a year after the spore germinates), the small plants can be transplanted into deep flats, each plant spaced about 6 inches (15 cm) apart, or into individual pots. They continue growing under lights until they are transplanted into the garden or, if grown on in flats, into their own individual 4-inch (10-cm) pots. It takes about 18 months to produce a fern in a 4-inch (10-cm) pot.

Pests
and
Diseases

The majority of the perennials described in this book are generally trouble-free. Even if they have pests or diseases listed in their entry in the encyclopedia section, these problems do not necessarily occur regularly. And among the pests and diseases expected regularly, some will not harm the plant in question and require no action on the part of the gardener. In general, the more highly bred the perennial, the longer the list of pests and diseases it has. Delphiniums, lupines, Chinese peonies (*Paeonia lactiflora*), asters, phlox, German bearded irises and chrysanthemums are notable examples. Indeed, more and more gardeners are avoiding such perennials, or planting them in small numbers, preferring trouble-free types.

The current trend in gardening is to turn away from chemical methods of pest control. Chemical controls are expensive, unpleasant to use and potentially dangerous to both the user and the environment. We often forget that the pesticides we use can also kill beneficial insects, such as ground beetles, butterflies and bees. Toxic chemicals produced during the manufacture of pesticides can also harm the environment. In addition, pesticides find their way into the food chain, threatening the health of animals right to the top of the chain, including such predatory birds as eagles, falcons and owls.

A study done in 1980 by the National Academy of Sciences in the United States showed that home gardens and lawns receive the heaviest pesticide applications of any land area in the United States. While this seems frightening, it offers us, as home gardeners, the chance to take control and make decisions that will have far-reaching effects.

In general, good horticultural practice will reduce the number of pest problems. Healthy plants will be less bothered by light infestations of pests. Consider the following pointers:

- Choose appropriate plants for each setting; for example, placing a plant that requires well-drained soil in a damp area invites problems.
- Space plants well to encourage good air circulation.
- If possible, choose disease-resistant cultivars. However, more work has been done to develop disease-resistant cultivars of bedding plants and vegetables than of perennials.
- Avoid overhead or evening watering of plants that are prone to leaf spots and molds.
- When growing perennials that are disease-prone, space them through the garden, rather than planting them in large groups. This will make it harder for the disease to move from plant to plant.
- Remove and destroy diseased leaves and flowers as soon as they are noticed. Place them in the garbage, not in the compost heap.
- Keep the area near plants tidy during the growing season to reduce the number of hiding and breeding places for slugs and snails.

Discussed in this chapter are the most common pests and diseases that you are likely to encounter on your garden perennials. Few greenhouse problems have been included. If, after consulting this listing, you still are unable to identify the problem, there are other sources of information available. In British Columbia, VanDusen and UBC Botanical Gardens both operate a phone-in question service, listed in the phone book. In Alaska, Washington and Oregon, the county extension agent will be able to offer advice on pest and disease problems.

Another source of information is the licensed pesticide dispenser at your local garden center. In British Columbia, Oregon and Washington, the law requires that anyone giving pesticide advice obtain such a license. Once the problem has been identified, be cautious about choosing a chemical solution until you have tried other methods. Organic gardening books in your public library may provide alternate solutions.

Insecticidal soaps available on the market are effective against soft-bodied pests, such as aphids, spider mites and whiteflies. They are of low toxicity, but because they do not have a residual effect, spray applications may need to be repeated more often than if more toxic chemicals were used. A study done in 1982 at the University of California found that a 1 percent solution of Ivory dishwashing liquid and water was as effective as insecticidal soap; you might wish to experiment with dishwashing liquid. To prevent damage to the foliage, either rinse the soapy solution off the plant with water several minutes after spraying, or spray a small part of the plant and wait four to five days to determine whether damage will occur.

If using any pesticides, please remember the following:

- Only use an insecticide if damage is seen. Do not spray regularly to prevent insect pests. Positive identification of the pest is imperative so that the appropriate insecticide can be selected.
- Use an insecticidal soap or an "organic" pesticide, such as pyrethrin (derived from the flower pyrethrum) or permethrin (a synthetic pyrethrin-like compound). Some products combine insecticidal soap and pyrethrin to produce a spray more effective than insecticidal soap alone. Do not use insecticidal soap on spurges (*Euphorbia*), western bleeding heart (*Dicentra formosa*) or maidenhair fern (*Adiantum pedatum*)—it will burn their foliage.
- Always read the label very carefully and follow instructions exactly.
- Wear rubber gloves, long sleeves and trousers. Launder your clothing and take a shower after spraying.
- Move away from the direction in which you are spraying to avoid inhaling spray droplets. If you have access to a respirator designed for use during spraying, use it.
- Do not spray when the bees are out foraging. The best time of day is just before the sun sets.
- Do not spray unless the air is still.
- Do not spray if you have any health problems or are pregnant.
- Store all chemicals and fertilizers out of the reach of children and pets in a locked, ventilated box or cupboard.

- Always store pesticides in their original containers to prevent accidental consumption.
- Do not spray with chemicals indoors; always take the plants outdoors.

APHIDS are insects with soft, pear-shaped bodies, which cluster in large numbers near the ends of new shoots and under leaves, causing them to curl. Usually green, gray, black or pink, they suck the sap of plants and produce a sweet substance called "honeydew." Ants often "farm" aphids, carrying them to infest new plants and collecting the honeydew. Black sooty mold may grow on this honeydew, causing the foliage to appear unsightly. If you see an army of ants marching up and down a plant's stems, look for aphids. Because aphids suck the sap, they may transmit viral diseases from plant to plant. If there are only a few aphids, they may easily be sprayed off with a strong jet of water or rubbed off by hand; wear gloves if you are squeamish. Use insecticidal soap or a combination of insecticidal soap and pyrethrin.

Aphids have many natural predators that may keep things under control without your intervention. Ladybird beetles and their young, which look like little blackish green dragons, prey on aphids. Parasitic wasps lay their eggs in the aphid and the wasps' larvae eat the aphid when they hatch. If you see a beige aphid "mummy" on the leaves, this is what has happened. Avoid spraying any pesticides if biological controls are working.

CATERPILLARS. Numerous caterpillars are found in the garden; they are all the larval stage of moths and butterflies and most feed on leaves. They attack only a few perennials and even on those do light damage. Handpicking is the easiest method of control. If spraying is necessary, use B.T. (*Bacillus thurengiensis*) or an insecticidal soap/pyrethrin combination.

CLUBROOT is a serious disease caused by a fungus in the soil. It affects members of the Brassicaceae family. These include vegetables such as cabbage, broccoli, brussels sprouts and cauliflower; and perennials such as mountain-gold (*Alyssum*), rock cress (*Arabis*), aubrietia, basket-of-gold (*Aurinia*), perennial wallflower (*Cheiranthus*) and candytuft (*Iberis*). To help prevent clubroot, plant only on well-drained soil and add several handfuls of dolomite lime to the planting hole. Cautious gardeners avoid the risk of introducing infected soil into their garden by growing the above-mentioned vegetables from seed, rather than buying

45

young plants. Once the fungus is in the garden, it is virtually impossible to eliminate. You must wait five to seven years before growing any Brassicaceae in infected soil.

CUTWORMS are large, to 2 inches (5 cm), hairless caterpillars that curl up when disturbed. They are the larval stage of many species of dark, night-flying moths. Some cutworms climb plants to feed on stems and fruit, some feed at surface level and some feed underground. Although they cause serious damage to some bedding plants and vegetables, damage to perennials is usually light. Scratch the soil around the plants to expose cutworms and dispose of them. You can handpick climbing cutworms at night, using a flashlight to see. Deter surface feeding cutworms by making 3-inch-high (8-cm-high) collars for plants from old paper milk cartons or toilet paper tubes and pushing these 1 inch (2.5 cm) into the ground around each plant. A mulch of wood ashes or pine sawdust around the base of each plant discourages cutworms. A spray of *Bacillus thurengiensis* on the plant parts the cutworms are consuming will also help.

DAMPING-OFF refers to a fungal attack which results in seeds failing to emerge or in the collapse of young seedlings. Always sow seeds in sterilized soil and do not sow too thickly. Once seedlings emerge, grow on at the recommended temperature and provide good air circulation.

EARWIGS are dark brown insects about 1 inch (2.5 cm) long with forceps-like pincers at the rear. They are most often found hiding in large, show-type chrysanthemums, where they sometimes eat the flowers and leaves. To trap earwigs, stuff newspaper into the bottom of a clay flower pot and invert over a wooden stake near the damaged plants. The earwigs climb up into the pot to hide, and the paper can then be burned the next morning to destroy them. In addition, for show mums trained to a stake, a band of vaseline around the stem of the plant and around the stake will prevent earwigs from climbing up. They can also be hand-picked when seen, but wear rubber gloves to avoid being pinched.

FLEA BEETLES are tiny, 1/8-inch (3-mm), black beetles that jump like fleas and are hard to spot. Damage—tiny holes in the leaves—is usually not serious enough to warrant attention; plants will normally outgrow the damage. If flea beetles are a cause for concern, use rotenone dust or spray.

GRAY MOLD. With the exception of peonies, gray mold (*Botrytis* spp.) is not a serious problem on most perennials, because it infects mainly old flowers and leaves in humid conditions. Spores are airborne. Keeping the garden well-groomed will help control gray mold on most plants.

Gray mold is, however, a serious disease of peonies and is also called peony blight. Damage is seen most often on foot-high (30-cm) shoots, which suddenly collapse. A brown or blackish rot may be observed at the base of the stem, and the presence of fluffy gray fungal spores may be seen early in the morning before the sun dries the dew. The flower buds may fail to open and leaf spots appear later in the summer. Good garden hygiene is critical. Plant peonies with their crowns at soil level and avoid mulching until well into summer. If your peonies are troubled by gray mold in unusually cold, damp springs, spray with benomyl as soon as the young tips emerge in the spring, and again two weeks later. Destroy any unhealthy-looking shoots. Cut down stems in early fall and put them in the garbage, rather than the compost heap.

LEAF MINERS, which commonly attack columbine and chrysanthemum, are the larvae of small flies. They tunnel inside leaves, making characteristic pale serpentine trails. While the damage is odd-looking, leaf miners do not generally harm ornamental plants grown in the garden. Pick off the infested leaves and put them in the garbage, rather than the compost heap.

LEAF SPOTS are caused by a number of fungi, and in the case of irises, both fungi and bacteria. They occur most often in bergenia, Christmas rose (*Helleborus niger*), tall German bearded iris, and the various species of pinks (*Dianthus*). While unattractive, they generally do not do serious harm to the plants. Practice good garden hygiene, removing infected leaves as soon as they are noticed and putting them in the garbage rather than the compost heap. Avoid overhead watering. For leaf spots of Chinese peonies (*Paeonia lactiflora*), see gray mold, above.

MITES, sometimes called spider mites, are an occasional pest on a few perennials. A telltale sign is the yellowing of older (bottom) leaves or a pale mottled look to the foliage. Often leaves fall off without even looking unhealthy. If you look under leaves, you may be able to see fine webbing, but it is best to use a magnifying glass to detect the mites themselves. If you watch carefully you can see them walking around. If you see tiny specks on the leaves, poke them to see if they run away—a sure sign they aren't dust! Control is often difficult. Increase air circulation if possible, by light pruning of stems for example. Mites are worse in hot, dry weather; increase humidity by misting the leaves, particularly the undersides, with water. Spray with insecticidal soap or sulfur weekly for several weeks.

NEMATODES are also known as eelworms. Most are thin, transparent, microscopic invertebrates that feed in the intercellular spaces and cause the disintegration of plant cells. They enter the plant through wounds, root tips or natural pores. Leaf nematodes infect florist's chrysanthemum, causing brown areas on the leaves between the veins. These nematodes spread in water on the leaves, so it is important to pick infected leaves and keep the foliage dry. Stem nematodes infect tall border phlox, causing swollen stems, deformed leaves and no formation of flowers. Seriously infected plants should be destroyed, and no susceptible plants should be grown in the same soil for several years.

POWDERY MILDEW is a fungus disease which leaves a white, powdery coating on shoots and upper leaf surfaces. It appears most often during warm, muggy summer weather on border phlox and bee balm (*Monarda*). Plants are also more susceptible if the soil is allowed to dry out. Try not to wet foliage when watering and never water in the evening. Spray every two weeks with sulfur. There is a flowable sulfur on the market now that is said not to clog your sprayer or leave the residue that wettable sulfur does. As a last resort, spray with benomyl.

ROOT ROT is a general term used when root tissues are attacked by various species of fungi. As the roots become damaged, the leaves and stems may look slightly droopy, yellowish and generally unhealthy. Root rot in perennials is generally attributed to inadequate drainage or overwatering. Dig the plant up, cut away infected or damaged tissue (often dark brown rather than healthy white roots), dust the roots with sulfur, replant it in a well-drained location and take care not to overwater until new, healthy roots form.

ROOT WEEVIL adults are 1/2-inch (1-cm), dull, gray-black beetles with a distinctive long snout. (Do not confuse them with the larger, shiny black ground beetles that are very beneficial in the garden.) They eat the edges of leaves, leaving characteristic notches along the margins. They do not eat holes in the middle of leaves. The perennials they prefer are mainly bergenia and primula. In areas of high weevil infestation, their white larvae may eat the roots of coralbells (*Heuchera*), × *Heucherella* and saxifrages. When fresh leaf-notching is noticed, go out at night with a flashlight and handpick the adults. A board laid over the surface of the soil will attract weevils as a hiding place; they can then be collected and flushed down the toilet. Sprays are expensive and not very effective.

RUST appears most often on chrysanthemums and dianthus. As with many plant diseases, healthy plants are most resistant. The symptoms are yellow, orange or reddish-brown raised spots on the undersides of the leaves. Pick off diseased leaves and put them in the garbage. Spray with sulfur.

SLUGS and SNAILS are gastropods (meaning stomach-foot), related to moon-snails and other aquatic animals bearing single, usually spiral, shells. Slugs do have rudimentary shells, but are certainly not as handsome as most other gastropods. Slugs are common all over the Pacific coastal region; the presence of snails varies by locale and seems to be on the increase. Both attack about two dozen of the perennials described in this book. They eat the new shoots of delphiniums and may kill the plants completely. With most other perennials, they eat the leaves, which may not generally be noticeable. In the case of hostas, if they eat the leaves while they are still furled, they exhibit a most annoying pattern of holes when they unfurl. If you are not sure whether leaf damage is caused by cutworms or slugs, look for shiny trails near the plants; they are a sure sign of slugs and snails.

Slug fences made of salt-impregnated plastic are safe, effective and nontoxic. A container of beer sunk into the ground will attract them and they will drown. A half-full beer bottle works well for this purpose and is inconspicuous. (One study showed that nonalcoholic beer was the most popular with these pests!) A board laid over the surface of the soil will attract slugs and snails as a hiding place; they can then be collected and flushed down the toilet.

The most common metaldehyde slug and snail baits are bran-based and thus are very attractive to pets and toddlers, especially the pellet types. They have been the cause of many pet poisonings, sometimes resulting in death.

THRIPS are chiefly greenhouse pests, feeding on roses, carnations (*Dianthus caryophyllus*), chrysanthemums, geraniums (*Pelargonium*), baby's breath (*Gypsophila paniculata*) and many other flowers. However, they can be a problem for Shasta daisies (*Chrysanthemum* × *superbum*) and other garden flowers during hot, dry weather. Adult thrips are tiny, yellow to gray, about 1/10 inch (2 mm) long and have two pairs of fringed wings. They are fond of pollen and enter flower buds before they are even open, causing the flower to abort. In addition to eating pollen, they will eat petals and, as a last choice, leaves. Thrips breed in nearby weeds, so keep the garden well-weeded if thrips are a problem.

VIRUS organisms are made up of genetic material and are not organized into cells as are other living organisms. There is debate as to whether they are "life" as we usually think of it, but they certainly have the ability to affect normal cell functions. There is presently no way to kill them without killing the plant. A plant that shows symptoms of a virus disease should be destroyed. Virus particles are spread from plant to plant by insects, nematodes and pruning tools. Symptoms include abnormal growth, such as stunting, deformed leaves, yellow streaks or rings on the leaves, or streaks in the flowers.

WHITEFLY is a serious pest in the greenhouse, particularly on chrysanthemums, and may be introduced into your garden with plants grown in a greenhouse. They look like tiny, delicate white flies. They hide under leaves and flutter about when the plants are moved. There are two species of whitefly. Sweet potato whitefly was not seen in the Pacific coastal region prior to 1987, and it is more difficult to eradicate than common greenhouse whitefly. In the greenhouse, try one of the following:

- Trap flies with automotive S.T.P. oil painted onto an 8-inch-square (20-cm-square) piece of yellow cardboard hung near plants. Commercial sticky traps are also available.
- Spray with permethrin or insecticidal soap weekly for several weeks.
- Introduce the parasitic wasp *Encarsia formosa* into the greenhouse. It can be purchased from a company specializing in biological control agents and is effective against both species of whitefly if the greenhouse is kept warm enough.

In the garden, spray with insecticidal soap or permethrin.

WILT DISEASES are caused by two genera of fungi—*Fusarium* and *Verticillium*—and most commonly affect Michaelmas daisies and chrysanthemums. These fungi, and the debris they produce inside the plant, clog up its water-conducting vessels. Young plants may suddenly collapse and die. On more mature plants, the leaves may turn yellow and wilt, beginning with the lower leaves. Initially, plants may only wilt at the end of the day and regain their turgidity by morning. A thin coating of pink fruiting bodies may be seen on the lower stem. There is no treatment and the infected plant should be removed. The disease persists in the soil for long periods of time and can be transmitted on shoes or tools. Do not throw diseased plants in the compost and do not plant susceptible species in the same place twice.

Encyclopedia
of
Perennials

T he following encyclopedia gives information on over two hundred species of popular perennials and their named cultivars. Plants are organized alphabetically by their botanical names. Descriptions include bloomtime (which can vary as much as three weeks, depending on the weather), height, spread and region of origin. Cultural requirements include light, soil, care and propagation, pests and diseases and frost hardiness. Only instructions specific to each entry are given; for general gardening information—on techniques for planting, staking, propagation and pest and disease control, for instance—refer to the opening chapters. The Quick Reference Chart at the back of the book summarizes important information and notes whether a plant is good for cutting and if it attracts butterflies and bees.

What's in a name?

The international organization for plant nomenclature—Taxon—assigns plants their botanical names and makes changes as required. Although often referred to as Latin names, many have Greek roots or are named after people or places. Gardeners often feel uncomfortable using botanical names at first, but with use they become less intimidating. Be reassured that even the experts vary in their pronunciations.

Genus and species. Each species of plant has a name with two parts, for example, *Hosta sieboldiana*. This system of "binomial nomenclature" was devised by the Swedish botanist Linnaeus during the late 1700s. The first part (in this case, *Hosta*) is the name of the genus to which this plant belongs. A genus (plural: genera) is a group of plants that are closely related. This generic name always has the first letter capitalized.

Although not always specified in the encyclopedia section, it is more and more common for the generic name to be used also as a common name; examples include chyrsanthemum, delphinium, hosta and geranium. These common names can be pluralized by adding "s" (hostas), but the botanical name cannot (for example, *Hostas* is incorrect).

The second name in the example (*sieboldiana*) is called the "specific epithet" and is not capitalized. The combination of the two names (*Hosta sieboldiana*) forms the name of the species. Names of both genus and species are either italicized or underlined.

Because the name of a species depends on the genus in which it was originally placed, you can see that if it is subsequently assigned to another genus, its name changes dramatically. An example is *Anemone pulsatilla*, which was formerly *Pulsatilla vulgaris*. This can be very frustrating for gardeners.

The word species is either singular or plural, but the abbreviation sp. represents a singular usage, while spp. represents a plural usage.

Common names. In the title lines of each encylopedia entry, common names are shown in double quotation marks. There are no regulations regarding common names. Each country, and sometimes region, has its own favorite common names for a plant. In English, the suffix *wort* is often seen in common names: bloodwort, lungwort, soapwort and spiderwort. Wort is an ancient word meaning plant.

Subspecies and varieties. Some plant species have naturally occurring subgroups that are consistently distinct enough to warrant an additional designation, either variety or subspecies (abbreviated var. and ssp.) depending on the botanical details. For example, *Adiantum pedatum* var. *subpumilum* is a dwarf variety of our native maidenhair fern that grows on the rock cliffs of northwestern Vancouver Island. When plants of this variety are grown in the garden, they retain their dwarf growth habit, indicating a genetic rather than environmental cause for their diminutive size.

Cultivars. Cultivated varieties—as opposed to those that occur in the wild—are called cultivars. (See also page 9 for a discussion of cultivars.) Cultivar names are not underlined or italicized, but are enclosed in single quotation marks. In 1959, Taxon ruled that new cultivar names must be in modern language, to avoid confusion between botanical and cultivar names. You will often see old cultivar names such as 'Alba' and 'Rosea'; they would not be accepted today.

Hybrids. Some plants result from crossing two unrelated plants. These two parent plants may be of two different species, two genera or they may be cultivars or even hybrids themselves. To signify that it is a hybrid, a multiplication sign (×) is used in the plant's name. (See also page 10 for a discussion of hybrids.)

If the parents of a hybrid are from two separate **species**, the multiplication sign is placed between the generic name and the specific epithet. If two parent species are known and their names combine neatly, these can be used to make the new specific epithet. For instance, *Primula* × *bullesiana* is a hybrid of *Primula bulleyana* and *Primula beesiana*. If a hybrid has many parents, or parents with cumbersome names or unknown parents, the × may be used with a completely new specific epithet. For example, *Digitalis* × *mertonensis* is a hybrid of *D. grandiflora* and *D. purpurea*. Alternatively, the specific epithet may be dropped altogether and only a cultivar name used. Examples include *Hosta* 'Frances Williams', *Artemisia* 'Powis Castle' and *Sedum* 'Autumn Joy'.

If the parents of a hybrid are from two different **genera** (a less common occurrence), a multiplication sign is placed in front of the generic name. For example, × *Heucherella alba* is a hybrid of *Heuchera* × *brizoides* and *Tiarella wherryi*.

In either case, the × is not italicized and need not be pronounced, unless you wish to say "cross" or "hybrid" instead of the ×.

Synonyms. In the encyclopedia entries, names shown in parentheses are synonyms that are in common usage, but are obsolete. Many books and catalogues still use these names, so they are included here for reference.

Hort. (horticulture abbreviated) after a plant's botanical name indicates that although the species often goes under this name in horticultural circles, the name in fact belongs to a different species. For example, *Arabis caucasica* is often sold under the name of an entirely different species, A. *alpina*. Merely listing A. *alpina* as a synonym would suggest that it is an obsolete name; listing A. *alpina* Hort. as a synonym alludes to the mix-up. Botanists often despair over horticulturists' use of plant names.

Family names. In each entry, the name shown in capital letters is the name of the plant family to which the genus belongs. It is not necessary to capitalize the entire family name and it should not be italicized. The family name can usually be recognized by the ending **aceae** attached to the stem of the name of a genus within the family. Thus, LILIACEAE, the name for the lily family, is composed of the stem Lili, from the name of a genus in the family, with aceae attached. Six family names, with which you may have been familiar, have changed in accordance with these rules. Old family names are used in many references, but you will see the new family names in botanical gardens.

Former family name	New family name	Examples of family members
COMPOSITAE	ASTERACEAE	chrysanthemum, yarrow
CRUCIFERAE	BRASSICACEAE	candytuft, aubrietia
GRAMINAE	POACEAE	all true grasses
LABIATAE	LAMIACEAE	bee balm
LEGUMINOSAE	FABACEAE	lupine
UMBELLIFERAE	APICACEAE	masterwort, sea holly

A brief glossary

In the interest of making descriptions easier to understand for most readers, the use of botanical terminology has been kept to a minimum. There are, however, a dozen or so words that are indispensable in describing plants, even for the occasional gardener.

Alternate. An alternate arrangement of leaves is one in which the leaves are attached singly to each leaf node, on alternating sides of the stem.

Basal leaves are those that arise directly from the base of the plant, often in a rosette.

Bracts are modified leaves that are sometimes associated with flowers or flower-like structures. The best known example is the poinsettia, whose brightly colored bracts superficially resemble floral parts.

Calyx and sepals. The calyx is the protective outermost whorl of floral parts and may not be present in all flowers. It is most familiar to gardeners as the covering over a flower bud. The calyx may be green or colored and may resemble or even replace the flower's petals. When the calyx is separated into sections, these are called sepals. Japanese anemone and Christmas rose are examples of flowers with showy sepals instead of petals.

Compound. Compound leaves are divided into distinct leaf-like sections called leaflets. The leaflets can be in a number of arrangements. See also palmate and pinnate.

Crown. The base of a plant, where the stem and roots meet, is often referred to as the crown.

Disk florets. See inflorescence, below.

Inflorescence. The flowering part of a plant is called its inflorescence. While flowers may be borne singly at the end of stems, an inflorescence is often made up of many flowers in a number of arrangements. The inflorescence may be a tall, slender spike. The flowers may be arranged on much-divided branches. One common arrangement is that of a daisy-like flower head. In this dense cluster of flowers, the flowers of the central disk are called **disk florets** and those of the outer ring are called **ray florets.**

Leaflet. See compound.

Opposite. An opposite arrangement of leaves is one in which the leaves occur two at each leaf node, on opposite sides of the stem.

Palmate means in the shape of an open hand. Leaves can be palmately lobed, the maple leaf on the Canadian flag for example, or they can be palmately compound, with a number of separate leaflets joined at the base.

Pinnate means in the shape of a feather. Pinnately compound leaves have a double row of leaflets along a central leafstalk.

Pistil and stamens. The pistil is the female reproductive organ of a flower and the stamens are the male, pollen-bearing reproductive organs of a flower. In flowers with both, the pistil is usually in the center of the flower, surrounded by the stamens.

Rhizomes are stems, usually horizontal, that grow at or under ground level and throw up a succession of stems or leaves at their tips. German bearded irises are an example of a perennial with rhizomes.

Ray florets. See inflorescence.

Sepal See calyx.

Stamens. See pistil.

References

Botanical classification is subject to constant examination and revision, resulting in occasional changes of nomenclature. For the sake of consistency *Hortus Third* has been used as a definitive reference in the preparation of this book. Because few named cultivars are included in *Hortus Third*, Graham Stuart Thomas's book *Perennial Garden Plants* and Ruth Clausen and Nicolas Ekstrom's book *Perennials for American Gardens* are also used as references. *Hortus Third* was written before the current interest in grasses developed, so Roger Grounds's *Ornamental Grasses* is used for information on grass nomenclature.

Encyclopedia of Perennials

Achillea filipendulina "fernleaf yarrow"
Achillea millefolium "common yarrow" "milfoil"
Achillea 'Moonshine'
Achillea ptarmica "sneezeweed" "sneezewort" ASTERACEAE
(Figure 1-1)

Most of the one hundred or so species of yarrow have finely dissected, aromatic leaves that are alternate or in basal rosettes. Some yarrows are handsome garden plants; some are borderline weeds. The genus is named for Achilles, who is said to have used the herb to treat his soldiers' wounds. Most make good cut flowers, and, if picked while fresh and dried in a cool place, will retain their color for months.

Achillea millefolium is native to Europe and western Asia. The names milfoil and *millefolium* come from the Latin for one thousand leaves, describing the finely cut foliage. The multitude of common names indicate its medicinal uses: sanguinary, staunch-grass, bloodwort and carpenter's weed. Yarrow was also used to treat headache, toothache, hypertension, dysentery and many more complaints. Indeed, it was said to grow in churchyards as a reproach to the dead, who wouldn't have ended up there if they had consumed yarrow broth daily. The Chinese credit yarrow with mystical properties. In the ancient Chinese book of divination, the *I Ching*, or *Book of Changes*, forty-nine yarrow stalks are used to foretell the future.

As a garden plant, common yarrow is not as interesting as its history. It grows to about 2 feet (60 cm) tall, with deeply divided, narrow, dark green leaves, to 8 inches (20 cm) long. Many small flower heads combine to make a flattened inflorescence of white, pink or red, up to 2 inches (5 cm) across. Plants tend to be untidy—in need of frequent lifting and dividing—and floppy. 'Cerise Queen', a seed strain with darker flowers, is often sold in garden centers, but unless you are interested in it as a cut flower, it is not garden worthy.

The Galaxy series, new *A. millefolium* hybrids from Germany, have recently added more interest to this group. They bloom for months in a new range of colors for this species, including pink and yellow. Their long-lasting blooms fade to buff, giving the plant a multi-colored effect. Cultivars include:

Name	Height	Flower Color
'Appleblossom' ('Apfelblute')	3 feet (90 cm)	pink
'Great Expectations' ('Hoffnung')	2 feet (60 cm)	sandstone yellow
'Salmon Beauty' ('Lachsschoenheit')	3 feet (90 cm)	salmon pink
'The Beacon' ('Fanal')	2½ feet (75 cm)	crimson red

Achillea filipendulina and its hybrids are classics for the perennial border. The species is a native of the Caucasus and has been cultivated for almost two hundred years. Its best cultivar is 'Gold Plate', a handsome plant reaching 4–5 feet (1.2–1.5 m) in height. The leaves are pale gray green, to 10 inches (25 cm) long, each divided into many toothed and lobed leaflets, giving a feathery effect. Hundreds of small yellow flower heads cluster to form a flattened inflorescence, to 6 inches (15 cm) across. Fernleaf yarrow blooms in July and August. Although tall, plants are slender, especially when young, so space them 18 inches (45 cm) apart, placing other bushier plants in front. They contrast well with

Salvia × *superba*, summer-blooming monkshood, delphiniums and border phlox.

Achillea 'Coronation Gold' is similar to 'Gold Plate', but, being shorter and bushier, is better for most gardens. It reaches 2^1/$_2$–3^1/$_2$ feet (.75–1 m) with smaller heads above slightly gray foliage. It may need supporting where the soil is moist and rich, but stands up nicely on its own in poor dry soil. A 1952 hybrid of A. *filipendulina* and A. *clypeolata*, it blooms June to September and the basal leaves are evergreen. Plant it with one of the shorter *Salvia* × *superba* cultivars, such as 'East Friesland'.

Achillea 'Moonshine'. About his outstanding hybrid, Alan Bloom writes:

> Some years ago I took seed of . . . [A. *clypeolata*, A. *taygetea*] and 'Schwefelblute' as a mixture, but very few of the resultant plants having flowered, survived the first winter. One survivor did not flower and remained just for its silvery foliage. It was in a rather shady place for two more years until with a vacant sunny space I divided the now large clump to fill it. The immediate result was a show of bright lemon yellow flowers, and the award of a name. Since then 'Moonshine' has become the most popular achillea hybrid ever introduced, for it retains its leafage so well, flowers freely, and is constitutionally strong. (Alan Bloom. *The Garden*. June 1979, page 247.)

'Moonshine' has ferny, silver foliage that is evergreen and it grows to 2 feet (60 cm) in height. It combines well with *Salvia* × *superba*, creating a softer contrast than the gold fernleaf yarrows.

Achillea ptarmica 'The Pearl' is supposed to have small, double, white flowers grouped into loose inflorescences. But, as it is usually sold in shops, it is generally not the true clone, but rather is a seed-grown imitation, often lacking its only redeeming characteristic, the double flowers. It is a sprawling, invasive perennial, worth planting only if the true double form can be obtained, and then best planted in a remote corner of the garden for a supply of cut flowers. The species is native to Europe and Asia. The gray leaves are narrow, to 4 inches (10 cm) long. It grows to 2^1/$_2$ feet (75 cm) high.

Bloomtime: All *Achillea* begin blooming in June/July and most continue until August/September. ('Moonshine' should be deadheaded when flowers fade for longest succession of bloom.)

Height: 2–5 feet (.6–1.5 m), depending on the species and cultivar.

Spread: A. *filipendulina*, 'Moonshine' and 'Coronation Gold': 18 inches (45 cm); A *millefolium* cultivars: 2 feet (60 cm).

Light and soil: All are best in full sun and well-drained soil to which some organic matter has been added. A. *millefolium* and A. *filipendulina* will tolerate poor, dry soil, and A. *ptarmica* will tolerate damp soil.

Care and propagation: As with many fuzzy-leaf plants, it is safest to plant in the spring, but one does not always have the choice. In good soil, the taller types may need staking. Propagate from seed (except named cultivars that are not true from seed) or by division.

Pests and diseases: Generally trouble-free.

Frost hardiness: To zone 3.

Aconitum species and hybrids "monkshood" "aconite" "helmet flower"
RANUNCULACEAE
(Figure 1-2)

Note: All parts of the plant are extremely poisonous.

Since ancient times, the various species of the deadly monkshood have figured prominently in human life and lore. In Greek mythology, the strong and brave hero, Hercules, undertook twelve labors as penance for killing his wife and children in a fit of insanity. His twelfth labor was to visit Hades and return with Cerberus, the many-headed dog who guarded the underworld. During the abduction, the furious animal spit venomous froth and where it fell to earth arose the poisonous monkshood. This event transpired on a hill named Aconitus, hence the generic name.

The juice from various species of monkshood was used throughout Europe and Asia as a poison in hunting; in war it was used to contaminate wells against advancing armies. *Aconitum vulpina* was used as a poison bait for wolves in France, Germany and Russia, explaining another common name: wolfsbane.

Despite warnings by successive generations of garden writers, monkshoods continue to be cultivated in gardens. In 1726, Richard Bradley mentioned a gentleman in France who perished from "eating of only six or seven of the Blossoms in a Sallet." (Which, by the way, shows us that eating flowers in salad was not invented in California in the 1980s!) Another writer—with a dry wit—wrote that to discard all kinds of monkshood would be "rather fastidious, inasmuch as the English are not so passionately attached to a vegetable diet as to eat garden herbage indiscriminately." After 250 years, the English still have a reputation for being less than adventurous in the salad department.

Monkshoods are easy to recognize from their unusual flowers. Borne along tall stalks, they look like the helmets of ancient Greek warriors. The flowers are pollinated by bumblebees. Their alternate leaves are glossy dark green and are palmately lobed, each section pointed and toothed. They are up to 6 inches (15 cm) across. They look similar to the leaves of delphiniums, a close relative.

In general, there are two groups of monkshoods: those that grow from tuberous roots and those with fibrous roots. A. *henryi* (native to China), A. *napellus* and A. *pyramidale* (both native to northern Europe) are three species with small tubers; they have been used to breed the cultivars most often sold. These species and their cultivars bloom in summer. Not even Alan Bloom, who has done much of the hybridizing, is sure which of his plants are closest to which species, so there is no point in being too concerned about the taxonomy here. Hybrids that fall into this group include the following:

Name	Height	Flower color	Bloomtime
A. × *bicolor*	3¹/₂ feet (1 m)	blue and white	June–Aug
'Blue Sceptre'	2–3 feet (60–90 cm)	blue and white	July–Aug
'Bressingham Spire'	2¹/₂ feet (75 cm)	deep violet blue	July–Aug
'Newry Blue'	5 feet (1.5 m)	deep blue	June–July
'Spark's Variety'	4–5 feet (1.2–1.5 m)	royal blue	July–Aug

Autumn-flowering monkshoods have larger tubers, up to 2 inches (5 cm) across. Their leaves are attractive for the summer months before the flowers open, especially if given the rich, moist soil and light shade they prefer. Most widely available (usually only by mail-order) is a native of eastern Asia, A. *carmichaelii*, often listed as A. *fischeri*. It has lavender blue flowers in September and October. The cultivars 'Arendsii' and 'Kelmscott' (worth seeing at the UBC Botanical garden in September) have flowers of a richer shade of blue. The fall monkshoods combine well with *Cimicifuga simplex*, *Polygonum amplexicaule* and *Sedum spectabile* and grow 4–6 feet (1.2–1.8 m) high.

The most common cultivar in the fibrous-rooted department is 'Ivorine', which Alan Bloom selected from a group of seedlings of yet another northern European species—A. *lycoctonum* (A. *septentrionalis*).

It has a neat habit, growing to about 3 feet (90 cm) and producing ivory flowers beginning in late May and continuing for weeks. It does not need as much dividing or require the rich soil of the tuberous-rooted types.
Bloomtime: See descriptions above.
Height: 2–5 feet (.6–1.5 m), depending on the cultivar.
Spread: 18 inches (45 cm).
Light and soil: The autumn-flowering monkshoods require part shade, the others full sun or part shade. Plant in moist or even wet soil with lots of organic matter.
Care and propagation: Despite their height, most monkshoods do not need staking, especially if rich soil is provided. They are most attractive with other perennials in front of them to hide their "knobby knees." The monkshoods grown from small tubers tend to become congested. About every three years in the fall, lift the plants. The tubers are round and point upwards. They should be divided and replanted 5 inches (13 cm) deep, with plenty of organic matter. The others may be left undisturbed for years.

Named cultivars should be propagated by division. The species can be divided or grown from seed; they need a 6-week cold treatment to break dormancy and may still take up to a year to germinate. Although seed of some named cultivars, 'Newry Blue' for example, is offered by seed houses, it will produce variable results.
Pests and diseases: Generally trouble-free, and not usually eaten by deer.
Frost hardiness: To zone 2.

Adiantum pedatum "maidenhair fern" POLYPODIACEAE
(Figure 1-3)

This species of the dainty maidenhair fern is native to North America and east Asia and flourishes in the forests of the Pacific coastal region. It is easy to recognize: its fronds have a wiry, shiny black stalk about 1–2 feet (30–60 cm) long. This stalk divides into a spray of 8 to 24 shorter stalks, each bearing two rows of bright green leaflets (pinnae). The effect is fresh and delicate, but the plants themselves are amazingly tough and easy to grow. Maidenhair fern combines well with dwarf rhododendrons and shade-loving perennials, such as hostas and hardy geraniums.

Adiantum pedatum var. *pumilum* is native to the coastal rock cliffs of northwestern Vancouver island. It grows to a diminutive 8 inches (20 cm) and is available from fern specialists. Avoid collecting native plants from the wild; the survival rate is low and many wild species have become endangered.

Bloomtime: Like all ferns, maidenhair does not bear flowers. It is grown for its beautiful foliage.

Height: The species grows to 2 feet (60 cm); *pumilum* grows to 8 inches (20 cm).

Spread: To 2½ feet (75 cm); 8 inches (20 cm) for *pumilum*.

Light and soil: Maidenhair fern flourishes in very shady places where few other plants will grow and can also be grown in light shade. It prefers moist soil with lots of organic matter, but established plants will tolerate a surprising amount of drought. It is not, however, tolerant of wind.

Care and propagation: Maidenhair fern requires little care other than cutting the dried fronds to ground level in the fall if desired. Propagation by division in autumn or spring is the easiest method for most gardeners. The rhizomes are quite strong—use a sharp knife or a small saw to divide them. Propagation from the spores is explained in chapter 5.

Pests and diseases: Generally trouble-free.

Frost hardiness: To zone 3.

Alchemilla alpina (A. *conjuncta*) "alpine Lady's mantle"
Alchemilla mollis and/or *Alchemilla vulgaris* "Lady's mantle" ROSACEAE (Figure 1-4)

Alchemilla mollis. Lady's mantle has beautiful soft gray green leaves, rounded and ruffled, up to 5 inches (13 cm) across. The common name, originally Our Lady's mantle, compares the leaves to the headdress worn by Mary, mother of Jesus, and was recorded as long ago as 1550.

Dew and raindrops caught on the leaves look like drops of quicksilver. To sixteenth-century alchemists, dew was considered to be magical; it was carefully collected from the leaves of Lady's mantle and used in various potions, hence the generic name *Alchemilla.*

The flowers—tiny, 8-pointed, lime green stars—appear in intricately branched inflorescences from June to August. Plants become a rounded mound 12–18 inches (30–45 cm) high. The form generally grown in gardens—larger than the common species—is thought to have been collected in Asia Minor in 1874. In the past few decades, English flower arrangers have done much to promote Lady's mantle. Its flowers are such an unusual color that they naturally lend themselves to floral and foliage associations, whether for vase or border.

The taxonomy relating to *Alchemilla* is confusing because this genus often reproduces asexually; seed is produced without cross-pollination, so seedlings are usually a clone of the parents. It is difficult to determine whether plant populations are different clones of one species, or two different species. This is the case with A. *mollis* and A. *vulgaris*.

Alchemilla alpina. The alpine Lady's mantle, native to the mountains of Europe, was grown in gardens before its larger cousin. Its leaves are palmately compound, with five to seven leaflets, each with small teeth at the tip. The undersides of the leaves are covered with a layer of shimmering, silky white hairs that peek around to the top side of the leaf, framing the leaf margins in silver. The flowers are a scaled-down version of Lady's mantle. Foliage looks fresh right up to the end of the summer.

Bloomtime: June to August.

Height: A. *alpina*: 5–8 inches (13–20 cm); A *mollis*: 12–18 inches (30–45 cm).

Spread: A. *alpina*: 12 inches (30 cm); A. *mollis*: 12–18 inches (30–45 cm).

Light and soil: Plant in full sun or light shade in a moist but well-drained soil. A. *mollis* tolerates damp soil and its foliage will scorch if grown in too much sun and dry soil.

Care and propagation: Cut flowering stems back to 1 inch (2.5 cm) above the soil line after blooming. (Some gardeners recommend cutting all the leaves back to ground level after flowering, top-dressing with a mixture of wet peat and bonemeal and watering well. It is a bit extreme, but will produce a new carpet of the lovely leaves.) Lady's mantle will self-seed if old flowers are not removed, which can be a blessing or a nuisance, depending on your point of view. Seedlings can easily be discarded, transplanted or given away. Plants may also be propagated by division in the fall or spring or grown from seed.

Pests and diseases: Generally trouble-free.

Frost hardiness: To zone 3.

Alyssum montanum "mountain-gold" "madwort"
Aurinia saxatilis (*Alyssum saxatile*) "basket-of-gold" "gold dust"
BRASSICACEAE
(Figure 2-5)

Very closely related, these two species both form a rounded clump of gray green leaves and are covered with bright yellow flowers in spring. Both are wonderful for trailing over retaining walls and for the front of a border, spilling onto a path. Their inflorescences are clusters of tiny, 1/4-inch (.6-cm) golden flowers, each with four notched petals.

Alyssum montanum, a native of Europe, has leaves up to 1 inch (2.5 cm) long with straight margins.

Aurinia saxatilis, native to both Europe and Turkey, has been in cultivation since before 1710. It was formerly placed in the genus *Alyssum*. It has narrow leaves up to 8 inches (20 cm) long with an undulating leaf margin. They are softly fuzzy and rounded at the tip. There are a number of named cultivars of this species. 'Compacta' has been grown in gardens since 1872 and is consistently dwarf even from seed. 'Sulphureum', also usually grown from seed, is sulfur yellow. 'Citrinum' is a cool lemony color, the double-flowered 'Flore Pleno' ('Pleno') is excellent, and there is a new clone named 'Sunnyborder Apricot' that has apricot flowers.

Bloomtime: April to May, with a few flowers in August and September if cut back after spring bloom.

Height: 10–18 inches (25–45 cm), depending on the species and cultivar (and whether or not it is pruned back after blooming).

Spread: 12–18 inches (30–45 cm).

Light and soil: Full sun and an average, well-drained soil. Both species tolerate dry soil.

Care and propagation: Easy to grow. Cut off old flower stalks after the blooms have faded, cutting about 1 inch (2.5 cm) into the stalks to encourage a compact habit and repeat bloom in the late summer and early fall. Propagate from seed (except for double-flowered and variegated cultivars) or from cuttings.

Pests and diseases: FLEA BEETLES, SLUGS and SNAILS.

Frost hardiness: *Alyssum montanum*: to zone 3; *Aurinia saxatilis*: to zone 4.

Anemone species and hybrids "Japanese anemones"
Anemone pulsatilla (*Pulsatilla vulgaris*) "pasqueflower" RANUNCULACEAE
(Figure 1-5 and 1-6)

Japanese anemones were given their common name by a German employee of the Dutch East India Company who lived in Nagasaki from 1682 to 1686. Dr. Cleyer described *Anemone hupehensis* var. *japonica*, which was in fact a variety of a Chinese species that had been grown in Japan for some time.

In 1844, the famous plant-hunter Robert Fortune sent live plants of the original Chinese species A. *hupehensis* to England. He had discovered them growing in the graveyards around Shanghai. Once it reached England, it was crossed with a Nepalese species, A. *vitifolia*. Most of the Japanese anemones grown in gardens today are descendants of this cross and are called A. × *hybrida*, also listed as A. *japonica* and A. × *elegans*.

Japanese anemones have handsome dark green leaves, some basal and some along the flower stalks. The leaves are attractive for most of the winter. The basal leaves of all Japanese anemones except A. *vitifolia* are palmately compound, up to 6 inches (15 cm) across, with three toothed and pointed leaflets. (Leaves along the stem may be lobed rather than compound.) A. *vitifolia*—meaning grape leaf—is appropriately named; its leaves resemble large grape leaves.

What appear to be petals of the Japanese anemones are actually sepals—true petals are lacking—and a beautiful ring of golden stamens surrounds a light green knob of pistils. All are excellent cut flowers, and even the knobby seed heads are attractive in flower arrangements. Flowers vary from single to double in various shades of white and pink, as follows:

Name	Height	Flower description
A. *hupehensis*	2¹/₂ feet (75 cm)	single; wide rose pink sepals
A. *hup*. var. *japonica*	2¹/₂ feet (75 cm)	double; narrow pink sepals
A. × *hybrida* cultivars (all have broad sepals):		
'Bressingham Glow'	2 feet (60 cm)	semidouble; rose red
'Honorine Jobert'	4 feet (120 cm)	single; white
'Prince Henry'	2 feet (60 cm)	single; deep pink
'Queen Charlotte'	2 feet (60 cm)	single; pink
'September Charm'	2¹/₂ feet (75 cm)	single; very large pink
A. *vitifolia*	3–4 feet (90–120 cm)	single; white

Anemone pulsatilla. This beautiful perennial was once common in its native Britain and Europe, but it is now rare in the wild. Pasqueflower was cultivated since before 1596, but was of no medicinal value and was therefore undervalued. Its one practical application was in the production of a green dye for dying Easter eggs.

In early spring, the pasqueflower sends up shoots covered with silky hairs that catch the dew and glisten in the sun. Its purple cups and golden stamens are simple yet charming, and it forms elegant fluffy seed heads that are decorative for months. Each flower has six pointed sepals. There are different color forms, including white and burgundy; many of the darker ones are hybrids with other species. The leaves are pinnately divided into linear segments and keep a remarkably long time in water— handy for adding to small bouquets.

Bloomtime: Japanese anemones: August to October; pasqueflower: April and May.

Height: Japanese anemones: 2–5 feet (.6–1.5 m). They do not reach their full height until at least the second season after planting, and it will vary a bit depending on light conditions. Pasqueflower: 12 inches (30 cm)

Spread: Japanese anemones: 1½–2 feet (45–60 cm). Plants gradually creep into the surrounding planting area, but I couldn't imagine a more welcome gate-crasher. Pasqueflower: 15 inches (38 cm).

Light and soil: Full sun or part shade in a well-drained soil to which plenty of organic matter has been added.

Care and propagation: Little care is required other than cutting down old stems. Leaves are evergreen in a mild winter, so this job can be delayed until the spring. It is best to leave new plants undisturbed for several years. Despite their height, Japanese anemones do not require staking. Propagate both Japanese anemones and pasqueflowers by division in fall or spring. Better still, for both resent being disturbed, take root cuttings in the late winter or fall. Pasqueflowers can be grown from seed; color forms will often come true from seed. Sow seed as soon as it is ripe (July) if possible. Species of Japanese anemones can also be grown from seed.

Pests and diseases: Japanese anemones may be bothered by APHIDS, CATERPILLARS, CUTWORMS, SNAILS and SLUGS. Pasqueflowers are generally trouble-free.

Frost hardiness: To zone 6; except A. *vitifolia*: to zone 7.

Anthemis tinctoria "golden marguerite" ASTERACEAE
(Figure 1-7)

Anthemis tinctoria is an easy front-of-the-border perennial that is excellent for cutting and useful for screening other plants such as monkshood, phlox and aster, which become untidy at their bases. The flower heads are daisy-like, with a yellow disk and a single row of white, golden or pale yellow ray florets. The foliage is gray green and finely cut. 'Grallagh Gold' is golden orange, 'Beauty of Grallagh' is gold and 'Moonlight' is pale yellow. 'E.C. Buxton' should be pale yellow (as it was introduced) but the ones sold are usually white. The species is native to Europe and has been cultivated for over four hundred years; the flowers yield a rich yellow dye. It is related to A. *nobilis*, the well-known chamomile.

Bloomtime: July and August.

Height: 2¹/₂ feet (75 cm).

Spread: 15–18 inches (38–45 cm).

Light and soil: Full sun and well-drained, not-too-rich soil, for best flower production.

Care and propagation: In rich soil, place woody twigs around the crown to support stems. Cut stems as the flower heads fade, to encourage more bloom. Cut away old stems before new ones emerge in spring, so that new stems can get lots of sun. Divide every second year, replanting the vigorous outer sections of the clump. This is the best method of propagation. Seedlings are not as good as the named parents, so they are usually discarded.

Pests and diseases: Generally trouble-free.

Frost hardiness: To zone 3.

Aquilegia hybrids "columbine" "granny's bonnet" RANUNCULACEAE
(Figure 1-8)

There are about seventy species of the distinctive and popular columbine in the wild in Europe, Asia and North America. They have fascinated gardeners since the Middle Ages and, because they are easy to hybridize and grow from seed, there are dozens of hybrids in cultivation. They make good cut flowers and work well in mixed borders or lightly shaded woodland setting. The small species are attractive in the rock garden.

The flowers of columbines are quite distinctive. Appearing at the end of the tall, branched stalks, the flowers have five alternating petals and petal-like sepals. The petals are flared at the front around the bright yellow stamens and taper into a hollow, backward-projecting spur. The whole effect is delicate and quite charming. The compound leaves, which cluster at the base of the plant and along the flower stalks, are divided into gray green, lobed leaflets. Many seeds are borne in the paper-like, tapering brown capsules.

The most common garden columbines are not true species, but hybrids of two or more species. Those with hooked spurs usually indicate derivation from A. *vulgaris*; those with long straight spurs from A. *caerulea* and A. *chrysantha*. Most hybrids are short-lived and need to be started again from seed every few years. Alternatively, allow seed pods to form and let plants seed themselves. Of the many seed strains, 'McKana's Giant Hybrids' are the most popular. They grow to 3 feet (90 cm) tall and have blooms in a wide range of colors, including white, pink, red, yellow and violet. Flowers are large, have long spurs and are often bicolor, having sepals and petals of two different colors.

'Music', a recent award-winning introduction from Germany, is a compact columbine that has the long spurs and grace of the taller hybrids, yet with strong, sturdy, wind-resistant stems. It reaches 18–20 inches (45–50 cm) and is available in six separate colors—blue and white, pink and white, red and white, yellow, red and gold, and white— and as a mixture.

'Spring Song Mixed' reaches the same height as 'McKana's Giant Hybrids' but is reported to be more vigorous and floriferous and to have a wider color range. Flowers sometimes have more than one row of petals and are excellent for cutting.

'Nora Barlow', introduced by Alan Bloom, is a double columbine that has no spurs. Flowers are red, white and green, and look more like small dahlias than columbines. Its height is 2 feet (60 cm) and it makes an effective cut flower. Ninety percent of the seedlings are true to the parent; they must be selected when blooming.

Not generally available from seed, 'Hensol Harebell' is a hybrid, possibly between A. *alpina* and A. *vulgaris*. It has deep blue flowers with incurved spurs, grows 24–30 inches (60–75 cm) tall, and blooms over a long period. Plants are long-lived, unlike many columbine hybrids. It self-seeds and seedlings vary in color. You are most likely to acquire it as a plant through mail-order catalogues, but it is worth hunting down this superb columbine.

In addition to the columbines discussed here, there are many excellent species available from seed catalogues.

Bloomtime: May to June, unless otherwise noted.

Height: 18–36 inches (45–90 cm), depending on the species or cultivar.

Spread: 18 inches (45 cm).

Light and soil: Moist but well-drained soil in sun or very light shade.

Care and propagation: Columbines require little care other than deadheading (although the seed capsules are also decorative), and cutting stems to the ground in late fall or early spring. They are easy to grow from seed. Sow seed as soon as you can get it—July and August from plants you have access to, or March if ordered from seed houses. (Seed from garden plants will not necessarily be true as plants hybridize easily.) The species are a bit trickier to grow from seed and may require a cold treatment to break dormancy. Clumps can also be divided in fall or spring, but because individual plants are fairly short-lived, seed propagation makes the most sense.

Pests and diseases: APHIDS, LEAF MINERS, POWDERY MILDEW and SPIDER MITES. Deer do not usually eat columbines.

Frost hardiness: To zone 5.

Arabis caucasica (*Arabis albida, Arabis alpina* Hort.)
Arabis × *arendsii* both called "rock cress" BRASSICACEAE
(Figure 1-9)

Arabis caucasica is a member of a team of trailing perennials that is perfect for creating a softer effect at the top of retaining walls and for adding color to rock gardens. It can also be grown at the front of a perennial border, especially trailing over onto a path. It blooms between March and May, with clusters of four-petaled flowers closely resembling those of its cousin aubrietia. The wild species, found on cliffs and rocky places from southern Europe to Iran, has clusters of small white flowers to 1¼ inches (3 cm) across. The small, gray green leaves are arranged in rosettes and have a few teeth along the margin.

The cultivar 'Flore Pleno' (or 'Plena') has double flowers that are good for cutting. The striking 'Variegata' has a margin of cream around each leaf, although it may revert to solid green.

Arabis × *arendsii* is one of the many outstanding perennials introduced by Georg Arends. He crossed A. *caucasica* with the pink-flowered A. *aubrietioides*, a native of the mountains in Turkey. The resulting hybrid was introduced in 1914 as A. *albida rosea*, a name often seen today. It is very similar to A. *caucasica* in foliage and habit. Seed strains include 'Spring Charm' (carmine) and 'Rosabella' (rose red).

Bloomtime: Most bloom March to May, some earlier and some later.

Height: To 9 inches (23 cm), depending on the species or cultivar.

Spread: 12–24 inches (30–60 cm).

Light and soil: Full sun or part shade in well-drained soil.

Care and propagation: Easy to grow—just trim the stalks of the faded blooms, cutting about 1 inch (2.5 cm) down into the leafy part of the stems to encourage compact growth. Propagate from seed (except 'Flore-Pleno' and 'Variegata'), by division, or from cuttings of nonflowering rosettes. Rock cress is not a long-lived perennial and may need to be replaced after several years.

Pests and diseases: Generally trouble-free, but rock cress is occasionally troubled by CLUBROOT and VIRUS diseases.

Frost hardiness: To zone 4.

Armeria maritima
Armeria plantaginea
Armeria pseudarmeria (A. *formosa*, A. *latifolia*) all called "thrift" "sea pink" PLUMBAGINACEAE
(Figure 1-10)

Growing as neat tufts and gradually spreading to form mats, thrifts have evergreen, grass-like leaves and globular inflorescences on strong stems. To 1 inch (2.5 cm) across, each is made up of dozens of tiny, five-petaled flowers in shades of pink, red or white, depending on the cultivar. At the base of each inflorescence is a distinctive, papery collar. Thrift is attractive year-round and can be used to edge borders, in rock gardens and in containers. All three species are native to Europe and attract butterflies.

Armeria maritima grows wild near the seashore (hence the name "sea pink"), its individual tufts spreading to form mats that stabilize the sand. It is the most common thrift in cultivation and was used in Tudor times to edge the elaborate knot gardens that were popular then. Its leaves are up to 4 inches (10 cm) long and the flowers sit atop 12-inch (30-cm) stems. This species is variable in nature and breeds freely with other species, so some of the cultivars for sale may be hybrids. 'Alba' is white,

'Dusseldorf Pride' is nearly red, 'Vindictive' is rose red, and 'Ruby Glow' is deep rose.

A. plantaginea has larger leaves, up to 10 inches (25 cm) long and ¹/₂ inch (1.3 cm) wide. The popular cultivar 'Bees' Ruby' (named after the British seedsman Bees) grows up to 24 inches (60 cm) tall with flower heads of bright ruby red, 1–1¹/₂ inches (2.5–4 cm) across.

A. pseudarmeria has leaves up to 10 inches (25 cm) long and ³/₄ inch (2 cm) wide. The seed strain 'Formosa Hybrids' gives a mixture of the common thrift colors, but also includes terra cotta shades, for gardeners preferring less vibrant red tones.

Note: Some taxonomists do not recognize A. *pseudarmeria* as a separate species, but group it with A. *plantaginea*.

Bloomtime: A. *maritima*: May to July; A. *plantaginea* and A. *pseudarmeria*: June to August.

Height: A. *maritima* is variable, 6–18 inches (15–45 cm); A. *plantaginea* and A. *pseudarmeria*: 2 feet (60 cm).

Spread: 12 inches (30 cm).

Light and soil: Full sun and a well-drained, preferably sandy soil that is not too dry.

Care and propagation: Remove blooms when faded. Thrifts can be propagated by division or from seed sown in spring.

Pests and diseases: Generally trouble-free and not usually eaten by deer.

Frost hardiness: A. *maritima*: to zone 3; A. *pseudarmeria* and A. *plantaginea*: to zone 6; ('Bees' Ruby': to zone 5).

Artemisia abrotanum "southernwood" "old man" "lad's love"
Artemisia absinthium "common wormwood" "absinthe"
Artemisia lactiflora "white mugwort"
Artemisia ludoviciana (A. *albula*)
Artemisia 'Powis Castle'
Artemisia schmidtiana
Artemisia stellerana "beach wormwood" "old woman" "dusty miller"
ASTERACEAE
(Figures 1-11 and 1-12)

Artemisia is the genus of the sagebrush; most are aromatic and native to dry areas of the northern hemisphere. All but two of the species described here are grown for their beautiful silver foliage.

A. abrotanum has been cultivated since before A.D. 25, when the Greek writer Dioscorides described it as having "very small leaves, as if it were . . . furnished with hair." Since that time, writers of all eras have praised its value in treating colds and asthma, in dying wool and in keeping moths away. It is native to Europe, and its name in Russian means God's tree.

Southernwood makes a rounded subshrub with fine, aromatic, light green leaves. It grows to about 3 feet by 18 inches (90 cm by 45 cm) and makes a good foil for plants with larger leaves or bright colors, such as red roses. Although southernwood's flowers are insignificant, sprigs of foliage last indefinitely in water (often rooting), their delicate foliage adding texture to arrangements. Prune off about two-thirds of the previous season's growth in spring to keep plants compact. Southernwood is hardy to zone 6.

A. absinthium, a native of Europe, has a fascinating history. Pliny the Elder, who lived in Verona from A.D. 23 to A.D. 70, records that even then it was made into the alcoholic beverage *Absinthes*. In the early 1900s, the liqueur absinthe was very popular in France, but was subsequently banned for health reasons because it was said to cause hallucinations and mental derangement.

A. absinthium is generally represented in cultivation by 'Lambrook Silver', a selection made by the English plantswoman Margery Fish. It grows to 2¹/₂ feet (75 cm). It has gray, much-divided leaves and tiny flowers, produced in July and August, that are wrapped in gray foliage. It is slightly floppy, so insert small branches into soil around the crown for the stems to grow through. It is frost hardy to zone 4.

A. lactiflora is an interesting green-leaf artemisia. It reaches 4–5 feet (1.2–1.5 m) and produces a branched inflorescence with hundreds of tiny off-white flower heads in August and September. You have to look hard to see the family resemblance here, but each small flower head is actually a cluster of a half-dozen or so individual florets, much as they are clustered in the disk of a daisy. The pinnately compound leaves are dark green, lighter beneath. The general effect is somewhat like a huge astilbe. White mugwort is a native of China and India. It doesn't usually need staking and makes an excellent back-of-the-border plant. It is hardy to zone 4.

A. ludoviciana is a North American species that grows to 3 feet (90 cm). It has narrow, silver gray leaves along the slender, erect, unbranched stems. The leaves are variable in shape—sometimes lobed. It is usually represented in cultivation by two cultivars. 'Silver King' has white fuzz on both surfaces of its leaves, which grow to 2 inches (5 cm) long. 'Silver Queen' is slightly shorter, with more fuzz on the leaves. The running roots can be controlled by dividing the clump every few years. Plants may flop in rich soil; insert small branches around the crown for the stems to grow through. It is frost hardy to zone 5.

A. 'Powis Castle' is thought to be a hybrid of A. *absinthium* and the beautiful, but less hardy, A. *arborescens* (zone 9). It makes a rounded plant, to 2–3 feet (60–90 cm) tall and 2 feet (60 cm) wide. The branches are somewhat brittle and break easily. Plant 'Powis Castle' in a place where it will not be damaged and stake with small branches. The aromatic leaves are divided many times into very fine segments—the plant looks like a mound of silver lace. Although it is frost hardy in the Pacific coastal region, it often becomes woody and less attractive in its second year. Because it is easy to grow from cuttings, it is worth starting with new plants every year or two. It rarely blooms, but the foliage lasts for a long time in water, making it useful for flower arranging. Do not prune the plant too hard in spring, or it may be damaged and not recover. Hardiness rating has not been firmly established, but it is probably hardy to zone 7.

A. schmidtiana shows its preference for hot, dry climates more than the other artemisias described here. A native of Japan, it forms a soft mound of thread-like silver leaves crowded along the branches. Although it is very beautiful, it often doesn't survive the winter dampness in most parts of the Pacific coastal region. This would be an excellent choice for drier parts of the region, such as the Gulf Islands. Its small flower heads, produced in September, are not noticeable because they are wrapped in silver foliage. Most common are 'Nana', to 3 inches (8 cm) in height and 'Silver Mound', to 12 inches (30 cm) in height. All are frost hardy to zone 4.

A. stellerana grows to 3 feet (90 cm) and has 1/4-inch (.6-cm) yellow flower heads in August and September. The leaves and stems are covered with fine white hairs, giving them the appearance of silver felt. The species is native to northeast Asia.

The cultivar 'Silver Brocade' is a 1990 introduction under the Plant Introduction Scheme of the UBC Botanical Garden. It is more prostrate than the species, to 6 inches (15 cm) high and 2 feet (60 cm) wide. The leaves are cut into wide lobes, somewhat reminiscent of oak leaves. It is excellent for rockeries and containers. Although not widely tested yet, it should be frost hardy to zone 3 or 4.

Bloomtime: All except 'Powis Castle' (which rarely blooms) bloom between July and September (see above). The only species grown for its flowers is A. *lactiflora*. The other species are sometimes trimmed back lightly when they begin to bloom, either because the flowers are unattractive or to increase bushiness, or both.

Height and spread: See above.

Light and soil: All, except A. *lactiflora*, require full sun and perfect drainage and tolerate dry soil. A. *lactiflora* grows in full sun or part shade and thrives with added organic matter and moisture.

Care and propagation: In general, artemisias are easy to grow. Plant the silver-leaf types in the spring if possible. As noted above, some tall species should be staked with small branches placed near the crown for the stems to grow through. Named cultivars can be propagated by division or from cuttings. Species can be grown from seed, division or cuttings; A. *abrotanum* becomes woody at the base and is not easy to divide, but cuttings root very easily.

Pests and diseases: Generally trouble-free.

Frost hardiness: See above.

Aster alpinus "alpine aster"
Aster amellus "Italian aster"
Aster × *frikartii*
Aster novae-angliae "Michaelmas daisy" "New England aster"
Aster novi-belgii "Michaelmas daisy" ASTERACEAE
(Figure 2-1)

The name given to this genus, and in turn to its family, is the Greek word for star and refers to its daisy-like flower heads. Many species of aster are from North America. Sent back to Britain and Europe in the late sixteenth and early seventeenth centuries, they touched off a flurry of aster hybridizing, resulting in some outstanding cultivars that are seen in gardens every fall. Although of no medicinal or culinary value, asters have always been enjoyed for their simple and colorful blooms. (Note: do not confuse perennial asters with the annual China asters—*Callistephus*.)

Aster alpinus is the early summer bloomer in the group (May and June) and is a native of the mountains of Europe and Asia. Plants grow to 6–12 inches (15–30 cm) in height and spread to 12–18 inches (30–45 cm) across. They have narrow gray green leaves up to 2 inches (5 cm) long. The flowers, generally one per stalk, are up to 2 inches (5 cm) across, in shades of lilac, reddish purple and white, with gold or yellow centers. Popular seed strains include 'Albus' (white), 'Dark Beauty' (violet blue) and 'Happy End' (bright pink).

Aster amellus, a native of Europe and western Asia, grows to 2 feet (60 cm) in height and blooms from August to October. Its leaves, up to 5 inches (13 cm) long are rough in texture and gray green, tapering to a point at both ends. The 2-inch (5-cm) flowers are usually in clusters in shades of blue, pink or violet. Some cultivars are floppy, but 'Violet Queen', compact at 16 inches (40 cm), and rosy lavender 'Nocturne', 32 inches (80 cm), are excellent.

Aster × frikartii is a hybrid of *A. amellus* and *A. thomsonii* (native to the western Himalayas). It has an attractive open growth habit—especially appealing to those who find the habit of some asters too congested—reaching 3 feet (90 cm) in height. Flowers are large and lavender blue, borne from July to October. It is considered by many to be the best of all the asters. 'Wonder of Staffa' is excellent, and the respected British horticulturist Graham Stuart Thomas recommends the cultivar 'Mönsch' as "not only the finest perennial aster; it is one of the best six plants; and should be in every garden."

The closely related *Aster × 'Flora's Delight'* is a hybrid of *A. amellus* and *A. thomsonii* 'Nanus'. Selected by Alan Bloom, it has gray green foliage and pale lilac flower heads with yellow disks.

Michaelmas daisies. *Aster novi-belgii* was described and identified by a German botanist in 1687 and named after New Netherlands—later to become New York City—where the seed was collected. Over the years, particularly in the early 1900s, hybridizing was done with *A. laevis* and the dwarf *A. dumosus*, and many cultivars were produced. The narrow leaves are dark green, pointed at each end, up to 7 inches (18 cm) long and not particularly attractive. Plants of the taller cultivars are lanky, so they are best sited in the garden with something in front of them and they should be staked. Unless kept moist, the bottom leaves will shrivel and fall off. This particular species and its hybrids are prone to wilt diseases.

Despite these negative traits, Michaelmas daisies remain popular with a great many gardeners. They bloom in a wide range of jewel tones—violet, wine red, carmine, light blue, rose pink—and seem to actually glow in the soft light of autumn. They also make excellent cut flowers and are readily available in garden shops in the fall. Buy them in bloom to get the shade that appeals to you the most.

The dwarf Michaelmas daisies, listed by some nurseries as cultivars of A. *novi-belgii* and others as cultivars of A. *dumosus*, have a rounded compact habit, suitable for the front of the border. Popular cultivars include:

Name	Height	Flower Color
'Heinz Richard'	12 inches (30 cm)	pink
'Lady in Blue'	9 inches (23 cm)	semidouble blue
'Professor A. Kippenberg'	14 inches (35 cm)	violet blue
'Snowcushion'	10 inches (25 cm)	white
'Starlight'	16 inches (40 cm)	wine red

A. *novae-angliae*, another species of Michaelmas daisies, is generally healthier than the A. *novi-belgii* group and has more attractive, gray green foliage. However, its blooms are not as good for cutting because they close at night. Bloomtime is September; some continue into October. Because it does not hybridize with other aster species as freely as A. *novi-belgii*, it has not produced as many cultivars. Some are:

Name	Height	Flower Color
'Alma Pötschke'	20 inches (50 cm)	bright pink
'Barr's Blue'	5 feet (1.5 m)	blue
'Harrington's Pink'	5 feet (1.5 m)	clear pink
'September Ruby'	4 feet (1.2 m)	rose carmine

Bloomtime and height: See above.
Spread: 15–24 inches (38–60 cm), depending on height.
Light and soil: All the asters described above appreciate full sun and moist but well-drained soil. A. *amellus* and A. × *frikartii* will also grow in part shade. Michaelmas daisies will tolerate wet soil. A. × *frikartii* needs excellent drainage, especially in winter.
Care and propagation: Use generous amounts of organic matter and a handful of all-purpose fertilizer when planting asters. Tall cultivars

definitely require staking and are best sited with a bushy type of plant in front of them, to hide their awkward stems. Even the dwarfs will flop a bit, so insert some twigs into the ground around the clumps in spring for a bit of support. Dig plants up every other year, remove some vigorous shoots from the outer edge of the clump and replant with a bucketful of compost. As Louis Liger wrote in 1706, "As this plant . . . [spreads] very fast, it will be proper every Three Years to remove it, lest it harass the Ground too much."

All perennial asters can be propagated by root division or cuttings. Species and seed strains can be grown from seed, but many named cultivars do not come true from seed.

Pests and diseases: CATERPILLARS, POWDERY MILDEW, ROOT ROT, SLUGS and SNAILS. A. *novi-belgii* is susceptible to WILT DISEASES, causing stems and leaves to wither, but leaving the leaves clinging to the stems. Eventually plants are killed completely.

Frost hardiness: To zone 4; except A. × *frikartii*: to zone 5.

Astilbe × *arendsii*
Astilbe chinensis 'Pumila'
Astilbe taquetii 'Superba'
Astilbe thunbergii 'Ostrich Plume' all called "astilbe" "false spirea"
SAXIFRAGACEAE
(Figure 2-2)

Ideal garden perennials, astilbes have many good points in their favor. Bearing fluffy tapering plumes composed of a profusion of tiny flowers on wiry stems, they bloom for weeks in summer. They are easy to grow, and despite the height of some cultivars, staking is not required. The flowers are attractive in arrangements.

The soft texture of astilbe's foliage adds to its effectiveness as a garden plant. The leaves arise from the ground on wiry stalks and are thrice divided, each division having three toothed leaflets. Foliage color, bright green in the white cultivars, often becomes progressively darker and reddish as the flower color moves through the pinks and reds.

A. × *arendsii.* Most of the astilbes seen in gardens are complex hybrids derived from four Asian species (A. *chinensis* var. *davidii*, A. *japonica*, A. *thunbergii* and A. *astilboides* Hort.). They are the result, in part, of work done at the Lemoine nursery in France, but they are mainly the product of the Georg Arends nursery in Germany in the early 1900s. They are usually grouped together as *Astilbe* × *arendsii*. A few cultivars of astilbe are not hybrids, but are derived from one species, A. *japonica*.

In all, there are dozens of named cultivars with differing characteristics. Unfortunately, many local nurseries label them merely "pink," "red" and "white," rather than giving the correct cultivar name. For this reason, you cannot be sure which cultivar you are getting. It is hoped that with the increased popularity of perennials and the increased sophistication of gardeners, nurseries will begin to use the cultivar names when labeling astilbes.

The following are some A. × *arendsi* cultivars:

Name	Height	Flower	Bloomtime
'Bridal Veil'	2^1/$_2$ feet (75 cm)	white; open, elegant	July–August
'Bressingham Beauty'	3^1/$_2$ feet (1 m)	rich pink	July–August
'Cattleya'	3 feet (90 cm)	pink	August–September
'Diamond'	2^1/$_2$ feet (75 cm)	white; slender	July–August
'Erika'	3 feet (90 cm)	clear bright pink	August–September
'Fanal'	1^1/$_2$ feet (45 cm)	dark red; dense, short	July–August
'Fire'	2 feet (60 cm)	bright coral red	August–September
'White Gloria'	2 feet (60 cm)	white; dense plumes	July–August
Some A. *japonica* cultivars:			
'Bonn'	20 inches (50 cm)	bright carmine pink	June–July
'Deutschland'	2 feet (60 cm)	white	June–July
'Europa'	2 feet (60 cm)	pale pink; elegant	June–July
'Montgomery'	2^1/$_2$ feet (75 cm)	bright red	July–August
'Red Sentinel'	2 feet (60 cm)	red; bronze foliage	July–August

Three other species of astilbe are represented in cultivation, although their cultivars may in fact be hybrids. All bloom in August and September.

A. *chinensis* 'Pumila' is a dwarf, growing to 10 inches (25 cm), with dense, lilac pink flower plumes. It makes an excellent ground cover.

A. *thunbergii* 'Ostrich Plume' has softly arching plumes of coral pink. It reaches 3 feet (90 cm) or more.

A. *taquetii* 'Superba' has dark reddish green, rounded leaves and narrow, erect plumes of light purple. It grows to 4 feet (1.2 m).
Bloomtime and height: See above.

Spread: 2–3 feet (60–90 cm); except A. *chinensis* '*Pumila*': to 1 foot (30 cm).

Light and soil: Full sun or part shade (the latter is best if the soil tends to be at all dry). They prefer moist—even wet—soil with lots of organic matter. Plants are amazingly tough, and even though the foliage may crinkle if watering is neglected during a hot spell, the roots may still be alive.

Care and propagation: Plants are heavy feeders and appreciate an extra handful of all-purpose fertilizer in the spring and again in the early summer. Soak deeply during dry spells in July and August. Staking is not required. Dig and divide every few years and replant with more organic matter. Tidy gardeners prefer to cut flower stalks down after blooming. The dried inflorescences can, however, look attractive in the winter and be cut down to ground level in the spring instead. The best method of propagation is division.

Pests and diseases: Generally trouble-free.

Frost hardiness: To zone 4.

Astrantia carniolica
Astrantia major
Astrantia maxima (A. *helleborifolia*) all called "astrantia" "masterwort"
APIACEAE
(Figure 2-3)

Although not widely grown, astrantias are delicate and charming perennials. From 1769–73, Reverend William Hanbury published his *Complete Body of Planting and Gardening* in sixpenny installments. Of *Astrantia major*, a woodland plant from Austria, he wrote, "being flowers of no great beauty, the very worst part of the garden should be assigned to them." How very wrong he was.

Astrantias are native to Europe. They are members of the dill family (APIACEAE) and have that family's distinct inflorescence made up of dozens of individual flowers on wiry stalks all joined together at the base. The inflorescence of astrantia is about 1 inch (2.5 cm) across; each individual flower is 1/8 inch (.3 cm) across. The inflorescence is surrounded by a collar of petal-like bracts—resembling a ballerina's tutu.

The handsome leaves of astrantia are midgreen and are divided into toothed leaflets. Astrantias add an element of softness to the border and make wonderful cut flowers.

A. carniolica reaches 12–18 inches (30–45 cm) in height and its bracts are shorter than its white flowers. It has three to five leaflets per leaf.

A. major, the most widely available astrantia, is easy to grow. Forming a neat, rounded clump of foliage, it bears dozens of greenish white or pinkish flowers. It has three to seven leaflets and the leaves are up to 6 inches (15 cm) across. It has been in cultivation since 1597. 'Shaggy' has long irregular bracts. 'Margery Fish' is very close to the species, but this name is often misapplied to 'Shaggy'. 'Rubra' has rose pink bracts. 'Sunningdale Variegated' ('Variegata') has a creamy border on the leaves when they first emerge, but it gradually changes to green by summer. Its leaf color is best in sun. *A. involucrata* is a synonym for *A. major* var. *carinthiaca*, which has larger bracts than the species.

A. maxima has three leaflets per leaf and the flowers are rose pink. The bracts are longer than the flowers and edged with sharp teeth.

Bloomtime: June and July.

Height: 2 feet (60 cm).

Spread: 15 inches (38 cm).

Light and soil: Full sun (provided the soil does not dry out) or part shade. Plant in moist—even damp—soil with plenty of organic matter. *A. maxima* needs more pampering in terms of rich soil and shade to look its best.

Care and propagation: Astrantias are easy to grow. Water well during dry spells in July and August to keep the foliage looking fresh. Cut old flower stalks after blooms have faded. Propagate from seed (except named cultivars that are not true from seed) or by division.

Pests and diseases: Generally trouble-free. Dark areas occurring on the leaves by late summer seem to be due to dryness. Some gardeners report that astrantias are deer-resistant.

Frost hardiness: To zone 4.

Aubrieta deltoidea "rock cress" "aubrietia" BRASSICACEAE
(Figure 2-4)

Aubrietia is a wonderful trailer for cascading over rocks and walls in the spring. It produces sheets of color in varying shades of purple. The flowers of aubrietia appear in small clusters. Each is up to 3/4 inch (2 cm) across, in shades of purple and rose lilac. The four petals are arranged in pairs, making the flowers resemble small butterflies. The leaves are gray green, to 1/2 inch (1.3 cm) long, with tiny hairs and teeth along the margin. Aubrietia is native to Sicily and also grows wild from Greece to Asia Minor.

Named cultivars, both seed strains and clones, may in fact be hybrids with other species of *Aubrieta*. In general, clones are superior to seed-grown plants. Some popular clones include 'Borsch's White' (probably the only white aubrietia), 'Castle Ekberg' (long-blooming, lavender blue), 'Dr. Mules' (heavy bloomer, dark royal blue), 'Gurgedyke' (showy reddish purple), 'Lamb's Brilliant' (large bright red flowers) and 'Indigo' (violet). Two double-flowered clones are 'Dawn' (rose pink) and 'Purple Heart'. 'Variegata' has a white leaf margin and blue flowers. In shops, clones are often sold in one-gallon (20-cm) pots.

Plants grown from seed often have less attractive foliage, but are also less expensive, a consideration if you require a large number of plants. In shops, seed-grown plants are usually sold in 4-inch (10-cm) pots. Seed strains include 'Royal Cascade' and 'Red Cascade'.

The genus *Aubrieta* was named for the French botanical illustrator, Claude Aubriet (1668–1743). It should really be pronounced oh-bree-et-a, but over the years it has ended up being pronounced oh-bree-sha, hence the difference in spelling between the common and botanical names.

Bloomtime: Most cultivars bloom in April and May, but some start later and bloom until late June.

Height: 4–6 inches (10–15 cm).

Spread: 12 inches (30 cm).

Light and soil: Best in full sun and a well-drained soil to which some organic matter and dolomite lime have been added.

Care and propagation: After blooming, cut back rock garden plants to encourage compact growth. On plants that are being allowed to trail over a wall, cut off only the old flower stalks.

All types of aubrietia can be propagated by division or (if even more plants are required) from cuttings. To make a cutting of a favorite plant, cut it back after it has bloomed and cover it with wet peat mixed with sand, perlite or vermiculite. In about August, when the new shoots emerge, remove the peat mixture and take 2-inch (5-cm) cuttings.

Species and seed strains can be grown from seed. Sow seed at room temperature or outdoors in a cold frame in February or March.

Pests and diseases: SLUGS and SNAILS.
Frost hardiness: To zone 4.

Bergenia cordifolia "heartleaf bergenia"
Bergenia crassifolia "leather-leaf bergenia" "pigsqueak"
Bergenia purpurascens all also called "elephant ears" "saxifrage"
SAXIFRAGACEAE
(Figure 2-6)

Bergenias are plants that arouse strong feelings in gardeners–some think they are great, others hate them. All bergenias are easily recognized by their large, rounded, waxy midgreen (redder in winter) leaves that emerge from thick trailing stems. The flowers and leaves of bergenia are suitable for bold floral arrangments.

Bergenia cordifolia, the most commonly available species, has been in cultivated since before 1779. The leaves are heart-shaped with a wavy margin, to 12 inches (30 cm) long. The leaves are attached to the thick, creeping stems by stalks as long as the leaves. The leaf margin is tinted red and the veins are prominent, being light pinkish white. Blooming in early spring, this native of Siberia and Mongolia produces an inflorescence that starts as a compact cluster of flowers, somewhat resembling a hyacinth, but lengthens to 15 inches (38 cm), carrying purplish pink bells with five petals each.

B. crassifolia was sent to the famous botanist Linnaeus from its native Siberia in 1760 by the physician to the Empress of Russia. It has smaller leaves than the previous species, to 8 inches (20 cm) long. The curious common name pigsqueak refers to the fact that if you rub a leaf between your fingers, it makes a squeaking sound.

B. purpurascens, a native of the Himalayas, China and Burma, was introduced into cultivation in 1850. It has narrow, erect leaves that turn deep mahogany red in winter.

Cultivars. There are many worthwhile named cultivars of these three; many are hybrids. If you dislike the purplish pink blooms of *B. cordifolia*, try to find 'Bressingham Silver', which has white flowers. 'Abendglut' ('Evening Glow') is a compact cultivar that grows to 9 inches (23 cm) high by 12 inches (30 cm) wide, with deep purple flowers. 'Bressingham Salmon' has salmon pink flowers and the leaves have a pink flush in winter. 'Morning Red' ('Morgenröte') is an excellent purplish red, reaching 15 inches (38 cm) in height. 'Purpurea'—one of English gardener

Gertrude Jekyll's favorites—maintains its purplish leaf coloration throughout the warmer months and has vivid magenta flowers on tall red stalks.

Bloomtime: Most bergenias bloom April to May, but some cultivars may bloom again in late summer. The foliage remains on the plant all winter.
Height: 9–24 inches (23–60 cm), depending on the species and cultivar (see above).
Spread: 12 inches (30 cm); except *B. purpurascens*: 24 inches (60 cm).
Light and soil: Plant in full sun or partial shade in almost any soil. Bergenias tolerate a wide range of soil moisture conditions, growing more slowly in dry soil and quickly in moist soils. The leaves will be larger on plants growing in the shade.
Care and propagation: Cut down flower stalks after blooms have faded. New plants may be made by division or from cuttings; break off a thick stem in winter, bury it in the ground, and it will root.
Pests and diseases: LEAF SPOT, SLUGS, SNAILS and WEEVILS.
Frost hardiness: To zone 4; except *B. cordifolia*: to zone 3.

Buphthalum salicifolium "sunwheels" "oxeye" ASTERACEAE
(Figure 2-7)

It is surprising that this perennial is not more widely grown, for it offers months of bloom on a neat, attractive plant for virtually no work. Sunwheels is an appropriate common name for its bright yellow, daisy-like flower heads, which are excellent for cutting. The neat 2-foot (60-cm) plants begin blooming in late May and, if deadheaded, continue until the fall. The narrow midgreen leaves are up to 7 inches (18 cm) long and alternate along the stems. Native to Central Europe, sunwheels can be used to make a ribbon of bright yellow along a path or driveway. They are often sold as *Inula* 'Golden Beauty'.

Bloomtime: Late May until late July if not deadheaded; until September if deadheaded.
Height: 2 feet (60 cm).
Spread: 12 inches (30 cm).
Light and soil: Happy in full sun and an average well-drained soil.
Care and propagation: Although not generally available in garden shops, sunwheels may be mail-ordered or easily grown from seed (listed by Thompson and Morgan). Little care is required other than deadheading to prolong bloom. If the soil is too rich, plants may need staking.

Plants can also be propagated from cuttings or by division.
Pests and diseases: Generally trouble-free.
Frost hardiness: To zone 3.

Campanula carpatica "Carpathian harebell" "tussock harebell"
Campanula glomerata "clustered bellflower"
Campanula persicifolia "peach-leaf bellflower"
Campanula portenschlagiana (*C. muralis*) CAMPANULACEAE
(Figures 2-8 and 2-9)
Easy to grow, blooming when many other perennials have finished, clear blues and whites that combine well with many other flower colors—all of the bellflowers have much to offer in the garden. There are about three hundred species of campanula in cultivation. Most are native to the Caucasus, Baltic and Mediterranean regions. One distinguishing feature of many campanula flowers is the central pistil, which flares out into three lobes. The following give you an idea of their diversity.

Campanula carpatica, native to the Carpathian mountains of Europe, forms a rounded clump, making it an ideal choice for the front of the border or for the larger rock garden. It has heart-shaped, toothed, midgreen leaves, up to 3 inches (8 cm) long. In July and August, flowers are held on wiry stems and are lilac blue, upward-facing bells, to 1½ inches (4 cm) across. They flare out into five pointed petals. Many excellent named cultivars are available, often sold as *C. turbinata*. Overall plant height for cultivars of this species ranges from 4–12 inches (10–30 cm). Two excellent and easy-to-grow seed strains are readily available—'Blue Clips' and 'White Clips'.

C. glomerata looks entirely different from *C. carpatica*. The flowers are deep purple and are clustered at the ends of the 18-inch (45-cm) stems. They are produced between May and July. The basal leaves are heart-shaped, to 6 inches (15 cm) long, including the thin leafstalk. Narrower, stalkless leaves alternate along the flower stems. It is excellent for cutting and makes a good companion for red peonies and the silver *Artemisia ludoviciana*. The species is native to Eurasia. Good cultivars for the garden include 'Superba', to 3 feet (90 cm); *C. glomerata* var. *dahurica*, to 2 feet (60 cm); and *C. glomerata* var. *acaulis* (meaning without a stem), to only 12 inches (30 cm) in height.

C. persicifolia, like C. carpatica, is easy to grow from seed and has almost identical blooms on a taller plant. The flowers are open bells of blue or white and are arranged in clusters along erect flower stalks, reaching up to 3 feet (90 cm) in height. The leaves are very different from C. carpatica, however, narrow and to 5 inches (13 cm) long. They are dark green and a bit glossy, with tiny teeth at intervals along the margin; there is no leafstalk—the base of the leaf wraps around the stem. Plants are slender, so several should be planted about 1 foot (30 cm) apart to make a clump. Peach-leaf bellflower is an excellent and long-lasting cut flower. The species is native to Europe and northeast Asia, but has been cultivated since before 1596. There are named clones with double blooms, grown since 1665, but the singles are very charming.

C. portenschlagiana grows to 6–9 inches (15–23 cm) high. Native to Yugoslavia, it spreads to form a bright green mat covered with tiny, blue star-like flowers from June to August, if deadheaded. The leaves are about 1 inch (2.5 cm) across, round or heart-shaped and toothed. Similar hybrids include C. 'Birch Hybrid' (C. portenschlagiana × C. poscharsky-ana), which has deep blue, bugle-shaped flowers and grows to 6 inches (15 cm) in height, and C. 'Stella', which has lavender blue flowers in 12-inch (30-cm) sprays.

Other species. There are many other excellent campanulas. However, be cautious about planting C. poscharskyana, which is very invasive—although drought resistant—and C. isophylla, which is sometimes sold as a garden perennial but is poorly suited to garden culture in the Pacific coastal region. Stems are brittle and the brown, faded flowers cling to the stems, rather than dropping neatly.

C. rapunculoides is quite beautiful but a terrible weed—almost impossible to eradicate. Its leaves are quite distinct from all of the above. They are 1–3 inches (2.5–8 cm) long, heart-shaped and tapering to a long point. It grows 2–4 feet (.6–1.2 m) in height. If you are growing exotic campanulas from seed, watch their leaves carefully. This species has been introduced to gardens accidentally through mislabeled seed.

Bloomtime: C. carpatica: July and August; C. glomerata: variable, between May and July; C. persicifolia and C. portenschlagiana begin to bloom in June and will continue through the summer if deadheaded.

Height: 4–36 inches (10–90 cm). See above.

Spread: C. carpatica and C. persicifolia: 12–15 inches (30–38 cm); C. glomerata: 1–2 feet (30–60 cm); C. portenschlagiana: 2–3 feet (60–90 cm).

1-1 *Achillea filipendulina*
'Coronation Gold'
fernleaf yarrow

1-2 *Aconitum carmichaelii*
'Kelmscott'
monkshood

1-3 *Adiantum pedatum*
maidenhair fern

1-4 *Alchemilla mollis*
Lady's mantle

1-5 *Anemone × hybrida*
'Honorine Jobert'
Japanese anemone

1-6 *Anemone pulsatilla*
pasqueflower

1-7 *Anthemis tinctoria*
'Grallagh Gold'
golden marguerite

1-8 *Aquilegia* hybrid
columbine

1-9 *Arabis caucasica*
rock cress

1-10 *Armeria maritima*
thrift

1-11 *Artemisia* 'Powis
Castle'

1-12 *Artemisia stellerana*
'Silver Brocade'
beach wormwood

2-1 *Aster novi-belgii*
'Lady-in-Blue'
Michaelmas daisy

2-2 *Astilbe × arendsii* 'Erica'
astilbe

2-3 *Astrantia major*
masterwort

2-4 *Aubrieta deltoidea*
aubrietia

2-5 *Aurinia saxatilis*
basket-of-gold

2-6 *Bergenia purpurascens*
bergenia

2-7 *Buphthalum salicifolium*
sunwheels

2-8 *Campanula carpatica*
'Blue Clips'
Carpathian harebell

2-9 *Campanula*
portenschlagiana
bellflower

2-10 *Catananche caerulea*
cupid's dart

2-11 *Centranthus ruber*
red valerian

2-12 *Cerastium tomentosum*
snow-in-summer

3-1 *Cheiranthus* 'Bowles Mauve' perennial wallflower

3-2 *Chrysanthemum × morifolium* florist's chrysanthemum

3-3 *Chrysanthemum × superbum* Shasta daisy

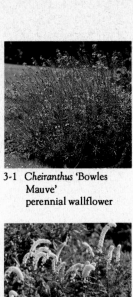

3-4 *Cimicifuga simplex* Kamchatka bugbane

3-5 *Coreopsis grandiflora* 'Sunray' coreopsis

3-6 *Coreopsis verticillata* threadleaf coreopsis

3-7 *Delphinium* hybrids delphiniums

3-8 *Dianthus deltoides* 'Flashing Light' maiden pink

3-9 *Dianthus plumarius* 'Rock Garden Mixed' cottage pink

3-10 *Dicentra* 'Luxuriant' hybrid bleeding heart

3-11 *Dicentra spectabilis* common bleeding heart

3-12 *Dictamnus albus* gas plant

4-1 *Digitalis purpurea*
common foxglove

4-2 *Doronicum* 'Madame
Mason'
leopard's bane

4-3 *Echinacea purpurea*
purple coneflower

4-4 *Echinops* species
globe thistle

4-5 *Eryngium alpinum*
sea holly

4-6 *Eupatorium purpureum*
joe-pye weed

4-7 *Euphorbia epithymoides*
cushion spurge

4-8 *Euphorbia griffithii*
spurge

4-9 *Festuca* species
blue fescue

4-10 *Gaillardia* × *grandiflora*
'La Portola'
blanketflower

4-11 *Geranium* × *magnificum*
hardy geranium

4-12 *Gypsophila paniculata*
baby's breath

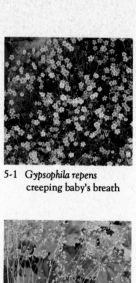

5-1 *Gypsophila repens*
creeping baby's breath

5-2 *Helleborus niger*
Christmas rose

5-3 *Hemerocallis* hybrids
daylily

5-4 *Heuchera × brizoides*
coralbells

5-5 *Heuchera* 'Palace Purple'
coralbells

5-6 *Hosta* 'Frances
Williams'
hosta

5-7 *Iberis sempervirens*
candytuft

5-8 *Incarvillea delavayi*
hardy gloxinia

5-9 *Iris sibirica*
Siberian iris

5-10 *Liatris spicata*
gayfeather

5-11 *Lobelia splendens* 'Queen
Victoria'
perennial lobelia

5-12 *Lupinus* hybrids
lupine

6-1 *Lysimachia punctata*
yellow loosestrife

6-2 *Lythrum salicaria*
'Firecandle'
purple loosestrife

6-3 *Miscanthus sinensis*
'Zebrinus'
Japanese silver grass

6-4 *Monarda didyma*
cultivar
bee balm

6-5 *Oenothera fruticosa*
'Fireworks'
sundrops

6-6 *Paeonia officinalis*
'Rubra Plena'
common peony

6-7 *Papaver orientale*
cultivar
Oriental poppy

6-8 *Pennisetum setaceum*
'Rubra'
fountain grass

6-9 *Penstemon* 'Evelyn'
beard-tongue

6-10 *Phlox paniculata*
border phlox

6-11 *Phlox subulata*
moss phlox

6-12 *Phygelius capensis*
Cape fuchsia

7-1 *Physostegia virginiana*
obedient plant

7-2 *Polemonium caeruleum*
Jacob's ladder

7-3 *Polygonatum ×*
hybridum
Solomon's seal

7-4 *Polygonum affine*
Himalayan knotweed

7-5 *Polystichum munitum*
sword fern

7-6 *Primula × bullesiana*
candelabra primula

7-7 *Primula veris*
cowslip

7-8 *Pulmonaria angustifolia*
blue cowslip

7-9 *Rudbeckia hirta*
'Marmalade'
black-eyed susan

7-10 *Salvia × superba* 'East
Friesland'
perennial salvia

7-11 *Saponaria ocymoides*
rock soapwort

7-12 *Saxifraga* 'Peter Pan'
mossy saxifrage

8-1 *Saxifraga × urbium*
London pride

8-2 *Scabiosa caucasica*
'Schöneste Spielarten'
pincushion flower

8-3 *Sedum sediforme*
rockery sedum

8-4 *Sedum spectabile*
fall border sedum

8-5 *Sempervivum* species
houseleek

8-6 *Silene schafta*
rose campion

8-7 *Silene vulgaris* ssp.
maritima
sea campion

8-8 *Solidago* hybrid
goldenrod

8-9 *Stachys byzantina*
lamb's ears

8-10 *Thalictrum*
rochebrunianum
lavender mist

8-11 *Tradescantia ×*
andersoniana 'Isis'
spiderwort

8-12 *Trollius × cultorum*
globeflower

Light and soil: Plant in full sun or part shade in a well-drained soil to which some organic matter has been added. C. *glomerata* and C. *persicifolia* will also do well in wet soil.

Care and propagation: Easy to grow. Cut off old flower stalks after the blooms have faded to extend bloom time. Propagate from seed (except named cultivars that are not true from seed) or by division.

Pests and diseases: Generally trouble-free.

Frost hardiness: C. *carpatica*, C. *glomerata* and C. *persicifolia*: to zone 3; C. *portenschlagiana*: to zone 5.

Catananche caerulea "cupid's dart" ASTERACEAE
(Figure 2-10)

A hardy perennial from the Mediterranean, cupid's dart blooms for months in the summer. It has attractive, narrow, gray green leaves and blue flowers with papery petals, similar to a cornflower. They are good fresh and dry cut flowers and give a soft, old-fashioned look to the front of the border.

Bloomtime: June to October.

Height: 18–30 inches (45–75 cm).

Spread: 12 inches (30 cm).

Light and soil: Full sun or part shade and any well-drained garden soil to which some organic matter has been added. Plants have a deep tap root that helps them grow in very dry soils (and may lead to root rot in wet soil).

Care and propagation: Plants are virtually care-free. They can be grown from seed and will bloom the first year if started early. They can also be propagated from root cuttings or division. Individual plants are not long-lived, but young ones appear to take their place so readily that you won't even notice.

Pests and diseases: Generally trouble-free.

Frost hardiness: To zone 4.

Centranthus ruber "red valerian" "Jupiter's beard" VALERIANACEAE
(Figure 2-11)

A handsome and easy-to-grow perennial, red valerian is an old-fashioned plant native to rocky areas of the Mediterranean and European Atlantic coasts. It has opposite, gray green, almost succulent leaves that attach directly to the stem (without a leafstalk). The leaf is rounded at the base and tapers gradually to a point. The leaf margin is without teeth and the leaves are up to 4 inches (10 cm) in length. Flowers appear in June atop 2- to 3-foot (60- to 90-cm) stems in dense clusters. Each individual flower is 1/2 inch (1.3 cm) long, having a tube that opens out into five tiny petals and a distinct spur at the base of the tube.

Plants bloom over a long period, longer if the soil is not dry. If old flowers are not removed, red valerian will seed itself in the garden, which can be a bonus or a nuisance, depending on your point of view. (Do not allow seedlings to grow in rock walls; the roots become strong enough to push the rocks apart.) The species is variable, with flowers being red, pink or (rarely) white. If you start plants from seed, you can then select a flower color that you like and propagate it vegetatively. Some of the blue reds are best planted with flowers of white, pale yellow or blue. There are several named cultivars: 'Albus' is white, 'Atrococcineus' is deep coppery red and 'Roseus' is pink. Butterflies are attracted to the flowers.

Red valerian should not be confused with the medicinal herb common valerian (*Valeriana officinalis*). The use of common valerian was promoted by the Arabs even before the tenth century, and tincture of valerian was still used in World War II to treat shellshock. Common valerian is taller than red valerian, has divided leaves and prefers damp soils.

Bloomtime: June to mid-July.
Height: 2–3 feet (60–90 cm). Poor soil produces more compact plants.
Spread: 12 inches (30 cm).
Light and soil: Red valerian grows in full sun or light shade and thrives on poor, well-drained soil to which some dolomite lime has been added.
Care and propagation: Little care is required, other than cutting down the stems in late October. Plants can also be propagated from seed (Thompson & Morgan lists it), and named cultivars from basal cuttings (take near the crown), root cuttings or division.
Pests and diseases: Generally trouble-free.
Frost hardiness: To zone 4.

Cerastium tomentosum "snow-in-summer" CARYOPHYLLACEAE
(Figure 2-12)

The delicate beauty of this perennial belies its tough nature. Snow-in-summer has clusters of 1-inch (2.5-cm) white flowers with five deeply grooved petals. The small leaves and trailing stems are covered in fine hairs, making them slightly fuzzy and silver. Snow-in-summer is too agressive to associate with more well-mannered plants, particularly in sandy soils. Let loose in your rockery, it will wend its way under the rocks and spring up to choke out unsuspecting neighbors. Its elastic roots are virtually impossible to pull out. Even in the open garden, it has been known to choke out small shrubs such as Japanese azaleas. The named cultivars 'Yo-Yo' and 'Silver Carpet', perhaps hybrids with *Cerastium biebersteinii*, are less invasive.

Snow-in-summer could be considered for a spot where nothing else flourishes—either a damp part of the garden or a very dry spot—under large coniferous trees, for instance. It tends to look tatty by late summer.

Bloomtime: May and June.

Height: 8 inches (20 cm).

Spread: 2 feet (60 cm) at least.

Light and soil: Full sun and any soil.

Care and propagation: Although very pretty, snow-in-summer is a borderline weed. Needless to say, it is easy to grow, surviving almost any treatment. Propagate from seed (except named cultivars that are not true from seed) or by division.

Frost hardiness: To zone 3.

Cheiranthus **'Bowles Mauve'** (*Erysimum* 'Bowles Mauve') "perennial wallflower" BRASSICACEAE
(Figure 3-1)

Given a mild winter, this perennial wallflower can be in bloom almost year-round. It produces small purple flowers at the end of ever-lengthening flower stalks; the old flowers drop neatly off and the new flowers just keep on coming. Eventually you will want to cut it back, as the flower stalks become too gangly, but it will soon be in bloom again. The four-petaled flowers, like those of the closely related aubrietia, resemble small butterflies. Plants are evergreen subshrubs; the narrow gray leaves are handsome and nicely set off the purple flowers. This clone does not set seed, suggesting that it is a hybrid. It was named after Edward A. Bowles, English gardener and writer, and is also called 'Bowles Variety'. Butterflies are attracted to the flowers.

Bloomtime: May to October, or longer, depending on the weather.

Height: 24–30 inches (60–75 cm).

Spread: 18 inches (45 cm).

Light and soil: Full sun and well-drained soil. It does very well on poor, sandy soil.

Care and propagation: Easy to grow. Cut back flowering stems in midsummer. Do not cut into woody tissue. To prevent plants from exhausting themselves, it is wise to renew them from cuttings every two years. Take cuttings of nonflowering shoots, making them as long as possible, in early July or October; insert the lower three-quarters of the cutting into a trench of soil in a semishady, out-of-the-way corner of the garden. Transplant July cuttings the following spring, October cuttings the following July. Cuttings can also be made in the greenhouse.

Pests and diseases: Generally trouble-free.

Frost hardiness: To zone 6. If severe frost is expected, mulch plants.

Chrysanthemum × *morifolium* "florist's chrysanthemum" ASTERACEAE
(Figure 3-2)

Chrysanthemums and fall go hand in hand. In rich shades of gold, red, bronze, violet and yellow, their flowers echo the colors of the falling leaves. The soft light of autumn sets their colors aglow, giving us a last burst of color before winter sets in.

Hybridizers have been tinkering with chrysanthemums since perhaps 500 B.C. in China. In her book, *Flowers and their Histories*, Alice Coats writes:

> In the fifth century there lived one T'ao Yuan Ming, who was such a noted breeder of this flower that after his death the name of his native town was changed to Chu-hsien, the City of the Chrysanthemums. The culture of the flower spread from China to Japan at the end of the fourth century, and in 797 it was made the personal emblem or badge of the Mikado, the use of which was limited to imperial purposes only .... Cultivation of the flower was permitted only in the imperial gardens and those of the nobility ....

Chrysanthemums of various forms began to trickle into Britain and Europe in the late 1700s and early 1800s and the precursor to the British National Chrysanthemum Society was formed in 1846. In the past 150 years, a fantastic number of mums have been developed by breeders in Britain, Europe, the United States and Japan. In fact, chrysanthemum fanciers in British Columbia buy their show mums from England.

The name *Chrysanthemum* × *morifolium* is used to designate this group of hybrids. They are assumed to be hybrids of at least four species from China: *C. indicum*, *C. japonense*, *C. makinoi*, and *C. ornatum*. All hybrid chrysanthemums have dark green, deeply lobed leaves, up to 6 inches (15 cm) long. The leaves are alternate along the stems and have a characteristic pungent aroma.

Some taxonomists place florist's chrysanthemum in its own genus, *Dendranthemum*.

Exhibition chrysanthemums. There are many different categories of chrysanthemums, including incurved, reflexed, spider, spoon, pompon, anemone-centered and single. Many cities in the Pacific coastal region have chrysanthemum clubs. These clubs usually hold one or two shows (for early and late cultivars) in the fall. Shows are an excellent place to learn more about the vast array of types and colors available. These show mums are not usually sold in garden shops, but can be purchased by mail order, or by joining a club and attending club sales. A club is also the best way to learn cultural techniques for producing the best blooms.

Very briefly, the routine followed by a chrysanthemum exhibitor is as follows. Basal cuttings are taken through the winter from clumps of mums that were dug in the fall and housed in a cold frame or cool greenhouse. After cuttings are made, last year's plants are discarded. Rooted cuttings are potted into larger pots as necessary through the winter and spring.

Early-blooming (September and October) cultivars are planted out into the garden in May. They are usually grown under a plastic-covered frame, to protect the heavy blooms from rain, and are staked and carefully pruned.

November-bloomers are grown through the summer in large pots set out in the garden. In October these will be brought into the greenhouse to bloom for the late show.

As with any specialty hobby, the good grower learns which techniques suit him or her best and learns the best ways to grow each different cultivar.

Chrysanthemums in the garden. As you have probably gathered, mums are not a "plant-and-forget" perennial. The key to growing good mums in the garden is to refresh plants annually, otherwise most cultivars will gradually fade away. In the spring, dig up plants and remove the young shoots—with attached roots—at the outside of the clump. Replant these, replenishing the soil with fertilizer and organic matter. Success with chrysanthemums in the garden also depends on which cultivars are planted. Newest is not always best in the chrysanthemum world. It is interesting that two perennial experts—Englishman Graham Stuart Thomas and eastern American Frederick McGourty—both make the same observation concerning garden chrysanthemums. They tell of driving around the countryside of their respective regions and seeing old chrysanthemum plants flourishing in gardens. But when they stop and inquire, the owners do not know the names of the cultivars, and they are apparently no longer available to gardeners. The emphasis on breeding in the past decades seems to have been to develop exhibition mums and mums for the greenhouse pot-flower industry. Long-lived, carefree garden chrysanthemums are not as easy to find.

There are basically three ways to buy chrysanthemum plants for the garden—from a garden center in the spring, from a garden center in the fall or from a mail-order nursery or club in the spring. Some mums you see in a garden center in spring have been brought into bloom artificially. Mums are "day-length sensitive," that is, blooming is initiated by shortening days in the fall. By using black-out cloth, growers can limit the amount of light plants receive, and trick them into blooming in May. If you buy mums in bloom in the spring, **remove the flowers and buds** and allow the plants to get a good summer's growth and then bloom naturally in the fall.

Chrysanthemums sold in bloom in the fall have not been forced into bloom. However, they may have been treated with one of several growth-regulating chemicals that cause the plants to have a more compact habit of growth than they would have otherwise. Left to their own devices in your garden, they will become much taller. They can be pinched two or three times during the summer to encourage bushiness. To do this, simply pinch off the growing tip of each shoot. As plants become more bushy, pinch growing tips evenly over the plant. Do not pinch after mid-July, or you may be removing the flower buds.

The third way to buy chrysanthemums is from a mail-order nursery or chrysanthemum club in the spring. Plants are sold as rooted cuttings and have not been tampered with by manipulating their bloom schedule or using growth hormones. This is the best way to buy mums and it coincides with the ideal planting time of late April/early May. The only disadvantage is that you cannot see the plants in bloom before you buy.

Some mail-order nurseries carry tried-and-true cultivars. 'Clara Curtis', which has clear pink, single flowers, grows to 32 inches (80 cm). (It is actually C. × *rubellum*, rather than C. × *morifolium*.) 'Mei-Kyo' has small lilac pink pompons and grows to 26 inches (65 cm). Both are hardy and reliable. Cushion mums (with rounded, compact form) also do very well in the garden, and come in a wide selection of colors.

A somewhat recent development is the crossing of C. × *morifolium* with C. *zawadskii* (C. *coreanum*) by Alexander Cumming of Bristol Nurseries in Connecticut. This strain has been dubbed the Korean hybrids and attractive plants can be grown from seed. They have been grown at the UBC Botanical Garden with success.

Most chrysanthemums require staking. It is also best to leave the old canes standing through the winter (curb your neatness instincts here!). They will protect the crown from rain and frost. An alternative method for overwintering crowns is to lift them and set them in soil in a cold frame for the winter, to be divided and replanted in late April.

Bloomtime: September to November, depending on the cultivar.

Height: 1–4 feet (.3–1.2 m), depending on the cultivar.

Spread: 1–2 feet (30–60 cm).

Light and soil: Full sun and well-drained soil enriched with organic matter. **Care and propagation:** Add generous amounts of organic matter and some all-purpose fertilizer to the soil when preparing the ground. Stake tall types. Keep well watered and fertilized through the summer months. Propagate by division or cuttings; grow seed strains from seed. See also notes above, depending on whether you are more interested in mums for cutting and show, or for garden decoration.

Pests and diseases: Alas, the list is long. Pests include APHIDS, EARWIGS, CATERPILLARS, CUTWORMS, LEAF MINERS, NEMATODES, SLUGS, SNAILS, THRIPS and (in the greenhouse), MITES and WHITEFLIES. Diseases include LEAF SPOTS, POWDERY MILDEW, ROOT ROT, RUST, WILT DISEASES, VIRUS and (in the greenhouse), GRAY MOLD. Luckily, they don't always get all of those afflictions.

Frost hardiness: To zone 4, at least.

Chrysanthemum × *superbum* (C. *maximum*) "Shasta daisy" ASTERACEAE (Figure 3-3)

Shasta daisies are cheerful plants and are excellent for cutting. Although usually sold as C. *maximum*, most plants in cultivation are thought to be a hybrid between two European species, C. *maximum* and

C. lacustre. Flowers are up to 4 inches (10 cm) across, with white ray florets and yellow disc florets. The coarse, dark green, toothed leaves are up to 20 inches (50 cm) long and taper to a point. Smaller leaves alternate up the flower stalks. Many Shasta daisies have been named over the years. Two dwarf strains, 'Little Miss Muffet' and 'Snow Lady', are easy to grow from readily available seed. They grow to 15 inches (38 cm) and 12 inches (30 cm) respectively. The seed strain 'Double Diener's' (Park) produces a mixture of singles, semidoubles and doubles—you have to do the selecting.

The most famous double cultivars are propagated from cuttings. They include the old 'Esther Read'; the more reliable 'Wirral Pride'; 'Cobham Gold', which is suffused gold; and 'Mt. Hood', with flowers up to 4 inches (10 cm) across. 'Aglaya' is a double with a long blooming time and fringed ray florets. All of the doubles grow to about 2 feet (60 cm) tall. 'Thomas Killen', of the same height, has large single blooms, often used in the florist trade.

Bloomtime: June to August.

Height: 12–24 inches (30–60 cm), depending on cultivar.

Spread: 12–18 inches (30–45 cm), depending on cultivar.

Light and soil: Best in full sun, but they tolerate part shade. Plant with plenty of organic matter and a handful of dolomite lime; keep soil moist during hot weather.

Care and propagation: Staking is not required as a rule. Cut off old flower stalks after the blooms have faded, and cut stalks down to the ground in the late fall. Every third year, lift and divide plants in spring or fall. Propagate from seed (except named cultivars that are not true from seed) or by division.

Pests and diseases: SLUGS and SNAILS.

Frost hardiness: To zone 5 (most cultivars).

Cimicifuga americana "American bugbane"
Cimicifuga japonica and *Cimicifuga japonica* **var.** *acerina*
Cimicifuga racemosa "bugbane" "black snake-root" "black cohosh"
Cimicifuga simplex (*C. foetida* var. *intermedia*) "Kamchatka bugbane"
Cimicifuga simplex **var.** *ramosa* (*C. ramosa*) RANUNCULACEAE
(Figure 3-4)

You will easily recognize this group of perennials from their unique white bottle-brush flowers. It is too bad that such beautiful plants have ended up with such unattractive English common names. Bugbane refers to the reputation of some species to repel insects. The German common name silvercandle is more descriptive and appealing. All have large, compound, deeply toothed leaves held on wiry stems. *Cimicufuga* plants are not always correctly named as to species, but all are excellent in the garden and for cutting, so you can't really go wrong.

Cimicifuga racemosa blooms in July, holding its narrow 2¹/₂-foot (75-cm) wands, dense with small white flowers, on erect, branching stems. It grows 3–8 feet (.9–2.4 m) tall and is native to the northeastern United States. C. *racemosa* has one pistil per flower, a good key to sort it out from the others, as names are often confused.

C. simplex, as the common name suggests, is native to western Asia. The inflorescences of this species tend to arch more than those of other species. There is usually only one inflorescence per stalk. C. *simplex* blooms in September and October, generally reaching 4 feet (1.2 m) in height. 'Elstead' is an outstanding English cultivar that has purplish buds and blooms later. 'White Pearl' (also sold by its original German name 'Armleuchter' and by 'The Pearl') has very large inflorescences and is much taller than the species.

C. simplex var. *ramosa*—called C. *ramosa* by some authorities—flowers later than the species, grows taller and the inflorescences are held erect. The cultivar 'Atropurpurea' was selected for its dark purplish foliage. It is, however, often grown from seed, and a high proportion of green-leaf plants result. 'Brunette' is one of several clones selected in Denmark and Germany for excellent mahogany foliage that contrasts well with the white flowers. It must be propagated vegetatively to be true. This is a slow process and the true cultivar is expensive.

C. americana is similar to C. *simplex* var. *ramosa* but is native to the eastern United States.

C. japonica and **C. japonica** var. *acerina* are native to Japan. The latter has glossy, maple-shaped leaves and is sometimes assigned to its own separate species—C. *acerina*. Both grow to about 4 feet (1.2 m) in height and bloom in August, often continuing into September.

Bloomtime: See above.

Height: 4–8 feet (1.2–2.4 m).

Spread: 2 feet (60 cm).

Light and soil: Best in a lightly shaded spot with rich, moist soil to which a lot of organic matter has been added. If planting in full sun, keep plants well watered.

Care and propagation: Easy to grow. Deadheading is not required as the seed heads are attractive. Cut stems down to the ground in late fall if desired. Propagate from seed (except named cultivars that are not true from seed) or by division.

Pests and diseases: Generally trouble-free.

Frost hardiness: To zone 3.

Coreopsis grandiflora "coreopsis"
Coreopsis verticillata "thread-leaf coreopsis" both called "tickseed"
ASTERACEAE
(Figures 3-5 and 3-6)

These two are unsurpassed for length of bloom—they are as colorful as any bedding plant, and yet they bloom again each year. The generic name derives from Greek and means "bug-like," descriptive of the tiny black seeds. Both are native to the southern United States, where *Coreopsis verticillata* was used to dye wool red.

The leaves of **C. grandiflora** are variable. Some are up to 6 inches (15 cm) long and are divided into three or five slender leaflets. Some leaves are not divided, but taper to a rounded tip. The leaves are midgreen and slightly rough to the touch, caused by tiny hairs on both surfaces. Blooms are borne singly on wiry stems about 8–10 inches (20–25 cm) long. They are golden-yellow and daisy-like, up to 2¹/₂ inches (6 cm) across. Each plant grows to 18 inches (45 cm) high and produces dozens of flower heads at once over a period of months. There are many named cultivars, but the new seed strain 'Sunray' produces beautiful plants. Flowers have a double row of ray florets and bloom from June to October. It was the first perennial to receive the European Fleuroselect Award (1980) and is easy to grow from seed. To top it off, the blooms last for several days when cut. 'Goldfink' ('Goldfinch'), introduced by German nurseryman Otto Walther, is an excellent dwarf cultivar that grows to only 8 inches high (20 cm) but spreads well. (C. *grandiflora* is very similar to C. *lanceolata* and may be confused with it in cultivation.)

The leaves of **C. verticillata** are also variable. Some leaves are not divided, but are long and slender, up to 2 inches by 1/8 inch (5 cm by .3 cm) wide. Other leaves on the same plant are similarly slender, but are divided into up to nine finger-like parts. The effect of the foliage is delicate and feathery, hence the common name thread-leaf coreopsis.

The blooms, which are borne in abundance through the summer, are 1¹/₂ inches (4 cm) across and look like yellow daisies with yellow centers. Plants grow to 2 feet (60 cm). 'Zagreb' grows to 12 inches (30 cm).

  Coreopsis 'Moonbeam' is a hybrid of C. *verticillata* and an unknown parent, but it looks like the other thread-leaf coreopsis types. It has pale yellow flowers with undertones of green.

Bloomtime: June or July to October.

Height: 8–24 inches (20–60 cm), depending on the species and cultivar.

Spread: 18 inches (45 cm); except 'Goldfink': 12 inches (30 cm).

Light and soil: Full sun in well-drained soil. Soil that is too rich may cause plants to be floppy. C. *verticillata* will tolerate damp soil.

Care and propagation: Easy to grow. With the named cultivars and seed strains, staking is not generally required. Cut old flower stalks off C. *grandiflora* as blooms fade. This is more of a chore for the thread-leaf types; it is worth doing if the plants are close at hand, but it is easier to shear the whole plant back by one-third in August. It will start to bloom again in a few weeks. Cut plants to ground level in late fall and, to encourage longevity, divide each spring—they bloom so profusely, they sometimes exhaust themselves.

  Propagate from seed (except named cultivars that are not true from seed) or by division.

Pests and diseases: SLUGS and SNAILS.

Frost hardiness: C. *grandiflora*: to zone 5; C. *verticillata*: to zone 3.

Delphinium hybrids "delphinium" RANUNCULACEAE
(Figure 3-7)

  The tall border delphiniums are in a class of their own in the perennial world. Reaching up to 8 feet (2.4 m) in height when pampered, their tall floral spires are made up of hundreds of individual outward-facing blooms. The colors are rich: white, cream, pale pinks and blues, sky blue, slate blue gray, indigo, mauve, violet and deep purple, and almost every shade of blue you can imagine. Most flowers are semidouble, giving a ruffled effect; many have a contrasting eye and some have what looks like a striped bumblebee at the center of the bloom. The large, deep green leaves are palmately lobed, the tips of the lobes sharply pointed. Delphiniums are reminiscent of a bygone day, when estate owners had huge perennial borders set off by yew hedges and wide lawns and a handful of gardeners to take care of them.

The tendency in recent years has been to develop delphiniums that are shorter and so need less staking and are more in scale with smaller city gardens. Even so, thoughtful attention should be paid to their place in the garden scheme, and they do demand more care than many perennials.

Hundreds of species of delphiniums are found throughout the world, usually in mountainous areas. It was not until the early 1600s that the first perennial delphinium was cultivated—D. elatum, a native of Europe and Asia. In 1629, John Parkinson wrote the first English illustrated book devoted primarily to ornamental plants; at that time, he was growing single and double forms of D. elatum. By the next century, this species was grown in gardens near D. formosum and D. grandiflorum, both from Asia. They hybridized spontaneously and their offspring were referred to as "elatum delphiniums."

Another hundred years later, from 1850 until the turn of the century, French nurseryman Victor Lemoine seriously pursued the hybridization of delphiniums. He produced hundreds of outstanding hybrids—in terms of both height and color—and they were introduced into Britain by James Kelway. The British firm Blackmore & Langdon was formed in 1901; they still lead the field today, with a stunning display each year at the famous Chelsea Flower Show in England. They have introduced hundreds of named clones, which must be propagated vegetatively. While developing even more beautiful flowers and colors, Blackmore & Langdon are also committed to maintaining the perennial nature of delphiniums.

Blackmore & Langdon hybrids do not, however, perform well in the California climate, and American breeder Frank Reinhelt worked to develop heat-tolerant delphiniums that could be grown from seed in separate colors. By using D. cardinale—a red delphinium from California—in his program, Reinhelt added dusky pink shades to the color range. Thus originated the Pacific Giant Series, a group of seed strains.

Because Reinhelt also used annual delphiniums in his breeding program, his original Pacific Giants were not truly perennial, but were usually grown as annuals. Most of the seed sold as Pacific Giants today is more perennial than earlier strains. Pacific Giants Series includes cultivars of separate colors, including white, light to dark blues, dusky pinks and lavender. They grow to 4–5 feet (1.2–1.5 m) high. Several shorter delphinium cultivars are available from seed houses, including 'Emerald

Mixed', to 2 feet (60 cm); 'Blue Fountains' and 'Magic Fountains Mixed', to 2½ feet (75 cm); and 'Standup', which grows to only 20 inches (50 cm). If you find the inflorescences of the Elatum hybrids too dense, try the Belladonna hybrids (Thompson & Morgan); they have graceful, more branching spires with wiry stems.

Many of the dwarf strains are excellent for cutting. Park Seed lists 'Green Expectations'—4-foot (1.2-m) plants bearing soft lime green blooms, much admired by flower arrangers.

Thompson & Morgan list 'Blackmore & Langdon Strain Mixed'. Logically, they should be more perennial in nature than the Pacific Giants Series. You are not likely to find them in stores as plants.

Bloomtime: June and July.

Height: 20 inches to 8 feet (50 cm–2.4 m), depending on the type.

Spread: 18–24 inches (45–60 cm).

Light and soil: Delphiniums need full sun and rich soil. Choose a site with as little wind as possible. (Contrary to popular thinking, a solid fence is not a good windbreak; it can create strong currents on its leeward side. A hedge is a better defence against wind.) Add an abundance of organic matter—ideally well-rotted cow or horse manure, or compost— to the planting hole, mixing it into the garden soil.

Care: After improving the soil in the planting hole with abundant organic matter, set the young plant in it. Sprinkle the rootball with a handful of bonemeal and cover the rootball with soil. Sprinkle the area near the young plant with a handful of 6-8-6, taking care not to let it touch the foliage or stems. Water well. The most important concern after planting is to protect the new shoots from slugs and snails. For the tall strains, or for the shorter ones in a windy site, staking will be required in about April. This arrangement will allow the stems to move, yet will still give support. If stems are more tightly corseted, the result will often be that the entire flower head cracks off. To encourage bushy plants, the central stem should be pinched out in April. On the other hand, it is best to confine young plants to only three stalks; established plants can support seven or eight stalks. Cut the others out at ground level. This thinning will help make each stalk sturdier.

Sprinkle a second handful of 6-8-6 in June and water in well. Remove faded blooms, cutting just beneath the old inflorescence. Do not cut the foliage down at this time. If new shoots appear later, you should then cut down the old foliage and allow the new shoots to develop and provide a second bloom.

In late October, cut all the foliage down to ground level. Gently remove the soil from around the crown and cover the crown with sharp sand to discourage slug activity. Delphiniums are heavy feeders, and responding to this need with a mulch of well-rotted manure in June and 6-8-6 in the spring and early summer each year will improve their longevity.

Propagation: The best method of propagation for the delphiniums grown in the Pacific coastal region is raising seedlings. The seed of delphinium ripens in late August and if sown immediately, it will germinate quickly. If not, it will become dormant. Therefore, if you have purchased seed later in the year, you must break dormancy by giving it a cold treatment. Mix the seed with a handful of perlite or vermiculite in a plastic bag, dampen, close the bag and put it in the freezer for 7 to 14 days. Scatter the contents of the bag over the surface of your seeding mixture and water gently. Light is required for germination. Keep in a cool place until seeds have germinated.

Sowing may be done in either March or July to August. Plants from a March sowing should be transplanted into individual pots in April, to be set out into the garden in late May.

Plants from a late summer sowing will be ready to transplant (with care—the roots are easily damaged) into the garden in late September. Alternatively, if you do not have a spot for them in the garden or if you wish to give some plants away, they can be potted into individual 4-inch (10-cm) pots and overwintered in a cold frame. If you have a cool greenhouse (a few degrees above freezing—no warmer), fall-sown seedlings that have been overwintered in a cold frame can be brought into the greenhouse in about December to give them a head start.

You can also germinate seed in a shady part of the greenhouse in January, rather than waiting until March. Germination will take about 4 weeks.

Plants can also be grown from cuttings, necessary for increasing named clones such as are grown in Britain. However, if the plants available in the Pacific coastal region are the shorter-lived Pacific strains, it seems pointless to propagate them from cuttings. As the technique is complicated and somewhat difficult, readers who require more information should refer to Colin Edwards's book, *Delphiniums The*

Complete Guide, for details.

Pests and diseases: As with other plants that have been highly bred, pest and disease problems increase. The worst pests, which probably have nothing to do with breeding, are SLUGS and SNAILS. As delphiniums begin to send up new shoots in February, you must take steps to prevent damage even before you are thinking about gardening. Edwards recommends an unusual treatment. Dissolve 2 ounces (60 g) of aluminum sulphate in 160 fluid ounces (4^1/2 L) of water and pour one quart (one liter) of this around each plant, taking care not to wet the foliage. Treatments should be made in October, February and May. According to Edwards, this treatment destroys adults and eggs of slugs and snails due to its astringent action, but is not harmful to other living creatures. Aluminum sulphate is used to acidify the soil to turn hydrangeas blue; it would be advisable therefore to sprinkle dolomite lime around these plants a few weeks after the slug treatment to sweeten the soil. Edwards does not comment as to the suitability of this treatment for other perennials.

LEAF SPOTS appear in damp, humid weather. POWDERY MILDEW causes a white dusting on the leaves in late summer. VIRUS diseases cause the leaves to be deformed and the plants to be stunted.

Frost hardiness: To zone 3.

Dianthus × *allwoodii* "carnation pink" "border carnation"
Dianthus deltoides "maiden pink"
Dianthus gratianopolitanus (*D. caesius*) "Cheddar pink"
Dianthus plumarius hybrids "cottage pink" "garden pink"
CARYOPHYLLACEAE
(Figures 3-8 and 3-9)

There are hundreds of species and hundreds more cultivars of dianthus grown in gardens. They are extremely popular in Britain and are gaining in popularity in the Pacific coastal region. By nature, they are most at home in sweet soils, a fact we need to take into consideration with our naturally acid soils.

Various dianthus have been in cultivation since ancient times. The Greeks wove dianthus blooms into garlands; the Christians believed that *D. caryophyllus* first sprang up from the tears of Mary, mother of Jesus. *D. plumarius* crossed the channel to England in the eleventh century with the Normans, perhaps as seed on imported building stone; they have grown on the walls of Rochester Castle since those days. The word "pink"—from the Old English pinca (point)—was first applied to these flowers because of the pointed teeth on their petal edges and only later became the name of a color.

True carnations, *D. caryophyllus*, are usually only grown in greenhouses as commercial cut flowers. Although often sold with bedding plants, they do not thrive as garden perennials.

All dianthus have narrow leaves, without teeth along their margins. Like most members of their family, including baby's breath, the stems are swollen at the leaf joints. Most are evergreen, remaining attractive in the winter.

D. × allwoodii. By crossing a cottage pink (*D. plumarius*) and a carnation (*D. caryophyllus*) in England in the 1920s, the Allwood brothers made a new race of dianthus, *D. × allwoodii* or carnation pinks. Like cottage pinks, carnation pinks have silvery leaves and form a mat 12–18 inches (30–45 cm) high. They produce many more blooms than cottage pinks, most in June and July, often with a repeat in fall. The blooms are also held on longer stems, so they can be cut. Carnation pinks are faster growing than cottage pinks and are inclined to be shorter-lived. However, they can be renewed from cuttings every few years. 'Doris' is one of the most popular, with large double flowers of soft pink with darker accents. It is very fragrant and long blooming. Lamb Nurseries in Spokane lists a good collection of named cultivars.

D. deltoides has green foliage that forms a low mat, usually to 6 inches (15 cm) high. It will tolerate dry soils, for it is native to dry pastures and woodlands throughout Europe and western Asia. Maiden pinks bloom from June to August. 'Flashing Light' has masses of single vivid magenta blooms set off by deep burgundy foliage and is a vigorous grower. 'Albus' has white flowers. If grown away from other dianthus, these cultivars produce seedlings similar to themselves. (There are forms with blue foliage, but those with green foliage are most often grown.)

D. gratianopolitanus is native to Europe and Great Britain. It is longer-lived than most dianthus and makes an excellent candidate for the rock garden. It has gray green leaves and forms a tight mat to 6 inches (15 cm) in height. 'Tiny Rubies' has fragrant, 1/2-inch (1.3-cm) bright pink flowers on 2-inch (5-cm) stems in May and June. The hybrid 'La Bourboulle' has fragrant, single pink flowers. 'Red Riding Hood' has red flowers.

D. plumarius, while rare in cultivation, is thought to be one parent of the popular cottage pinks. It is native to eastern and central Europe. The narrow leaves are silvery and form a mat to 10–15 inches (25–38 cm) in height. Blooming in June, cottage pinks are especially popular in Britain, where much of the breeding has been done, and many cultivars have been named. More and more are becoming available here in the Pacific coastal region. One of the best is 'Pike's Pink'. It has beautiful double flowers of clear pink, with a serrated edge to the petal and a touch of dark pink at the center. Seed mixtures, 'Spring Beauty' for instance, produce some excellent plants, all with the same wonderful foliage, a variety of flower colors and a mixture of single and doubles. Favorite plants can then be propagated vegetatively.

Bloomtime and height: See above.

Spread: 1–2 feet (30–60 cm).

Light and soil: Dianthus do best in full sun, except for maiden pinks, which grow well in part shade. Soil should be well drained and enriched with well-rotted manure (not peat). Add a few handfuls of dolomite lime and bonemeal to the planting hole and scatter more in the fall.

Care and propagation: Do not set plants too deeply into the soil, as the stems may rot. If planted in spring, water well during dry spells the first summer. Do not mulch. In fall, clear away fallen leaves, to ensure good air circulation. The new growth on dianthus begins along last year's stems, so do not cut plants back hard in the fall or they may not recover.

Propagate from seed (except named cultivars that are not true from seed) or by division. Pinks are easy to grow from seed; while resulting plants will be variable, favorites can be propagated vegetatively. Ideally, seed should be sown in the spring, but can be sown as late as July. Cuttings should be made in July. Stems can also be layered.

Pests and diseases: APHIDS, CATERPILLARS, THRIPS and LEAF SPOT. Some gardeners report dianthus to be deer-resistant.

Frost hardiness: *D. × allwoodii* and *D. plumarius* are hardy to zone 4; *D. deltoides* is hardy to zone 3; *D. gratianopolitanus*, to zone 5.

Dicentra eximia "fringed bleeding heart"
Dicentra 'Luxuriant'
Dicentra spectabilis "bleeding heart" FUMARIACEAE
(Figures 3-10 and 3-11)

The old-fashioned bleeding heart (**Dicentra spectabilis**) looks like a plant someone dreamt up. It never fails to delight and surprise, especially springing up from some shady corner of the garden.

From the elegant foliage arise arching stems dripping rosy red heart-shaped flowers. Each 1-inch (2.5-cm) heart has a red droplet of flattened, extending petals falling from it, hence the melancholy common name. The compound leaves are blue green with a gray green reverse, up to 12 inches (30 cm) long (including the leaf stalk) and divided into several leaflets. This Asian species was introduced to Britain in 1810, lost and then reintroduced in 1846. It became so popular that in 1878, according to one writer, "its gracefully drooping spikes of heart-shaped pink flowers have become so familiar to many as a wallpaper pattern, that further description will be needless." There is also a white cultivar ('Alba') available, but the rosy pink is a classic. Both grow to 3 feet (90 cm). After producing this show in April and May, old-fashioned bleeding heart dies back to ground level. If the soil is rich and moist, it will remain in leaf longer, but by August it has usually left a gap in the garden scheme.

D. eximia, a native to the eastern United States, makes a ferny mound of foliage and bears mauve heart-shaped flowers from May to September. Like common bleeding heart, this species also has a white cultivar, also named 'Alba'; it is exquisite, particularly if you are not fond of mauve.

D. 'Luxuriant' is a hybrid of *D. eximia* and our Pacific coast native, *D. formosa*. It is one of the longest-blooming perennials, with bright rosy red flowers from May to October, making an excellent front-of-the-border plant. It also has handsome ferny foliage.

Bloomtime: See above.

Height: *D. spectabilis*: 3 feet (90 cm); *D. eximia* and 'Luxuriant': 12–18 inches (30–45 cm).

Spread: 12 inches (30 cm); except *D. spectabilis*: 18 inches (45 cm).

Light and soil: Full sun or light shade in a well-drained soil to which a lot of organic matter has been added. Give old-fashioned bleeding heart protection from the wind.

Care and propagation: Old-fashioned bleeding heart sometimes requires staking, particularly if grown in a lot of shade. Cut stems down to the ground after they wither if desired. Propagation can be done from seed (except for 'Luxuriant'), root division or root cuttings.

Pests and diseases: Generally trouble-free.

Frost hardiness: To zone 3.

Dictamnus albus (*D. fraxinella*) "burning bush" "gas plant" RUTACEAE
(Figure 3-12)

This handsome member of the citrus family is slow to develop and not in every shop, but it is a solid addition to the perennial or mixed border. It wins points for leaf, flower, fruit and fragrance. Throw in good manners and a long life span, and you'll find it worth hunting for.

The common names refer to this plant's curious reputation: the pungent, somewhat lemony oils it emits are said to be flammable on a still warm evening if a match is held at the base of the ripening seed pods. Flame will flicker around the seed heads, but the plant will not be harmed. Such oils are also exuded when the roots are cut.

The plant grows to 4 feet (1.2 m) and has thick, waxy, pinnately compound leaves with five to thirteen leaflets. Each leaf is up to 9 inches (22 cm) long; each individual leaflet to 2½ inches (6 cm). They are dark green and the tiny oil glands, a characteristic of the citrus family, show as dots when the leaves are held to the light. (These oils can cause severe dermatitis on susceptible individuals.)

The flowers are borne individually along an upright flower stalk. The five-petaled flowers have one prominent, drooping petal and ten long, showy stamens. The fruit capsules are star-shaped in section. Despite the specific name (*albus* means white), the flowers of the species are not always white, but can be pink and pale purple. There are several named forms: 'Purpureus' (var. *ruber*) is pale purple with dark reddish purple veins and tiny reddish purple speckles underneath the petals; 'Alba' is pure white; 'Rubra' is rosy red.

Burning bush is native from southern Europe to northern China. It was grown commonly in London gardens in the early 1700s and was well known to gardeners then.

Two unrelated plants share the common name burning bush, both for their fall color: *Kochia scoparia* forma *trichophylla*, an annual; and *Euonymus alata*, a shrub.

Bloomtime: June and July.

Height: 2–4 feet (.6–1.2 m).

Spread: 18 inches (45 cm). Burning bush will eventually spread up to 3 feet (90 cm), so plant it near neighbors that can be moved.

Light and soil: Plant in full sun and well-drained soil with added organic matter and dolomite lime. It is tolerant of dry soil. Give some thought to the planting site, as older plants should not be disturbed.

Care and propagation: Plant with care, so as not to disturb the rootball. Staking is not required. Once established, burning bush is virtually care-free. Cut stems to the ground in late fall. Grow new plants from fresh seed, one per pot, in August or September. Keep seeds refrigerated in moist peat for 4–6 weeks before sowing. Germination, at a cool 55°F (13°C), will take 1–6 months.

Pests and diseases: Generally trouble-free.

Frost hardiness: To zone 2.

Digitalis ferruginea "rusty foxglove"
Digitalis grandiflora (*D. ambigua*) "yellow foxglove"
Digitalis × *mertonensis*
Digitalis purpurea "common foxglove" SCROPHULARIACEAE
(Figure 4-1)

Note: All parts of the plant are poisonous.

Foxgloves have striking inflorescences, made up of a spire of pendulous tubular blooms. The name digitalis was given to the genus in the sixteenth century because the shape of the flowers bears such a close resemblance to that of a finger—if you slip your fingertips into the flowers, they fit neatly. The "glove" part of the common name continues this theme, but origin of the prefix "fox" is obscure. Handsome plants for the woodland garden or border, several species are the source of the heart drug digitalis.

Digitalis purpurea. The frequency with which the common purple and white foxgloves spring up uninvited in our gardens would lead one to believe they are native to the Pacific coastal region. They are, however, native to the western Mediterranean. This species is actually a biennial but becomes a short-lived perennial under ideal conditions. It also seeds itself if the flower stalks are allowed to mature, and you can move the rosettes to where you want them. It forms a rosette of large, basal, midgreen leaves, at least 1 foot (30 cm) long. They taper from a rounded base to a long point and have scallops along the margin. In June and July, the plant sends up dramatic flower stalks 3–5 feet (.9–1.5 m) tall. Common foxglove was grown in gardens in Britain as long ago as the 1400s.

There are a number of interesting seed strains. 'Foxy' blooms the first year from seed and should be treated as an annual. The blooms of

'Excelsior' are held almost horizontal. 'Giant Shirley' is noted for the height of its inflorescenses. Reaching up to 6 feet (1.8 m), 3 feet (90 cm) of this is hung with blooms. 'Apricot Beauty' gives an alternative to the purple shades. Thompson & Morgan lists 'Alba', a white that comes true from seed if kept away from other shades.

D. ferruginea is biennial or a short-lived perennial. In July, it bears yellowish flowers, heavily veined with red brown. The leaves of rusty foxglove are to 7 inches (18 cm) long and it is native to Europe and western Asia. It grows to 3–4 feet (.9–1.2 m) in height.

D. grandiflora, also native to Europe and western Asia, has yellow flowers on 3-foot (90-cm) stalks in July and August. A true perennial, it has shiny leaves to 10 inches (25 cm) long.

D. × mertonensis is a hybrid between *D. grandiflora* and *D. purpurea*. It has coppery pink blooms from June to September and reaches 3 feet (90 cm). The evergreen leaves are large and toothed. It is also perennial. Despite the fact that it is a hybrid, it comes true from seed.

Bloomtime and height: See above.

Spread: *D. × mertonensis* and *D. grandiflora*: 12 inches (30 cm); *D. ferruginea*: 18 inches (45 cm); *D. purpurea*: 18–24 inches (45–60 cm).

Light and soil: Sun or partial shade in ordinary soil.

Care and propagation: Little care is required other than to cut down the faded flower stems. Despite their height, they do not generally need staking. Plants will often bloom again in fall. Propagate from seed sown from April to June, in pots or in the ground. Do not cover seed, as light is required for germination. Set plants in their position in the garden in the fall.

Pests and diseases: Generally trouble-free and not usually popular with deer.

Frost hardiness: *D. purpurea* and *D. ferruginea*: to zone 4; *D. grandiflora*: to zone 3; *D. × mertonensis*: to zone 5.

Doronicum austriacum
Doronicum cordatum (*D. caucasicum*, *D. columnae*) both called
"doronicum" "leopard's bane" ASTERACEAE
(Figure 4-2)

The peculiar name leopard's bane dates from ancient Greek herbals, but no one is quite sure which plant the writers referred to, as they neglected to describe even the flower. The plant was apparently used to poison leopards.

Doronicums are valued for their bright yellow, daisy-like flower heads, appearing in spring, when few other daisy-like flowers or tall perennials are in bloom. The ray florets are long and slender.

The leaves of **Doronicum austriacum** are heart-shaped, bright green and hairy, with teeth along the margin. The basal leaves have a long leafstalk, while those along the stems clasp the stem. The plant grows to 4 feet (1.2 m) and bears 2-inch (5-cm) flowers in April and May, usually several per stem. It is native to Europe.

Doronicum cordatum is similar but shorter, to 2¹/₂ feet (75 cm), and the flower stems usually bear only one one bloom per stem. It is native to Europe and Asia. 'Magnificum' has larger flowers and grows to 2 feet (60 cm). 'Spring Beauty' is double, resembling a dandelion. Cultivars of D. cordatum are listed under D. orientale in some catalogues, so watch for this usage in garden shops. 'Madame Mason' is probably a hybrid between D. cordatum and D. orientale. It is an excellent cultivar, growing to 18 inches (45 cm) and forming an attractive clump of heart-shaped, rather smooth,leaves. It combines well with Dicentra spectabilis and is delightful with red and white tulips.

Both species of leopard's bane are excellent for cutting.

Bloomtime: April to May.

Height: 1–2 feet (30–60 cm).

Spread: 1 foot (30 cm); except 'Madame Mason': 1 feet (45 cm).

Light and soil: Full sun or light shade in soil containing much organic matter. **Care and propagation:** Doronicums are easy to grow. Keep well watered during dry spells. Deadhead regularly and plants may bloom again in fall. Cut stems to ground in late October. Propagate from seed (except named cultivars that are not true from seed) or by division.

Pests and diseases: Generally trouble-free and not usually popular with deer.

Frost hardiness: To zone 4.

Echinacea purpurea (*Rudbeckia purpurea*) "purple coneflower"

ASTERACEAE

(Figure 4-3)

The striking blooms of the purple coneflower are borne on stems up to 4 feet (1.2 m) high. Unusual for members of the daisy family, the light purple ray florets (up to 3 inches/8 cm long) reflex dramatically from the disk, which looks like a deep orange pincushion. It sounds like an unlikely combination, but as one gardening friend says, "They clash well." The sandpapery, dark green leaves are variable in shape. The basal leaves are heart-shaped, up to 10 inches (25 cm) long, and are carried on an even longer leafstalk. There are teeth along the margin. The leaves along the stems taper to a long point and the teeth are much reduced. The species is native to the eastern United States and the generic name is derived from the Greek for hedgehog. 'Bright Star' (which has more horizontal ray florets), 'Earliest of All' and 'Robert Bloom' are good cultivars. 'White Lustre' (which may be a hybrid) has creamy white ray florets.

Bloomtime: July to September if deadheaded regularly.

Height: 3–4 feet (.9–1.2 m).

Spread: 18–24 inches (45–60 cm).

Light and soil: Best in full sun, but coneflower will tolerate light shade. Average garden soil that is well drained is suitable. (If planted in soil that is too rich, staking may be required.)

Care and propagation: Coneflowers are easy to grow. Keep them dead-headed. Mature plants are best left undisturbed, so the best method of propagation for named cultivars is root cuttings. Plants can also be grown from seed, but will be variable. 'White Swan' blooms the first year from seed sown indoors in March.

Pests and diseases: Generally trouble-free.

Frost hardiness: To zone 3.

Echinops species "globe thistle" ASTERACEAE
(Figure 4-4)

You will recognize a globe thistle right away by its ball-shaped inflorescence made up of over a hundred silvery purple flowers that look like tiny blue stars. These striking blooms are held above dark green, jagged leaves that alternate along the stems. The leaves are silvery underneath due to a covering of fine white hairs and are up to 5 inches (13 cm) long. There are prickles at the tip of the leaf lobes. The white stems are strong and do not need to be staked. Globe thistles are a welcome addition to any garden because of their ease of care and their unique appearance. They are native to dry, rocky places in Europe and the Middle East.

The nomenclature surrounding this genus is somewhat confusing. The globe thistle in general cultivation in the Pacific coastal region is usually named *Echinops ritro*. It reaches at least 4 feet (1.2 m) in height, but the true *E. ritro* grows to only 2 feet (60 cm). The plant commonly grown in the Pacific coastal region is probably either *E. exaltatus* or *E. humilis*.

Bloomtime: July and August.

Height: See above.

Spread: 2 feet (60 cm).

Light and soil: Plant in full sun in average, well-drained soil. Globe thistles also do well in poor, dry soil.

Care and propagation: Globe thistles require little care, except to remove the old stems once the flowers have finally shattered. Cut stems to ground level in late fall, or sooner if foliage looks untidy. Propagate by seed, or division in fall or spring. Globe thistles are excellent for flower arranging and drying. To dry them, pick the stalks before the tiny flowers are fully open, or they will shatter. Bees are attracted to globe thistles. Some gardeners find that globe thistle seed themselves prolifically, becoming a nuisance; in other gardens, they do not seed themselves at all.

Pests and diseases: Generally trouble-free and not usually popular with deer.

Frost hardiness: To zone 3.

Eryngium species and hybrids "sea holly" APIACEAE
(Figure 4-5)

Sea hollies have striking flowers of metallic blue, each looking like a cone set off by a ruff of lacy divided bracts. They begin to bloom about July, and because the flowers are everlasting, the effect remains attractive until the fall if the weather is not too wet. The sea hollies are excellent as cut flowers and for winter decoration indoors.

The taxonomy of this genus is confused, but descriptions of the most widely available sea hollies follow.

Eryngium alpinum is one of the most beautiful sea hollies, both for its 1$\frac{1}{4}$-inch (3-cm) blue or white flowers, which have one of the fullest and laciest ruffs of any species, and for its foliage. The toothed basal leaves are heart-shaped and held on a long leafstalk. This species grows to 2$\frac{1}{2}$ feet (75 cm) and is native to Europe.

E. amethystinum has 1/2-inch (1.3-cm) blue flowers. Its leaves are egg-shaped, broader towards the end of the leaf, and divided along the edges. It grows to 2 feet (60 cm) and is native to Europe. Plants sold under this name may in fact be *E. planum*.

E. bourgatii has 3/4-inch (2-cm) blue flowers. Its basal and stem leaves are deeply cut. This excellent garden plant grows to grows to 2 feet (60 cm) and is native to the Pyrenees.

E. maritimum has 1-inch (2.5-cm) pale blue flowers. Its basal leaves are rounded and silver green; its stem leaves are palmate and deeply cut. Growing to 1 foot (30 cm) in height, it is native to Europe and Britain but has naturalized on sand dunes in the eastern United States. It prefers hot, dry, sandy soil.

E. × oliveranum has 1 1/2-inch (4-cm) blue flowers and its leaves are rounded and deeply cut. It grows to 3 feet (90 cm) and its parents are most likely *E. alpinum* and *E. planum*.

E. planum has 1/2-inch (1.3-cm) pale blue flowers, more useful for cutting than for garden impact. Its leaves are rounded and heart-shaped. It grows to 3 feet (90 cm) and is native to eastern Europe and Asia.

E. variifolium has 3/4-inch (2 cm) blue flowers and glossy dark green leaves with prominent, light green veins, giving a marbled effect. Its flowers are not as striking as those of some others, but its foliage is excellent. It grows to 2 feet (60 cm) and is native to North Africa.

E. × zabelii. Thrown in under the name *E. × zabelii* are a number of outstanding hybrids of *E. alpinum* and *E. bourgatii* and miscellaneous named cultivars. They are not as readily available as the species. In general, they have 1-inch (2.5-cm) blue flowers and reach 2 1/2 feet (75 cm) in height.

With all species of *Eryngium*, plants and seed are sometimes sold under the incorrect name, a problem in horticulture; don't be surprised if the plant you buy or grow from seed is not what you had hoped for.

Bloomtime: July to August or September.

Height: 1–3 feet (30–90 cm), depending on the species and cultivar (see above).

Spread: 18 inches (45 cm); except *E. bourgatii*, *E. maritimum* and *E. variifolium*: 12 inches (30 cm); *E. amethystinum*: 24 inches (60 cm).

Light and soil: Full sun and ordinary, well-drained soil.

Care and propagation: Some sea hollies may need light support in windy locations. For winter decoration indoors, cut flowers while they are fresh.

Pests and diseases: Generally trouble-free, but some species may get MITES.

Frost hardiness: To zone 5; except *E. alpinum*: to zone 3; *E. amethystinum*: to zone 2.

Erysimum 'Bowles Mauve' see *Cheiranthus* 'Bowles Mauve'

Eupatorium coelestinum "mist flower" "hardy ageratum" "boneset"
Eupatorium purpureum "joe-pye weed" ASTERACEAE
(Figure 4-6)

For height without staking and fluffy blooms in late summer, these two distinctive border perennials have a lot to offer. The genus, which includes European species of little garden interest, is named for Mithridates, a eupator (king) in the ancient land of Pontus, now part of Turkey. He was particularly interested in poisons and their antidotes.

E. coelestinum has beautiful foamy-looking blue flowers and coarsely toothed leaves up to 3 inches (8 cm) long. Native to the eastern and southern United States and the West Indies, it combines well with goldrods and is appreciated by butterflies and bees.

E. purpureum has rigid, hollow, maroon stems, with leaves in groups of threes. The leaves are up to 6 inches (15 cm) long and taper to a point at both ends. They are dark green with teeth along the margin. The stems divide at the top into many wiry flowers stalks with hundreds of clusters of small purplish pink flowers, giving a fuzzy effect. The flowers last for weeks in water and the fluffy seed heads are also attractive.

Joe-pye weed is native to the eastern United States and was used by the Indians and later by European settlers to produce a red dye and to induce perspiration to break a fever. It is still used today by British and European herbalists. The origin of the name joe-pye is obscure.

Bloomtime: August and September.

Height: Mist flower: 2 feet (60 cm); joe-pye weed: 6–8 feet (1.8–2.4 m).

Spread: Mist flower: 2 feet (60 cm); joe-pye weed: 3 feet (90 cm).

Light and soil: Sun or part shade in moist but well-drained soil.

Care and propagation: Easy to grow. Mist flower may need dividing every few years if it spreads too widely. Cut stems to the ground in late fall if desired.

Pests and diseases: Generally trouble-free.
Frost hardiness: Mist flower: to zone 6; joe-pye weed: to zone 3.

Euphorbia epithymoides (*E. polychroma*) "cushion spurge"
Euphorbia griffithii "spurge" EUPHORBIACEAE
(Figures 4-7 and 4-8)

This genus is known to all because of one member: the poinsettia (*Euphorbia pulcherrima*) which has become synonymous with the winter holidays. As most people know, the showy part of the poinsettia, and of other euphorbias, is the brightly colored bracts. The actual flowers are small, to ¼ inch (.6 cm). All euphorbias have milky sap, which can be severely irritating to some people's skins. They make good cut flowers, but let the stems stand in water before arranging them, to rinse away the milky sap.

E. epithymoides, a native of Europe, grows to 18 inches (45 cm) and forms a rounded evergreen plant. It has oblong, dark green leaves, to 2 inches (5 cm) long, which turn red in the fall. Cushion spurge produces sulfur yellow bracts in April and May and combines well with *Doronicum* spp. It is long-lived and a carefree perennial.

E. griffithii, an Asian species, grows to 3 feet (90 cm) and produces its vivid orange red bracts in May and June. It has slender deep green leaves to 3½ inches (9 cm) long, without teeth and with a pink midrib. The cultivar 'Fireglow' ' .s even more brilliantly colored bracts than the species. As the summer goes on, the bracts turn green and the plant becomes a mound of neat greenery for the rest of the summer. Spurge spreads by rhizomes and seeds itself, but is not invasive.

Bloomtime: *E. epithymoides*: April and May; *E. griffithii*: May and June.
Height: *E. epithymoides*: 18 inches (45 cm); *E. griffithii*: 3 feet (90 cm).
Spread: *E. epithymoides*: 18 inches (45 cm); *E. griffithii*: 2 feet (60 cm).
Light and soil: Full sun or light shade in ordinary soil; the colors are more intense in poor, dry soil. *E. griffithii* tolerates damp soil.
Care and propagation: Easy to grow. Cut off old flower stalks after the blooms have faded to keep plants bushy. Propagate by seed (except for named cultivars), division or 3-inch (8-cm) basal cuttings.
Pests and diseases: Generally trouble-free.
Frost hardiness: *E. epithymoides*: to zone 3; *E. griffithii*: to zone 5.

Festuca species "blue fescue" POACEAE
(Figure 4-9)

A waxy coating along the slender leaf blade of blue fescue gives it a vivid hue that is very attractive in the garden. There is great variability among plants for sale under this name. The best ones are compact and intensely blue. Other plants are taller growing and tend toward floppiness; some are a less vivid shade of blue. Use blue fescue in the rock garden, as an edging or even as the centerpiece for a small container filled with annuals.

Grasses are difficult to identify, even for botanists. According to Roger Grounds, the author of *Ornamental Grasses*, a detailed and erudite work, the blue fescues are usually misnamed in the horticultural trade; blue fescue is most often sold under the name *Festuca ovina* var. *glauca*, a nonexistent plant. The true species in cultivation and their characteristics are summarized on the following chart (height includes the flower stalks).

Species	Height	Leaf color	Bloomtime	Inflorescence
F. amethystina	18 inches (45 cm)	blue	June-July	6 inches (15 cm) long
F. caesia	12 inches (30 cm)	very blue	June-July	short, thick
F. glacialis	6 inches (15 cm)	blue green	July-August	short, thick
F. rubra	12 inches (30 cm)	blue	May -June	very narrow

Grounds adds that *Festuca caesia* is "a densely tufted plant without runners; *rubra* forms a looser tuft with quite long tillers." *F. amethystina* is "generally of larger, looser habit, a less glaucous blue and a relatively larger and more spectacular inflorescence. A densely tufted perennial . . . with short rhizomes." All four species are native to Europe; *F. rubra* also grows wild in North America, Asia and North Africa.

Many outstanding clones of blue fescue have been selected; while few are readily available, look for them in mail-order catalogues.

Bloomtime: May–August, depending on the species.

Height: 6–18 inches (15–45 cm), depending on the species.

Spread: 6–12 inches (15–30 cm), depending on the species. When used as a ground cover, space plants 6 inches (15 cm) apart.

Light and soil: Best in full sun and a well-drained soil to which some dolomite lime has been added. Tolerates dry sandy soil.

Care and propagation: Blue fescues generally require little care, other than division of the larger-growing species to keep them looking tidy. Propagate from seed (except named cultivars that are not true from seed) or by division.

Pests and diseases: Generally trouble-free.

Frost hardiness: To zone 4.

Gaillardia × *grandiflora* "gaillardia" "blanketflower" ASTERACEAE (Figure 4-10)

Most of the gaillardias in cultivation are hybrids of two species: *Gaillardia aristata* (a perennial native to western Canada and the U.S.) and G. *pulchella* (an annual from the eastern and southern U.S.). Because of the annual parent, they are not long-lived.

Gaillardia has showy, daisy-like flower heads, up to 4 inches (10 cm) across, in rich gold and burgundy shades. Excellent for cutting, they bloom over a long period, even if not deadheaded. The foliage is a soft gray green. Leaf shape is variable; the lower leaves are usually lobed, but the leaves along the stems do not always have lobes. The stems of gaillardias tend to sprawl, but newer named cultivars are compact and less floppy. 'Goblin' grows to only 10 inches (25 cm) and has red and yellow blooms. 'Golden Goblin' is the same height, but with all-gold flowers. 'Burgundy' is all one shade of deep red and grows to 20 inches (50 cm). Most named cultivars of *Gaillardia* are grown from seed, with the result that plants of the same name are rarely identical.

Bloomtime: June to October.

Height: 10–30 inches (25–75 cm), depending on the cultivar.

Spread: 10–18 inches (25–45 cm), depending on the cultivar.

Light and soil: Best in full sun, but they tolerate light shade. For longest-lived plants, choose a spot with well-drained, even dry, soil. Do not add fertilizer or organic matter. Add sand if your soil is high in clay or peat.

Care and propagation: Easy to grow. Insert twiggy branches around the stems for extra support, especially for taller cultivars. Deadhead if desired, although the seed heads are not unattractive. Propagate by division or from seed.

Pests and diseases: The leaves may get POWDERY MILDEW in humid summers.

Frost hardiness: To zone 3.

Geranium species and hybrids "hardy geranium" "cranesbill"
GERANIACEAE
(Figure 4-11)

Until only a few years ago, most gardeners only associated the name geranium with the popular bedding plants having brightly colored flowers and leaves with a pungent aroma. It turns out, however, that those cheerful blooms belong to the genus *Pelargonium* and that true geraniums (in the genus *Geranium*) are a different group entirely. Also called hardy geraniums, they are long-lived perennials with blooms in soft shades of white, pink, mauve, purple and blue. Troubled by few pests or diseases, they are easy to grow, and some bloom for months on end. They are generally happy in sun or shade and in quite a range of soil conditions. Once you have grown true geraniums, you will wonder how you managed without them. Many are suited to the rockery or trailing over retaining walls; the larger ones are excellent in a sunny border, or in a shady border with hostas and ferns. Many species and cultivars are grown in gardens, but the following are some of the most popular. All have five petals.

Geranium cinereum. Dwarf compact plants best suited to the rock garden, this species and its cultivars have a scattering of flowers from May to October. 'Lawrence Flatman' (lilac) and 'Ballerina' (pale lilac) both have deep purple veins. They have small, rounded leaves with scalloped edges and long leafstalks. Plants grow to 4–6 inches (10–15 cm) and spread 12 inches (30 cm). They are hardy to zone 5, but protect them from drying winter winds even in warmer zones.

G. dalmaticum is an excellent trailer, gradually building up a clump to 2 feet (60 cm) across and 4 inches (10 cm) high. Plant it at the top of a retaining wall for a softening effect. Grow this geranium for its foliage. Attractive year-round, it takes on bright tints in the fall. Leaves are 3/4 inch (2 cm) across, round in outline but divided into five toothed lobes. They have a long leafstalk and are aromatic. The pink flowers appear in June and July. G. *dalmaticum* is hardy to zone 4.

G. endressii cultivars are the longest-blooming geraniums. They start blooming in May and continue until September—and not just a few blooms scattered over the plant, but enough to make a good show. The stems are a bit lax, but not unattractively so. 'A.T. Johnson' reaches 12 inches (30 cm) in height and is silvery pink. 'Wargrave Pink', to 18 inches (45 cm) high, has clear pink flowers. Flowers of both are about 1 inch (2.5 cm) across, with notched petals. The five-lobed, toothed, midgreen leaves are soft and fuzzy. They do well in shade, part shade and sun, and are evergreen. Plants spread to 18 inches (45 cm) and are hardy to zone 4.

G. 'Claridge Druce' is a hybrid between the previous species and an unknown parent. It is extremely vigorous and has magenta pink flowers from May to August. It grows to 18 inches (45 cm) in height and spread. Despite the fact that it is a hybrid, it comes true from its own seed and will spread to fill large areas, especially effective under trees. 'Claridge Druce' spreads to 18 inches (45 cm) across and is hardy to zone 3. (Note: some taxonomists list both 'Claridge Druce' and 'A. T. Johnson' as cultivars of G. × oxoniensis, a hybrid of G. endresssii and G. versicolor.)

G. 'Johnson's Blue' is an outstanding blue geranium, very showy in July and August. It is a hybrid between G. pratense and probably G. himalayense. The leaves make an elegant mound to 15 inches (38 cm) high and wide. Its leaves are 2–8 inches (5–20 cm) across and divided into seven narrow segments. It is hardy to zone 5.

G. macrorrhizum is a handsome plant with good foliage and a full rounded habit, 15 inches (38 cm) high by 2 feet (60 cm) wide. The leaves have five to seven deep lobes and are aromatic when crushed. The leaves are somewhat evergreen, and take on reddish tints in the fall if grown in the sun. The plant makes a good ground cover. The flowers are 3/4–1 inch (2–2.5 cm) across, in clusters, from April to May. The species is native to Europe. 'Ingwersen's Variety' is named for the English nurseryman, Walter Ingwersen, who discovered it. It has flowers of soft rose pink. 'Album', also discovered by Ingwersen, has white flowers. All are hardy to zone 3.

G. × magnificum is a hardy geranium that has been grown in the Pacific coastal region for many years—you often see handsome, well-established plants in older gardens. It shows off its purple flowers with darker purple veins from late May to early July. These flowers have a notch in the outer edge of each petal—a good identifying characteristic. (Another is that G. × magnificum doesn't set viable seed, for it is a sterile hybrid of G. ibericum and G. platypetalum, and, incidentally, is sold often under both of the parents' names.) It has 2-foot (60-cm) red stems, with fine, white hairs. The soft, fuzzy leaves, to 4 inches (10 cm) across, are divided into five toothed lobes. After the bloom has finished, the stems flop over; cut them off and within a few weeks the plant will fill in with handsome new foliage that will remain neat and full all summer and fall. G. × *magnificum* will spread to 2 feet (60 cm) and is hardy to zone 3.

G. *renardii* has beautiful foliage of soft, textured gray green, with rounded lobes. It has an excellent habit, growing to 15 inches (38 cm) by 30 inches (75 cm) across. A perfect front-of-the-border plant to complement others, it has pale lavender flowers with purple veins, between May and July. It is hardy to zone 4.

G. *sanguineum*, bloody cranesbill, and its cultivars form a rounded clump of gray green leaves, each leaf having five to seven lobes and long, pointed teeth. It grows to 6–9 inches (15–23 cm) by 18 inches (45 cm) wide. The species has flowers in shades of reddish purple. 'Album' is white and is an excellent plant to brighten a semishady spot. 'Glenluce' is light pink; G. *sanguineum* var. *lancastriense* (also sold as 'Striatum') is light pink with crimson veins. All bloom June to September and are hardy to zone 4.

All of the species mentioned above are native to Europe, with the following exceptions. G. *himalayense* is from Turkestan, India and Tibet. G. *pratense* and G. *sanguineum* are native to Europe and Asia. G. *ibericum* is native to Asia. G. *platypetalum* and G. *renardii* are both native to the Caucasus, the former also extending into Armenia and Iran.

Bloomtime: Between April and October, depending on the species and cultivar (see above).

Height and spread: See above.

Light and soil: All do well in part shade or full sun in ordinary garden soil. G. *macrorrhizum* tolerates damp soil.

Care and propagation: Easy to grow. As noted above, G. × *magnificum* should be cut back after flowering to encourage a compact clump of foliage. This may be done for the G. *endressii* cultivars too—although they never stop blooming, they may be more open than you prefer.

Pests and diseases: Generally trouble-free, but watch for SLUGS and SNAILS.

Frost hardiness: To zones 3 to 5 (see above).

Gypsophila paniculata "baby's breath"
Gypsophila repens (G. *prostrata*) "creeping baby's breath"
CARYOPHYLLACEAE
(Figures 4-12 and 5-1)

At first glance, these two species are quite different: baby's breath is a border perennial of generous proportions; creeping baby's breath forms a delicate carpet for rock gardens and retaining walls. On closer inspection, the generic resemblance is apparent. Both have slender, matte gray green leaves that are arranged in opposite pairs along wiry stems. Characteristic of members of the carnation family, these species have a swelling along the stems at each leaf node. Both have tiny, 1/4-inch (.6-cm) flowers with five petals.

Gypsophila paniculata. Once established, baby's breath looks like a cloud of white foam for three months in late summer. It is wonderful for flower arranging—especially for those of us who are not gifted at this art—because it fills in so nicely. Its leaves are up to 3 inches (8 cm) long. Although individual flowers are tiny, they appear in the hundreds on intricately branched stems. Baby's breath is particularly useful for filling in above plants that die down in summer, such as Oriental poppies and bleeding heart. The species is native to Europe and Asia. In the past, named cultivars of baby's breath were propagated commercially by grafting, which made them relatively expensive, but they are now being propagated by a technique known as tissue culture.

'Bristol Fairy' (developed by the American nurseryman Alex Cummings at Bristol Nursery in Connecticut) and 'Perfecta' ('Bristol Fairy Perfect') grow to 2¹/₂–3 feet (75–90 cm) and have double white flowers. The double, rosy pink 'Flamingo' may be a form of the Korean and Chinese species G. *oldhamiana.* It grows to 2 feet (60 cm). The semiprostrate, pale pink 'Rosy Veil' grows to 15 inches (38 cm), and is possibly a hybrid with G. *repens* 'Rosea'. The seed strain 'Double Snowflake' produces about 60 percent doubles.

G. repens is a delightful European native, great for the rockery and for tumbling over retaining walls. Its leaves are a smaller version of those of its cousin and, despite its delicate looks, it is an easier plant to grow. It grows up to 6 inches (15 cm) in height and gradually spreads to form a mat up to 2 feet (60 cm) across. From June to August, it produces a myriad of tiny pink ('Rosea') or white ('Alba') flowers. The contrast against a rock wall is delightful.

Bloomtime: Late June to early September.

Height: G. *paniculata:* 15–36 inches (38–90 cm); G. *repens:* 6 inches (15 cm).

Spread: 2–3 feet (60–90 cm).

Light and soil: Full sun. *Gypsophila* means lime-loving, so add several handfuls of dolomite lime to the soil when planting, and top-dress with dolomite each fall.

Care and propagation: Baby's breath can be capricious. It is one of the few plants I have grown that seems to flourish or perish with no apparent reason for either. It can take several years to develop a full plant, but it is worth waiting for. Stake taller cultivars. Divide or transplant baby's breath only as absolutely necessary. Propagate named varieties from cuttings or try the seed strain.

Creeping baby's breath is easy to grow and can be divided or grown from cuttings.

Pests and diseases: Generally trouble-free.

Frost hardiness: To zone 3

Helleborus niger "Christmas rose"
Helleborus orientalis **hybrids** "Lenten rose" RANUNCULACEAE
(Figure 5-2)

If I had to pick one favorite plant in my garden, it would probably be **Helleborus orientalis**. It was presented to me many years ago by a woman who divided it in full bloom. At the time I hardly knew what it was. It forgave that rough treatment and settled in for the duration. Each year in February or March—just as the attraction of our mild Pacific coast winters is beginning to wear thin—it throws up dozens of saucer-shaped, dusky purple blooms held high over the thick, leathery, dark green leaves. The flowers transform into interesting seed capsules. The leaves are evergreen and form a handsome mound for the summer and fall, looking a bit tatty by late winter, when a new set is produced. The only attention I give it (other than compliments) is to cut away last year's faded foliage as the new appears. It also seeds itself—not enough to be a nuisance, but enough to let me know it feels at home.

Botanists believe that plants cultivated under the name of *Helleborus orientalis* are in reality hybrids with five other species. Plants are variable, producing blooms of cream and purples, some with attractive speckles inside.

H. niger, the Christmas rose, gets more attention than the Lenten rose because of its earlier bloomtime, but it is a more difficult plant to grow well. It is slow to establish and is subject to a fungal disease on the leaves. It produces beautiful white saucer-shaped blooms from December to March.

The showy floral parts of both the Lenten and the Christmas rose are sepals, not petals. The leaves are palmately compound, with five to seven leaflets. All are native to Europe or Asia Minor. Named cultivars of both are available in Britain, but not generally in our area.

Both species of *Helleborus* make good cut flowers. If you pick the young flowers, float them in a bowl of water. Or wait until the sepals become papery and use the whole stems. Sear the stems in boiling water, and they will last longer.

Bloomtime: *H. niger*: December to March; *H. orientalis*: February to March.

Height: *H. niger*: 12–18 inches (30–45 cm); *H. orientalis*: 18–24 inches (45–60 cm).

Spread: 18 inches (45 cm).

Light and soil: Plant in part or full shade. Fuss more over the soil for *H. niger*, adding a lot of organic matter.

Care and propagation: Although the old leaves look tattered by late winter, leave them on to protect new leaves and flower buds from late frosts. Cut them away when plants begin to bloom. Propagate from seed (except named cultivars that are not true from seed) or by division. Seed does not germinate readily.

Pests and diseases: *H. niger*, in particular, gets LEAF SPOT.

Frost hardiness: To zone 3.

Hemerocallis lilioasphodelus (*H. flava*) "yellow daylily" "lemon daylily"
Hemerocallis hybrids "daylily" LILIACEAE
(Figure 5-3)

The name *Hemerocallis* means beautiful for one day, for each lily-like bloom is open for one day only.

Daylilies are a life-saver for gardeners to our east, for they are able to withstand both cold winters and blazing hot, humid summers and survive, still looking comparatively unscathed in late summer. This solid performance has resulted in a hybridizing craze in the eastern United States, and hundreds of new daylily cultivars are registered each year. They are easy to grow, with lovely lily-like blooms in every imaginable shade of yellow, pink, cream and red. They have virtually no pests and diseases, are not usually invasive, and have attractive strap-like foliage. But in the Pacific coastal region, where there is a great wealth of suitable plant material, a few daylilies would probably be plenty for most gardens. Some cultivars make large clumps of foliage and only bloom for a few weeks, not really justifying the space they take, unless you have a very large garden to fill up. The flowers of cultivars with double blooms do not open well during damp weather.

Hemerocallis lilioasphodelus has been cultivated since before the 1600s. It is native to Siberia and Japan, blooms in May and is very fragrant. It is the one of the few species of daylily that are readily available from several mail-order lists.

Hemerocallis **hybrids** bloom sometime between June and October; length of bloomtime varies with the cultivar. Because there are so many cultivars and availability varies with retailer, either buy plants in bloom, if possible, or read catalogue listings for the ones that sound appealing. Look for cultivars that are floriferous, meaning that they produce a lot of flowers, and ones that have a long bloom period. If possible, get plants that hold their blooms well above the foliage, and ones that have attractive foliage as well. For most gardens, the smaller plants are more suitable; the larger ones don't always have many more flowers.

One of the best of the new cultivars—and much sought after—is 'Stella d'Oro'. It has a very long season of bloom, virtually continuous from June until the frost. It is a neat plant, growing to 22 inches (55 cm), with dozens of canary yellow blooms.

Bloomtime: May to September, depending on the species and cultivar (see above).

Height: Most cultivars grow 18 inches to 3 feet (45–90 cm), but some unusual cultivars reach up to 6 feet (1.8 m).

Spread: 15–18 inches (38–45 cm).

Light and soil: Full sun or part shade in average garden soil. They will tolerate damp and dry soil, but the leaves look tatty by the end of summer in very dry soil.

Care and propagation: Easy to grow. Remove faded flowers, particularly with the large-flowered hybrids, to keep them tidy-looking. Cut back flower stalks when finished and cut leaves a few inches above ground level in the fall if necessary (some kinds are evergreen). If clumps become overcrowded, divide the root ball and replant. Propagate species from seed or division, named cultivars by division. Seed strains are also

122

available. Commercially, daylilies are sometimes propagated by tissue culture.

Pests and diseases: Generally trouble-free.

Frost hardiness: *Hemerocallis* hybrids: to zone 3 (the evergreen kinds are slightly less hardy); *H. lilioasphodelus*: to zone 4.

Heuchera × *brizoides* "coralbells"
Heuchera 'Palace Purple'
× *Heucherella* **'Bridget Bloom'** SAXIFRAGACEAE
(Figures 5-4 and 5-5)

Most of the coralbells grown in gardens are hybrids of *Heuchera micrantha* (native from B.C. south to California), *H. sanguinea* (Mexico and Arizona) and possibly *H. americana* (the midwestern U.S.). Even in the wild, various species hybridize, making identification difficult.

Heuchera × *brizoides*. Coralbells have gray green leaves with large scallops and small teeth along the margin. Leaves are up to 2 inches (5 cm) across and form an evergreen clump to 8 inches (20 cm) high by 12 inches (30 cm) across. Borne on wiry stems (not always as erect as one would wish) are clusters of 1/2-inch (1.3-cm) red, white, greenish white, or pink bells. The effect is open and airy, like many members of the saxifrage family. Coralbells blooms from May to July. Clones with strong, erect stems and blooms of various shades have been named, but they are most readily acquired by mail-order. Many have been developed by Alan Bloom. Some cultivars are 'Chatterbox' (rose pink), 'Chartreuse' (light green), 'Red Prince' (red) and 'Snowflake' (white). 'Bressingham Hybrids' is a seed strain that produces mixed colors.

H. 'Palace Purple', found at Kew Gardens in England, is an exciting cultivar that is quite different from other coralbells. It is a handsome plant, with deep, slightly puckered, mahogany leaves that form a large, richly textured mound up to 18 inches (45 cm) high. Cream flowers, held on 2 1/2-foot (75-cm) stalks, appear from July to October. It is a superb companion to many other perennials and is a selected form of *H. micrantha* var. *diversifolia*.

× *Heucherella alba* **'Bridget Bloom'** is a bigeneric hybrid (that is, a hybrid of plants from two different genera—most hybrids are of two species from the same genus). It was developed in Alan Bloom's nursery in England. One of the nursery staff had tried to cross the newly discovered species *Tiarella wherryi* with a *Heuchera* hybrid. After two years with no results, he planted them next to each other, and the bees managed to produce one seedling. 'Bridget Bloom' is similar to *Heuchera* × *brizoides*, but it is more delicate and the leaves have lobes that are more pointed. Each flower has both pale pink and white petals.

All of the above are excellent for flower arranging.

Bloomtime: *Heuchera* × *brizoides* and × *Heucherella*: May to July; *H.* 'Palace Purple': July to October.

Height: 1–2 feet (30–60 cm).

Spread: 12 inches (30 cm).

Light and soil: Sun or light shade in a well-drained soil to which some organic matter has been added.

Care and propagation: Easy to grow and long-lived. Coralbells has a tendency to become somewhat woody at the base. After blooming, dig plants and pull apart individual clumps with fibrous roots attached. Freshen the soil with organic matter and replant, setting the crowns well down into the soil, firming well and watering in.

Propagation of coralbells can also be done from seed, but characteristics of flower color and height will vary. 'Palace Purple' is most often grown from seed; select seedlings with the best dark red coloration. These plants can then be propagated by division. 'Bridget Bloom' does not produce seed and can only be propagated vegetatively.

Pests and diseases: Generally trouble-free, but I have seen the larvae of ROOT WEEVILS demolish the roots under the surface of the ground. If you have an infestation of weevils in the garden, keep an eye on your coralbells.

Frost hardiness: To zone 3; except *H.* 'Palace Purple': to zone 4.

Hosta species and hybrids "hosta" "funkia" LILIACEAE
(Figure 5-6)

Unsurpassed for the drama of their foliage, hostas add substance to the shady border. Their large, heart-shaped leaves can be glossy green, yellow, blue or have interesting variegations of white and green, or yellow and green. Leaf size ranges from several feet (1 m) long on plants mounding up to waist height, to diminutive gems with leaves only 4 inches (10 cm) long. Teamed up with ferns, astilbes and hardy geraniums, hostas add a rich textural contrast to the shady border.

In addition, hostas are easy to grow. They are very hardy (at the slightest frost, their leaves collapse, but the roots survive extreme cold), may be divided and transplanted with impunity and, except for their attractiveness to slugs and snails, are pest- and disease-free. Hosta leaves and flowers are both valuable for arranging.

Understandably, as part of the current perennials craze in North America, there has been a boom in hosta hybridization. One large catalogue from the midwestern U.S. lists 90 different hostas, second only to the 113 different daylilies they list. While most Pacific coast gardeners wonder why there is so much fuss about daylilies in the east, they usually perk up when it comes to hostas.

Confusion over taxonomy reaches new heights in the hosta world. Extensive research has been done by the late Dr. Fumio Maekawa and Dr. Noboru Fujita, who between them have spent over twenty-five years studying hostas in the wild in Asia. Hostas are primarily native to Japan, with a few species in China and Korea. Although there are over one hundred hostas sold with botanical names made up of the generic name and the specific epithet, for example *Hosta lancifolia*, it seems that there are probably only about twenty true species of hostas in all. These species are extremely variable, so that what were thought to be many species are actually a few highly variable species. Also, most of the hundred types sold with "latinized names," as hosta specialist Paul Aden refers to them, are actually seedlings originating in gardens, not in the wild.

The following species/hybrids/cultivars are the most readily available in our region. The height refers to the height of the foliage, not the flower stalks.

'August Moon' has large gold leaves that keep their color through the summer. In July, white flowers with a touch of mauve are held well above the foliage. Plant in shade to three-quarters sun. It grows to 20 inches (50 cm) high.

'Frances Williams' is a mutation of the blue *H. sieboldiana*. It has a creamy border along the margin of its large leaves. It was discovered in 1936 in a bed of seedlings at Bristol Nursery, Connecticut, by landscape architect Frances Williams. She was a hosta enthusiast, and, after buying that one plant, gradually sent divisions of it around the world. It was named for her in 1962, seven years before her death, and is the most popular hosta in the U.S. It grows in shade to one-half sun and reaches 32 inches (80 cm) in height.

'**Golden Tiara**' is a lovely small hosta with a striking chartreuse border. An award winner, it is a good edger. 'Golden Tiara' grows in shade to three-quarters sun, reaching 15 inches (38 cm) in height.

'**Halcyon**' makes a graceful clump of bright, silver gray leaves and bears heavy clusters of smoky lilac flowers in July and August. Plant in shade to one-half sun. It grows to 18 inches (45 cm) high.

'**Honeybells**' (a selection of H. *plantaginea*) has green leaves and fragrant purple bells in July and August. It grows in shade or sun, to 2 feet (60 cm), with the flower stalks reaching 3 feet (90 cm) in height.

'**Krossa Regal**' makes a huge, vase-shaped specimen over the years. Growing to 32 inches (80 cm) in height, it has large, wavy, blue leaves with lilac flowers on 4- to 5-foot (1.2- to 1.5 m) stalks in August and September. A handsome plant, it grows in shade to one-half sun.

'**Pearl Lake**' is noted for a profusion of lavender flowers over a medium-sized mound of blue green leaves. It blooms in July and August and grows to 15 inches (38 cm) in height. It is an award winner and grows in shade to three-quarters sun.

'**Royal Standard**' has large, glossy green leaves and wonderfully fragrant white flowers on 3-foot (90-cm) stems in August and September. It is a hybrid of H. *plantaginea*. The flowers smell like lilies (they are members of the same family). It grows to 28 inches (70 cm) in height. Plant in shade or full sun.

'**Sum and Substance**' is disliked by east coast slugs and snails on account of its thick, waxy leaves. If our Pacific coast slugs terrorize your garden, give it a try! It is a handsome plant, with large, glossy yellow leaves and tall stalks of lavender flowers in July. An award winner, it grows in one-quarter to full sun and reaches 26 inches (64 cm) in height.

'**Wide Brim**' is a relatively new cultivar that has received good reviews. It has broad, strongly ribbed, blue green leaves with wide, irregular margins of cream and golden yellow. Excellent in clumps, as a specimen or in a container on the patio, it produces lots of lavender flowers in July and August. Plant in shade to three-quarters sun. 'Wide Brim' attains 18 inches (45 cm) in height.

H. crispula has wavy leaves of dark green with white margins. Many lavender flowers are held on 3-foot (90-cm) stalks in late June and July. Plant in shade to one-half sun. It grows to 15 inches (38 cm) high.

H. decorata (also sold as 'Thomas Hogg') has broad, cream-edged leaves and lilac flowers in June and July. It grows in shade to one-half sun, reaching 18 inches (45 cm) in height.

H. fortunei cultivars form rounded mounds to about 15 inches (38 cm) high. They have pale purple flowers on tall flower stalks from June or July to August. 'Aureo-marginata' ('Obscura Marginata'or 'Gold Crown') has a yellow edge to the leaf. 'Albo-marginata' ('Silver Crown') has a white margin that remains all summer. The leaves of 'Albo-picta' ('Picta') unfurl yellow with a dark green margin; the yellow gradually darkens until the leaf is all dark green by late summer. This group grows in shade to three-quarters sun.

H. lancifolia has slender, glossy green leaves and light purple flowers on tall stalks from July to October. It is a very tough, even drought resistant, plant, and the foliage looks fresh all summer. Plant in shade to one-half sun. It grows to 12 inches (30 cm) high.

H. plantaginea and its cultivar 'Grandiflora' have fragrant, pure white flowers in August and September. The leaves are glossy green. Plant in a warm spot to encourage early flowering. It is ideal for a conservatory, where its fragrance can be enjoyed. It grows in shade or sun, reaching 2 feet (60 cm) in height.

H. sieboldiana **'Elegans'** is widely grown, although the leaves of some of the newer blues remain fresher looking for longer through the summer. It has puckered, blue green leaves and develops slowly into a huge mound up to 4 feet (1.2 m) high. It has stumpy flower stalks bearing thickly clustered white flowers in July and August. Plant in shade to one-half sun.

H. undulata **'Variegata'** has small leaves with white splashes and streaks in the center. The green margin is very wavy, with the leaf twisting especially at the sharply pointed tip. It grows to 10 inches (25 cm) in height and has pale purple flowers in July and August. It grows in shade to one-half sun.

Bloomtime: See above.

Height: The plants described here range from 1–4 feet (.3–1.2 m) in height. Plants as small as 5 inches (13 cm) can be ordered from specialist growers.

Spread: Allow 18 inches (45 cm) for small types such as 'Golden Tiara'. Large hostas such as *H. sieboliana* 'Elegans' can spread up to 5 feet (1.5 m) across in 5 years.

Light and soil: Shade to full sun, depending on the species or cultivar. If you are planting them under trees that drop petals, such as flowering cherry, or leaves, such as cedar, keep in mind that hostas with glossy leaves remain tidier looking. Hostas with blue leaves tend to hold the debris; not only is it messy, but it spoils the blue coating on the leaf. Hostas prefer moist soil with abundant organic matter, but some cultivars are more drought tolerant than others. All grow in damp soil. In general, if the soil is moist, more sun will be tolerated.

Care and propagation: Hostas are easy to grow. All that is required is to keep the slugs and snails at bay and tidy up the old leaves and flower stalks in fall. The waxy coating ("bloom") that causes the blueness on some hosta leaves can easily be destroyed by being rubbed or hit too hard with water. It also lasts longer through the summer if the surrounding humidity is high, such as by a pond. Gold-leaf hostas tend to have better color in some sun. Hostas with thick, glossy leaves are generally more drought tolerant.

Commercially, many hostas are now being propagated by tissue culture, a technique that can produce an enormous number of new plants each year. This should increase availability of some types and ideally decrease prices. For the home gardener, division is the only practical method for increasing clones. It is possible to slice off a pie-shaped wedge from an old hosta clump, making sure that it has several buds, rather than lifting the whole clump to divide it. Hostas are easy to grow from seed (although not all types set seed), but the seedlings are not usually the same as the parent. For example, 'Frances Williams' produces viable seed, but in my experience, the seedlings were all blue and lacked the contrasting margin.

Pests and diseases: SLUGS and SNAILS.

Frost hardiness: To zone 3.

Iberis sempervirens "evergreen candytuft" BRASSICACEAE
(Figure 5-7)

An outstanding evergreen subshrub, candytuft is a must for the large rockery or for trailing over a retaining wall. It can also be used at the front of a border. Candytuft bears clusters of tiny white flowers, each to 1/4 inch (.6 cm) across, in May and June. The narrow, dark green leaves of candytuft are to 1 inch (2.5 cm) long. Unlike its spring-blooming companions, aubrietia and phlox, it remains attractive year-round, gradually spreading to form a compact mat 9 inches (23 cm) high by 18–24 inches (45–60 cm) across. It is found growing wild in limy soils in southern Europe. All forms seem satisfactory, but there are a number of more-compact named cultivars. 'Little Gem' grows to 6 inches (15 cm) and 'Snowflake', brilliant white, grows to 8 inches (20 cm).

Bloomtime: May and June.

Height: 6–9 inches (15–23 cm).

Spread: 18–24 inches (45–60 cm) across.

Light and soil: Full sun in average garden soil. They tolerate poor soil.

Care and propagation: Easy to grow—just remove faded blooms after flowering has finished. Propagate from seed (except named cultivars that are not true from seed) or by division.

Pests and diseases: Generally trouble-free.

Frost hardiness: To zone 3.

Incarvillea delavayi "hardy gloxinia" BIGNONIACEAE
(Figure 5-8)

The exotic appearance of hardy gloxinias would lead you to suspect that they aren't hardy, but looks are deceiving. Related to the catalpa tree and the showy vine campsis, hardy gloxinia has showy, bright pink tubular flowers that flare out into five lobed petals. Each flower is up to 3 inches (8 cm) long, with yellow and purple markings in the tube. Although not related, they do resemble the popular houseplant *Gloxinia*, a member of the African violet family (Gesneriaceae). Several flowers cluster at the end of 2- to 3-foot (60- to 90-cm) stalks. These are held above a mound of handsome, pinnately compound leaves. The leaves are up to 1 foot (30 cm) long, and each has up to nine pairs of leaflets and one odd leaflet at the end. Hardy gloxinia is native to China and Tibet.

Bloomtime: May to July.

Height: 2–3 feet (60–90 cm). Flowering begins on short flower stalks, and these become taller as the summer progresses. Plant hardy gloxinia at the front of the border, so the leaves can be seen through the summer.

Spread: 15 inches (38 cm).

Light and soil: Full sun and rich, well-drained soil that does not dry out while the plants are in bloom.

Care and propagation: New growth of hardy gloxinia emerges in late spring; mark plants to prevent accidental damage to clumps while they are still dormant. Plants are not easy to divide successfully; attempt it in spring if necessary. Mulch each fall with organic matter, but pull the mulch back from the emerging shoots in spring to discourage slugs.

Pests and diseases: SLUGS and SNAILS.

Frost hardiness: To zone 5.

Inula 'Golden Beauty' see *Buphthalum*

Iris × germanica
Iris × germanica var. florentina "orris"
Iris pallida 'Variegata'
Iris siberica all called "iris" and "flag" IRIDACEAE
(Figure 5-9 and cover photograph)

There are about two hundred species of iris, most native to the north temperate zone and they have been a source of interest to people for thousands of years. Most irises have a characteristic flower shape: three flower parts held aloft are called the "standards"; the three drooping flower parts are called the "falls." The iris emblem has decorated the scepters of kings and rulers through the ages, its three standards representing faith, wisdom and valor.

The ancient Greeks named the iris after the goddess of the rainbow, because irises have flowers of almost every color. The Greeks planted irises on the graves of women, because one of the duties of the goddess Iris was to lead the souls of dead women to the Elysian Fields.

It was the symbol of the Gauls as early as the first century A.D., but was not actually used on the banner of France until 1294. In France, it was called Fleur-de-Lys or "the flower of Louis," Louis being the name taken by a long line of French kings from A.D. 814 to the French Revolution.

Many irises are in cultivation, and they have varying needs. *Iris pseudoacorus*, for example, is quite happy standing in a foot (30 cm) of water year-round, while *I. unguicularis* must be grown in a warm position in very quickly draining soil.

Irises can be divided into two types, according to their roots, which can be rhizomes or bulbs. The ones described here are the most commonly available of those with rhizomatous roots.

I. × germanica is an ancient plant, whose parents and place of origin are unknown. It is thought perhaps to have originated in the Mediterranean region and is itself one parent of a complex group of hybrids.

Known as German or bearded iris for the beard-like tuft on its falls, it has showy flowers in every imaginable shade and color combination except bright red. To give an idea of the diversity, the American Iris Society recognizes seven categories of flower types. A self is a flower of a single color. A bicolor has standards of one color and falls of another. A plicata has a two-toned effect on each standard and falls. A bi-tone has two shades of the same color, and a blend shows subtle variegation of a single color. A variegata is a brown and yellow combination and an amoena is a bicolor with either standards or falls being white. In addition, standards and falls may be ruffled. The beard may be the same color as the falls, but it is often of a contrasting color, adding another touch of interest. Each flower does not last long, either cut or in the garden, but for showiness, they are unrivaled.

The plants themselves are easy to grow, putting up with poor soil and little care. They have attractive gray green leaves, but these are subject to an unattractive fungal leaf spot disease. To draw attention away from their late-summer foliage, set plants in small groups in the middle of a mixed border. When one sees them in bloom from late May to June, it is tempting to dream of a border composed of an iris of every color possible, but they bloom for such a short time and look so tattered by late summer that it is more realistic to use bearded irises in small doses with other perennials and shrubs.

There are so many cultivars and they seem to come and go so quickly that your best bet is to check out the selection at a good garden center or order them from an iris specialist. Some are sweetly scented. Remember that the tall cultivars require staking. Best for most gardens are those of intermediate height, 16–27 inches (40–68 cm), or less.

I. × *germanica* var. *florentina* and *I. pallida*. These two irises have been in cultivation since ancient times because their rhizomes, dried and powdered, are the source of the perfume ingredient orris. *I.* × *germanica* var. *florentina*, also called *I. florentina* by some botanists, has beautiful white flowers. The purple *I. pallida*, a native to Austria, is most often seen as its striped cultivar, 'Variegata'. Both seem somewhat resistant to the unattractive leaf spot disease that afflicts their showier relatives and are heartily recommended. They grow to about 2 feet (60 cm) and need half of that to spread. *I. pallida* has two variegated forms, one with white and one with yellow; sometimes both appear under the name 'Variegata' and sometimes the yellow is called 'Aurea-variegata'. Both are fine for the front of a border.

Siberian irises are derived from *I. siberica* (native to Central Europe and Russia) and *I. sanguinea* (Manchuria and Japan). Their flowers have the same standard-and-falls arrangement as the above types, but, being a bit smaller and more graceful, they combine more easily with other perennials. Siberian irises are beardless and are therefore in a separate taxonomic section from the German bearded iris. They have healthy, bright green, grass-like leaves that die to the ground in winter. Providing excellent cut flowers, Siberian irises can be grown either in the border or at the edge of water. Bloomtime is early to mid-June. Plants grow up to 3 feet (90 cm). Cultivars have been named, but plants are often sold in shops as purple, white or blue. Look to mail-order sources for wine reds and yellows as well as many blues and whites. Many references say they tolerate shade; in my experience, this results in no bloom.

Bloomtime: Late May to June.

Height: Up to 3 feet (90 cm), except for the shorter cultivars of German bearded irises.

Spread: 12 inches (30 cm); except Siberian iris: 24 inches (60 cm).

Light and soil: Plant in full sun. *I.* × *germanica* and *I. pallida* and their relatives prefer a handful of dolomite lime and very well-drained, dryish soil; the Siberians flourish with lots of organic matter and moist soil.

Care and propagation: The bearded hybrids are generally divided after blooming, and if you order them by mail, they will probably be shipped in summer. To plant, dig a hole and at the bottom of it, make a cone of soil. Set the rhizome on the top of the cone, which should be high enough that the rhizome will be just at soil level. Spread the roots down over the cone and replace the soil. You should still be able to see the horizontal rhizome, which likes to creep over the soil surface and "sunbathe." Remove flower stems after blooms have faded and tidy up the leaves through the summer.

Siberian irises, like most other perennials, are best divided in spring or fall and should be planted about 1 inch (2.5 cm) deep in good soil. Mulch well and avoid cultivating near the plants, for the roots may be damaged. Deadhead after blooming and cut stems down to the ground in late fall.

Pests and diseases: Irises are attractive to SLUGS and SNAILS, which can make a mess of the leaves. They also get a fungal LEAF SPOT. If ignored, the leaves will shrivel up by late summer, sooner than they would otherwise,

but the plants are apparently not harmed in the long run.
Frost hardiness: To zone 3.

Liatris **species and cultivars** "gayfeather" "blazing star" ASTERACEAE
(Figure 5-10)
Gayfeathers grow wild in the United States and Canada. Their inflorescences are tall, erect spires packed with dozens of clusters of small flowers having long, ribbony stigmas; the overall effect is fluffy. Flowers open from the top of the inflorescence down and are usually purple or rosy purple. All species have white representatives. All have long (to 1 foot/30 cm at the base), narrow, shiny, grass-like leaves. All work well in the border (take care when combining the purple ones with other colors) and make great cut flowers.

Liatris aspera (*L. scariosa* Hort.) grows to 6 feet (1.8 m) and its flower clusters are well spaced, elegantly showing each off. It is highly recommended and drought tolerant.

L. pycnostachya grows to 4 feet (90 cm), with strong, mauve pink flower spikes up to 2 feet (60 cm) long. It enjoys moist soil in summer.

L. scariosa, to 3 feet (1.2 m), is drought tolerant and needs well-drained soil, especially in winter. The cultivar 'White Spire' is the best white gayfeather. There is also a white seed strain called 'Gloriosa'.

L. spicata, to 3 feet (90 cm), is the most adaptable in terms of soil conditions, growing in average to dry soil. The most common gayfeather cultivars are of this species. 'Kobold' is a dwarf form, to 2 feet (60 cm), with dark purple flowers. 'Floristan White' and 'Floristan Violet' were developed for the florist trade and have especially long inflorescences. They grow to 3 feet (90 cm).
Bloomtime: July to September.
Height: 2–6 feet (.6–1.8 m), depending on the species and cultivar.
Spread: 12–18 inches (30–45 cm), depending on height.
Light and soil: Full sun. See notes above for soil recommendations.
Care and propagation: Mulch plants to keep the soil moist. Fading flowers can easily be removed from the top of the spike. After the first flush of bloom in July, cut finished flower stalks at the base. More flowers may be produced later in the summer. Named cultivars should be divided in spring and species can be grown from seed or divided. *L. aspera*, *L. pychnostachya* and *L. scariosa* 'Gloriosa' are all listed by Thompson & Morgan.

Pests and diseases: SLUGS and SNAILS.
Frost hardiness: To zone 3.

Lobelia cardinalis "cardinal flower"
Lobelia splendens (*L. fulgens*) "perennial lobelia" LOBELIACEAE
(Figure 5-11)

Perennial lobelias are short-lived, but are so striking in the garden that it is worth planting them nonetheless. They have asymmetrical scarlet flowers held atop tall stems. Each flower consists of a tube that opens into two upper and three lower lobed petals. They make striking cut flowers. The alternate leaves are up to 6 inches (15 cm) long, are pointed at each end, and have small teeth along the margin.

Lobelia cardinalis has dark green or reddish leaves and is native to the eastern and central United States. It grows to 4 feet (1.2 m) in height and blooms in July and August. There are white and pink cultivars, but they are not readily available.

L. splendens is indeed splendid, particulary its cultivars 'Bees Flame' and 'Queen Victoria'. They have beet red foliage and scarlet flowers—such a rich color that it stirs the imagination to think of wonderful color combinations with other perennials. The taxonomy is somewhat confused in this genus, and these two may in fact be hybrids. They grow to 3 feet (90 cm) and the leaves are a bit downy. They bloom from August until late October.

Bloomtime: July to October, depending on the species.
Height: 3–4 feet (.9–1.2 m).
Spread: Plants are slender, spreading to 1 foot (30 cm); plant at least three in a group for impact.
Light and soil: Full or part sun. *L. cardinalis* will take full shade. Both prefer rich, moist soil.
Care and propagation: Mulch plants to keep the soil moist. Stems are brittle and break easily; stake to prevent damage. Both *L. cardinalis* and 'Queen Victoria' can be grown from seed, which is listed by Thompson & Morgan and Park. Plants can also be divided.
Pests and diseases: SLUGS and SNAILS.
Frost hardiness: *L. cardinalis*: to zone 2; *L. splendens*: to zone 7; 'Bees Flame' and 'Queen Victoria': to zone 4. They do have a habit of vanishing in the winter in the Pacific coastal region, despite the hardiness

listing. Mulch plants heavily to buffer against fluctuating temperatures. Remove mulch in spring to discourage slugs.

Lupinus hybrids "lupine" FABACEAE
(Figure 5-12)

Lupines have the same flower structure as fellow members of the pea family. The upper petal, called the standard, is folded back, and the lower petal, called the keel, is compressed. These flowers are arranged on tall spikes. The most commonly grown garden lupines are the Russell lupines, hybrids thought to be of *Lupinus polyphyllus* and *L. arboreus*, two species from western North America. These plants come in many beautiful colors, and often have standards and keels of two different colors. Lupines also have very beautiful leaves that are palmately compound, with many silky leaflets.

The biggest drawback to growing lupines in the Pacific coastal region is the aphids they attract—the largest you are likely to encounter. In no time they cover the flower spike in the hundreds, and spraying them only results in an unsightly mess. Furthermore, lupines are short-lived and require staking.

Bloomtime: May to July.

Height by spread: 3–5 feet (.9–1.5 m) by 2 feet (60 cm).

Light and soil: Full sun or light shade in average soil.

Care and propagation: Cut down flower stalks when the flowers have faded, for a repeat bloom in the fall. Propagation is easiest from seed. Alternatively, take cuttings close to the crown, preferably with a piece of the crown attached, in March or April.

Pests and diseases: APHIDS, POWDERY MILDEW, ROOT ROT and VIRUS.

Frost hardiness: To zone 4.

Lysimachia punctata "yellow loosestrife" PRIMULACEAE
(Figure 6-1)

Yellow loosestrife has a reputation for being invasive, but if you are handy with the spade and don't mind taking the time to divide it every second year, it has a lot to offer. It is tall but doesn't need staking. Its bright yellow, starlike flowers are a cheerful sight in June and July and it is bothered by few pests and diseases.

Yellow loosestrife has 3-foot (90-cm) stems bearing deeply veined, gray green leaves. Rounded at the base and tapering to a point, they are up to 3 inches (8 cm) long, decreasing in length as they ascend the stems. In the axils, where leaf meets stem, there are whorls of bright yellow flowers that look like stars. Each 3/4-inch (2-cm) flower is cup-shaped, with five pointed petals. About eight flowers on short stalks radiate from the stem at one place—like the spokes of a wheel. There are a dozen or so of these whorls ascending each stem.

Yellow loosestrife is native to Europe. The common name loosestrife is also used for the genus *Lythrum*, but was originally applied to this genus. It is a translation of the generic name, *Lysimachia*, and two explanations have been put forward as to its origin. Pliny, a naturalist from Verona in the first century A.D. claimed that a branch of loosestrife laid across the backs of a pair of quarreling oxen would calm them. Alternatively, the genus may have been named after Lysimachus, King of Thrace.

Bloomtime: Early June to mid-July.

Height: To 3 feet (90 cm).

Spread: 18–24 inches (45–60 cm).

Light and soil: Full sun or part shade in ordinary garden soil. Yellow loosestrife will flourish in damp soils and will tolerate dry soil in a bit of shade.

Care and propagation: Little care is required other than cutting down the stems after plants have finished blooming. Propagate by division or from seed.

Pests and diseases: Generally trouble-free.

Frost hardiness: To zone 4.

Lythrum salicaria
Lythrum virgata both called "purple loosestrife" LYTHRACEAE
(Figure 6-2)

The flowers of loosestrife are borne in tall rosy purple spires. The two most common species are native to Europe and Asia and are very similar. Both have narrow, tapering leaves to 4 inches (10 cm) long, arranged alternately along square stems. The leaves of *Lythrum salicaria* are rounded at the base and have minute hairs, while those of *L. virgatum* are pointed at the base and hairless. Cultivars of *L. virgatum* include 'Morden Pink' (pink, with larger flowers), 'Morden Gleam' and 'Morden Rose', all selected at the Morden, Manitoba, research station of Agriculture Canada. All three reach about 3 feet (90 cm). 'Firecandle' is tall, to

5 feet (1.5 m). A cultivar of L. *salicaria*, 'Robert' is a dwarf form, growing to 2 feet (60 cm).

Bloomtime: June to September.

Height: 2–5 feet (.6–1.5 m).

Spread: 18 inches (45 cm).

Light and soil: Best in full sun, but they will bloom even in light shade. Loosestrifes can adapt to a wide range of soil conditions, from average garden soil to wet soil.

Care and propagation: Loosestrife is easy to grow. Cut down flower stalks when finished and cut stems down in fall if desired. Propagate from seed (except named cultivars that are not true from seed) or by division or from cuttings.

Pests and diseases: Generally trouble-free.

Frost hardiness: To zone 3.

Miscanthus sinensis (M. *japonicus*, *Eulalia japonica*) "Japanese or Chinese silver grass" "eulalia grass" POACEAE
(Figure 6-3)

This large ornamental grass makes a bold statement in the garden. Combined with shrubs, placed at the back of a perennial border or filling an odd corner, *Miscanthus sinensis* and its cultivars are outstanding. The plants make an attractive rustling sound in a breeze.

In warm regions of the world, this east Asian species grows to 13 feet (3.9 m) high, but it usually reaches only 6 feet (1.8 m) in the Pacific coastal region. Individual leaf blades are up to 3 feet (90 cm) long and 1 inch (2.5 cm) wide. It is a clump-forming grass and not invasive. Of slender, upright growth, it blooms in October and November. When the blooms first open, they look like shimmering zigzags. If the fall weather is dry, they fluff out, resembling 12-inch (30-cm) feather dusters. Alternatively, cut them and let them fluff in the warmth indoors.

Use miscanthus as you would a tall shrub in the border or for a summer screen. Unlike many tall perennials, they are good-looking right to the ground and don't leave a gap in the border when cut back after blooming. This makes them ideal for adding height to a narrow border, as well as for use at the back of a wide border.

There are several excellent named cultivars, which are grown more than the species.

'Gracillimus' (maiden grass) has narrower, 1/2-inch (1.3-cm) leaf blades of sage green with a fine silver midrib; it grows to 5 feet (1.5 m) in height. The overall effect is more graceful than the species.

'Silberfeder' ('Silver Feather') is much like the species, except it is reported to be more free-flowering.

'Variegatus' (also called M. s. var. *foliis striatus* or M. s. var. *vittatus*) has creamy white stripes that run lengthwise up the leaf blade. It reaches about 5 feet (1.5 m) and produces pale pink flowers that fade to beige. (In zones colder than 7 it doesn't always flower.)

'Zebrinus' is also variegated. It is a handsome plant with creamy bands running across the leaf blade at irregular intervals. The variegation develops after the leaves have unfurled. The flowers have a hint of rosy red and the plants reach 7 feet (2 m) to the tips of the blooms. 'Strictus' (sometimes listed as 'Zebrinus Strictus') is a shorter version of 'Zebrinus'.

Bloomtime: October to November.

Height: 4–7 feet (1.2–2 m).

Spread: 3 feet (90 cm).

Light and soil: Full sun or light shade and an average to wet soil.

Care and propagation: Easy to grow. No staking is required. The dried stems add winter interest to the garden—cut them down in March before new growth begins. Propagate from seed (except named cultivars that are not true from seed) or by division.

Pests and diseases: Generally trouble-free.

Frost hardiness: To zone 4; except 'Silberfeder': to zone 5; 'Variegatus': to zone 6 or 7.

Monarda didyma
Monarda fistulosa both called "bee balm" "oswego tea" "bergamot"
LAMIACEAE
(Figure 6-4)

These two species of bee balm, both native to eastern and southern North America, are similar in appearance. Both have square stems—a feature of the mint family, to which they belong–and leaves in pairs along the stems. Oval at the base and tapering to a point, leaves are up to 4 inches (10 cm) long, with teeth along the margin. They are matte midgreen, with a pungent, mint-like aroma. Each individual flower is about 1¼ inches (3 cm) long with the two lips characteristic of the mint family. Dozens of these flowers are crowded together at the end of each stem. The odd flower also appears in a leaf axil on its own. In the wild,

M. *didyma* has vivid scarlet red flowers while those of M. *fistulosa* are bright lavender and smaller.

Named cultivars of M. *didyma* include 'Cambridge Scarlet', popular since before 1913; 'Adam' (rosy red and more compact than 'Cambridge Scarlet'); 'Croftway Pink' (clear rose pink); 'Mahogany' (dark reddish mahogany); and 'Prairie Glow' (salmon red). Hybrids of the two discussed here include 'Magnifica' and 'Prairie Night' (both purplish) and 'Snow Maiden' ('Schneewittchen'), which is white. Named cultivars do not come true from seed, but unfortunately, many bee balms are grown from seed and then given a label of the closest named cultivars. For example, many different shades of red bee balm are sold as 'Cambridge Scarlet'.

'Marshall's Delight', new from the Morden, Manitoba, research station, is a mildew-resistant hot pink, better than 'Croftway Pink'.

Bloomtime: July to September.

Height: 2–3 feet (60–90 cm).

Spread: 15 inches (38 cm).

Light and soil: Full sun or part shade in moist soil to which a lot of organic matter has been added. To discourage powdery mildew, plant in a spot that has good air circulation. M. *didyma* and its cultivars tolerate damp soil.

Care and propagation: Easy to grow. Bee balms can look untidy by the end of summer, so plant them in the middle of the border where they are not as noticeable. Divide every second year, replanting the younger outer portions of the clump. Propagate from seed or division; named cultivars from division.

Pests and diseases: POWDERY MILDEW.

Frost hardiness: To zone 3 or 4; 'Marshall's Delight': to zone 2.

Oenothera fruticosa (O. *tetragona*) "sundrops" ONAGRACEAE
(Figure 6-5)

This lovely perennial is native to the eastern United States and produces its golden, cup-shaped flowers in profusion from June to September. The leaves of sundrops are shiny midgreen, narrow and taper to a long point. The species is very variable, resulting in taxonomic confusion. One of the most popular cultivars is 'Fyrverkeri', translated into English as both 'Fireworks' and 'Illumination'. It has red stems and flower-buds and reddish green leaves. It forms a rounded mound to 20 inches (50 cm) high, a perfect candidate for the rock garden or front of the border. The stems die back to the ground in autumn. Other species of *Oenothera* flower only in the evening, but the name evening primrose is sometimes, confusingly, used for all members of the genus. Avoid the biennial species—for example the evening primrose *O. biennis*—as they become weedy and seed themselves all over.

Bloomtime: June to September.

Height: 6–24 inches (15–60 cm), depending on the cultivar.

Spread: 12 inches (30 cm).

Light and soil: Full sun in ordinary, well-drained soil. Sundrops tolerate poor soil.

Care and propagation: Easy to grow. Water during dry spells and cut stems to the ground in fall. Propagate by division or make cuttings of soft, nonflowering shoots. Species can also be grown from seed.

Pests and diseases: Generally trouble-free.

Frost hardiness: To zone 4.

Paeonia lactiflora "Chinese peony"
Paeonia officinalis "common peony" "May-flowering peony"
"Memorial Day peony" PAEONIACEAE
(Figure 6-6)

Traditional garden perennials, peonies are exceedingly long-lived. It is not uncommon for Pacific coast gardeners to be growing peonies that have been in their families for two or more generations. Peonies are the only genus in their family, which is closely related to the buttercup family, RANUNCULACEAE. They have thickened, tuberous roots. The new leaves of most peonies are rich burgundy when they unfurl in the spring. They are compound, divided into leaflets of irregular shape, and 3–5 inches (8–13 cm) in length. They are shiny dark green above and gray green underneath.

Paeonia officinalis. A native of Europe, this species is the first peony to bloom, with flowers opening in May. It has given rise to hundreds of named cultivars. Most often seen are three doubles: 'Rubra Plena' (red), 'Rosea Superba Plena' (pink) and 'Alba Plena' (white). 'Rubra Plena' was first introduced in the sixteenth century. All look like ruffled pompons to 4 inches (10 cm) across. After the flowers have finished, the leaves remain attractive in the garden until the fall.

P. lactiflora is a native of China, Tibet and Siberia and had been hybridized and selected by Chinese and Japanese gardeners since 500 B.C., long before it was introduced to Europe in 1784. The popularity of peonies in the Orient is demonstrated by their frequent use in Oriental art and fabric design.

There are three types of blooms, often up to 6 inches (15 cm) across. **Singles** have one row of petals, and the central cluster of dozens of yellow (sometimes red) stamens is visible. They are generally only available from a specialist. The flowers do not last as long in the garden or cut as those with fuller flowers, but they are very beautiful in their simplicity.

Japanese or anemone-flowered peonies have two or more rows of petals surrounding a pouf of petal-like structures (stamenodes). These are sometimes the same color as the petals, and sometimes of a contrasting color. For example, 'Akashigata' has bright rose pink petals and pink and gold stamenodes at the center. 'Jappensha-Ikhu' has dark red petals with yellow stamenodes and 'Leto' is white with canary yellow stamenodes.

Double peonies have many petals and the effect is of a pompon. They come in shades of red, pink, yellow and white. Some have flecks of a second color. The following are excellent cultivars.

Cultivar (date introduced)	Flower color	Comments
'Albert Crousse'	soft shell pink	strong growing
'Auguste Dessert'	rose red with silver	strong stems
'Baroness Schroeder'	blush white	fragrant
'Felix Crousse' (1881)	deep rose red	floriferous
'Festiva Maxima' (1851)	white with red flecks	fragrant
'Karl Rosenfeld' (1908)	very deep red	fragrant
'Kelway's Glorious' (1909)	lacy white	fragrant
'Laura Dessert' (1913)	white with lemon flush	fragrant
'Sarah Bernhardt' (1906)	pale pink	fragrant

As you can see by the dates of introduction, 'Festiva Maxima' and 'Felix Crousse' have been cultivated for over a century.

The above peonies are often referred to as herbaceous peonies, because they die to the ground each winter. *P. suffruticosa* is the parent of innumerable woody peonies, often called tree peonies, although they behave more like shrubs than trees.

Peony flowers are good for cutting; leave at least three sets of leaves on the plant below where you cut, to avoid weakening the plant.

Bloomtime: *P. officinalis* cultivars: April–May; *P. lactiflora* cultivars: June–July.

Height: 2¹/₂ feet (75 cm).

Spread: 2–3 feet (60–90 cm).

Light and soil: Full sun is preferable. They will tolerate light shade, but may not bloom as well or have sturdy stems. They grow well in average garden soil to which some organic matter has been added.

Care and propagation: Peonies resent disturbance and may take a year or two to begin blooming well after being planted, transplanted or divided. Ideally, give careful thought to where you will plant peonies, so they will not have to be moved soon. Plant crowns so that the new buds are an inch (2.5 cm) below the soil surface. Add bonemeal and dolomite lime to the bottom of the planting hole. Staking is usually required. Cut stems to ground level in late fall, but if any sign of leaf spot is seen, do not throw them in the compost heap. Mulch plants annually in late April with compost or well-rotted manure and water well during dry spells.

Propagate by division in September. If you are given an old clump, divide it into crowns with 3–5 buds on each before replanting.

Pests and diseases: The most serious disease of peonies is GRAY MOLD, also called peony blight. It does not affect *P. officinalis* as much as it does *P. lactiflora*. Try peonies if you are looking for deer-resistant plants.

Frost hardiness: To zone 2.

Papaver orientale "Oriental poppy" PAPAVERACEAE
(Figure 6-7)

These showy poppies are hardy, long-lived and easy to grow. They produce large, showy, bowl-shaped blooms in shades of brilliant orange red, dark red, pink, orange, white and bicolors. Many petals have a striking black blotch at the base and some are ruffled and cut. The flowers are up to 4 inches (10 cm) or more across. Oriental poppies have large, coarse, hairy leaves and hairy stems. The foliage dies away after the plants finish blooming and emerges again in fall. The foliage is evergreen through the winter. To fill in the gap left by Oriental poppies in late summer, plant fall asters, baby's breath, or bedding plants such as cosmos or marguerite daisies nearby. The species is native to southeast Asia. There are many named cultivars and they seem to change frequently, so

142

your best bet is to consult your garden center or a mail-order catalogue. If cutting the flowers, sear them in hot water before arranging.

Bloomtime: Late May to early June.

Height: 2–3 feet (60–90 cm).

Spread: 3 feet (90 cm).

Light and soil: Full sun and average, well-drained garden soil.

Care and propagation: Easy to grow. Stake stems and cut them down to ground level after blooming. The whole plant will become dormant during late summer. Divide after blooming. Plants can also be propagated from root cuttings taken in winter. There are a number of seed strains available.

Pests and diseases: Generally trouble-free and not usually eaten by deer.

Frost hardiness: To zone 3.

Pennisetum alopecuroides
Pennisetum setaceum both called "fountain grass" POACEAE
(Figure 6-8)

Both of these species of fountain grass add a new dimension to the garden. The bottle-brush-like flower heads, borne for months on end, bob and dance in the wind. They add softness and movement—a touch of the prairie to the civilized city garden. They are also excellent for flower arranging and they dry well.

Pennisetum alopecuroides is native to Asia. It grows to 3 feet (90 cm) and has narrow gray green leaf blades that are rough to the touch. They arch out from the stems (properly called culms) to 18 inches (45 cm) long. The inflorescence is like a buff bottle brush, to 6 inches (15 cm) long and 2 inches (5 cm) across, appearing in September and October, remaining attractive well into the winter. 'Hameln' is a dwarf cultivar, growing to 2 feet (60 cm).

P. setaceum, from Africa, is similar, but the inflorescence is longer and slimmer, to 8 by 1¼ inches (20 by 3 cm), and nodding. The handsome cultivar 'Rubrum' has mahogany leaf blades and dark red inflorescences. It blooms from July to October. *P. setaceum* is hardy to zone 8, meaning that it could be killed in a hard winter in the Pacific coastal region, but it is so decorative for such a long period that it is worth the risk.

Bloomtime: *P. alopecuroides*: September and October; *P. setaceum*: July to October.

Height: 2–3 feet (60–90 cm).
Spread: 2 feet (60 cm).
Light and soil: Full sun and an average, well-drained garden soil.
Care and propagation: Easy to grow. Cut stems to ground level in late fall. Mulch plants of P. *setaceum* well for winter protection or dig and over-winter in a cool greenhouse. Propagate from seed (except named cultivars that are not true from seed) or by division.
Pests and diseases: Generally trouble-free.
Frost hardiness: P. *alopecuroides*: to zone 5 or 6; P. *setaceum*: to zone 8.

Penstemon campanulatus hybrids "penstemon" "beard-tongue"
SCROPHULARIACEAE
(Figure 6-9)

Two hybrids of *Penstemon campanulatus*, probably crossed with P. *hartwegii*, are excellent for Pacific coastal region gardens. They produce elegant stems with tubular, foxglove-like blooms along them from June until late September. The slender, pointed leaves, to 4 inches (10 cm) long, are bright green. 'Evelyn' is pink and 'Garnet' is a deep rich red that combines well with all colors. P. *hartwegii* was discovered in the high mountains of Mexico by plant hunters in the early nineteenth century. P. *campanulatus* is also native to Mexico.

A different group of penstemon hybrids—for example, 'Skyline Mixed'—are frequently sold with bedding plants and are not perennial.
Bloomtime: June to late September.
Height: 2 feet (60 cm).
Spread: 12–18 inches (30–45 cm).
Light and soil: Full sun and average, well-drained garden soil.
Care and propagation: Cut stems down to a few inches (8 cm) above ground level in the fall and mulch with evergreen boughs for winter protection. Propagate by division or cuttings.
Pests and diseases: Generally trouble-free.
Frost hardiness: To zone 8.

Phlox maculata "border phlox"
Phlox paniculata (P. *decussata*) "border phlox"
Phlox subulata "moss phlox" "moss pinks" POLEMONIACEAE
(Figures 6-10 and 6-11)

The genus *Phlox* contains sixty-six species, but the phloxes most often seen in gardens are cultivars of three species native to the eastern United States. The flower buds of all three are long and pointed, and the petals wrap around each other, like a closed umbrella. The flowers have a long tube-like corolla that flares into a plate-like arrangement of five overlapping petals.

P. paniculata is a tall plant with billows of bloom in summer and fall. The thick, pointed, dark green leaves are opposite, up to 6 inches (15 cm) long and without teeth along their margin. The flower color is naturally variable and hundreds of color selections have been named over the past century. Flower colors include orange, white, lilac, and every imaginable shade of pink and red, often with a contrasting eye (flower center). Individual flowers are to 1½ inches (4 cm) across and are borne in pyramid-shaped clusters at the tops of the stems. Heights vary from 2 to 4 feet (.6–1.2 m). Excellent selections have been named in Britain, Europe and North America; specific availability will vary greatly depending on the origin of plant material. It is worth the extra effort to get good named cultivars. Some of the newer ones are more resistant to powdery mildew, a serious problem on some cultivars. Flowers are pretty but not at all long-lasting when cut.

P. maculata is a similar species but the individual flowers are smaller, the clusters are cylindrical in outline and plants stay below 3 feet (90 cm) in height. Only two cultivars are generally available: 'Alpha' is lilac pink and 'Omega' is white with a lilac eye. It does not need staking as cultivars of *P. paniculata* often do, and it seems resistant to nematodes.

P. subulata. Moss phlox is similar in flower but very different in habit, being a mat-forming rockery perennial that brightens the garden in April and May. Because moss phlox blooms the same time as aubrietia, they are often confused; but moss phlox has five petals and aubrietia has four. There are named cultivars of moss phlox, but those most often sold are labeled pink, red, white and blue and are very pretty. The foliage of moss phlox resembles that of needle evergreens—leaves are glossy bright green, to ¾ inch long by 1/16 inch wide (2 cm by 15 mm), often much smaller, and pointed at the tip. Leaves are arranged in bundles.

Bloomtime: Border phloxes: July to September; Moss phlox: April and May.

Height: Border phloxes: 3–4 feet (.9–1.2 m); moss phlox: 6 inches (15 cm).

Spread: Border phloxes: 18–24 inches (45–60 cm); moss phlox: 24 inches (60 cm).

Light and soil: Border phloxes grow well in full sun or part shade; moss phlox prefers full sun. Plant all in well-drained soil to which a lot of organic matter has been added.

Care and propagation: All are easy to grow. Mulch border phloxes annually with compost or well-rotted manure and keep plants well watered to discourage powdery mildew. Deadhead after blooming and cut stems down to the ground in late fall. Propagate by division, re-planting only young outer portions. Plants can also be propagated by 3- to 4-inch (8- to 10-cm) stem cuttings taken in March. If nematodes are present on the plant, propagate by making 1/2-inch (1.3-cm) root cut-tings in March—they will be free of nematodes. The original plant should then be destroyed and the young plants planted in a different part of the garden.

Moss phlox is best left to its own devices. It doesn't die to the ground in winter and sometimes looks untidy, but it greens up as soon as spring comes. Cutting it back hard can be fatal. Propagate by cuttings in July. Alternatively, stems will often layer themselves, or can be encouraged to do so; once roots have formed, they can be detached from the original plant in early spring or fall.

Pests and diseases: SLUGS and SNAILS feed on the stems and leaves of both types of phlox. NEMATODES may infest *P. paniculata*, causing young shoots to die and older leaves to be distorted. POWDERY MILDEW causes a white powdery coating on the leaves of border phlox in summer.

Frost hardiness: To zone 3.

Phygelius aequalis
Phygelius capensis
Phygelius × *rectus* all called "Cape fuchsia" SCROPHULARIACEAE
(Figure 6-12)

Cape fuchsias are evergreen subshrubs in their native South Africa, but are most often grown as perennials in the Pacific coastal region. They are valued in the garden for their exotic-looking flowers in sunset colors and their length of bloom. At first glance, they resemble fuchsias. Their flowers are teardrop-shaped and have prominent stamens. The leaves are opposite, rounded at the base and tapering to a point. Despite these similarities, Cape fuchsias are not members of the fuchsia family, but rather of the same family as snapdragons, foxgloves and penstemons.

Phygelius capensis has a striking inflorescence: the nodding flowers are arranged in airy tiers, held out from the main stalk on short stems. Each flower is about 1½ inches (4 cm) long, with a slightly curved, tubular corolla that flares out into five recurved lobes. In the wild, flower colors range from pale orange to deep red. Yellow is rare.

This species was introduced into cultivation before 1855. The scarlet-flowered cultivar commonly grown then was named 'Coccineus'. Botanical illustrations from the time show a different plant from the orange red 'Coccineus' sold today. The 'Coccineus' sold today is, however, considered to be the hardiest Cape fuchsia in cultivation.

In mild areas, try growing this species against a south-facing wall—if the spot is warm enough, the plant will develop a permanent structure of branches.

P. aequalis, which usually has dusky pink or salmon flowers, was introduced into cultivation much later than its cousin and is not as hardy. It differs from *P. capensis* in a number of ways. Its flowers are larger than those of *P. capensis*, to 2½–3 inches (6–8 cm), and the petals do not reflex when fully open. Its flowers are held more closely to the flower stalk and they have straight corolla tubes. Its leaves are broader. However, some botanists believe this is simply a variety of *P. capensis*, rather than a separate species. The cultivar 'Yellow Trumpet' has beautiful, creamy yellow flowers.

P. × rectus is the name given to hybrids of the two species above. The first of these, made in England in 1969, is 'African Queen', which is pale red with orange red lobes and a yellow throat. 'Winchester Fanfare' is reddish pink with scarlet lobes and a yellow throat. Although these two hybrids are not widely grown here in the Pacific coastal region, a lovely hybrid made by Dr. Gerald Straley at the UBC Botanical Garden has proved as hardy as *P. capensis*. It has soft apricot blooms and is often sold at the Alpine Garden Club sales.

Bloomtime: July to October.

Height: 2–3 feet (60–90 cm).

Spread: 18–24 inches (45–60 cm).

Light and soil: While at their best in a warm spot in full sun, Cape fuchsias will also tolerate light shade. Plant in well-drained soil that does not dry out in summer to encourage a well-developed root system. This will increase winter hardiness.

Care and propagation: Keep well watered during dry spells. Mulch in the fall to protect roots from the cold. If planted in the fall, mulch very well to protect the roots from frost. Cut stems to the ground in April. Divide plants every few years if they become untidy and produce fewer flowers. If you have a greenhouse, make insurance cuttings in case of a severe winter. Propagate from seed (except named cultivars that are not true from seed) or by division.

Pests and diseases: Generally trouble-free.

Frost hardiness: *P. aequalis*: to zone 7; *P. capensis*: to zone 6.

Physostegia virginiana "obedient plant" "false dragonhead" LAMIACEAE (Figure 7-1)

This attractive, clump-forming perennial blooms in late summer and fall, adding color to the garden and providing cut flowers for the home. Like other members of the mint family, obedient plant has opposite leaves on square stems. Flower buds, like bright green beads, pack the top 8–10 inches (20–25 cm) of stem. These open, from bottom to top, into asymmetrical, tubular flowers of pink or white. The curious common name of this perennial refers to the fact that if you push the flowers to the side of the flower spike, they will remain there and not spring back. Leaves are toothed, pointed, and up to 5 inches (13 cm) long. The species is native to the eastern United States and Canada.

Cultivars grown are shorter than the 4 feet (1.2 m) of the species. 'Rose Bouquet' (also translated from the original French name 'Bouquet Rose' as 'Pink Bouquet') is lilac pink and grows to 3–3¹/₂ feet (.9–1 m). 'Vivid' is deep rose and shorter, to 20 inches (50 cm). Neither are easy shades to blend with other flower colors, particularly yellow or orange. 'Alba', to 3¹/₂ feet (1 m) and 'Summer Snow', to 2¹/₂ feet (75 cm), are both white and combine well with all colors. 'Alba' forms particularly attractive seed pods after blooming.

Bloomtime: July and August.

Height: 20 inches to 4 feet (.5–1.2 m).

Spread: 2 feet (60 cm), at least. Plants spread more rapidly in moist, slightly acid soil.

Light and soil: Full sun or part shade in ordinary garden soil. On rich soil, light staking may be required.

Care and propagation: Easy to grow. Keep well watered during dry spells. This handsome perennial is not obedient about staying in one spot—dig and divide every second year to keep it from spreading too much, replanting vigorous outer portions. Propagation can also be done by cuttings.

Pests and diseases: Generally trouble-free.

Frost hardiness: To zone 3.

Polemonium caeruleum "Jacob's ladder"
Polemonium foliosissimum POLEMONIACEAE
(Figure 7-2)

Lovely, five-petaled, lavender blue flowers produced over a long period and attractive foliage borne on erect stems make these two species of *Polemonium* good garden perennials. The leaves are pinnately compound, suggesting the ladder that the angels climbed in Jacob's dream in the Bible, hence the common name. The generic name has an interesting history. *Polemos* means war, and according to Pliny the Elder, two kings battled about which one of them first discovered *Polemonium caeruleum*.

P. caeruleum, a native of Europe and Asia, grows to 3 feet (90 cm) or more in height. It blooms from April to July, bearing tall clusters of 1-inch (2.5-cm) blue flowers with orange stamens. Leaves have nineteen to twenty-seven leaflets, and the terminal leaflet is distinct from the others. This species is short-lived, but seeds itself readily. The variety *lacteum* (var. *album*) has white flowers and grows to 2 feet (60 cm); its seedlings are usually white.

P. foliosissimum, native to the Rocky Mountains, grows to 3 feet (90 cm) and has eleven to twenty-five leaflets. The five end leaflets often merge together. It produces its lilac blooms from early June to September. This species is long-lived and does not seed itself as prolifically as *P. caeruleum*.

The cultivar 'Blue Pearl', listed under various species, is most likely to be a cultivar of *P. reptans*, a North American native. 'Blue Pearl' reaches 15 inches (38 cm) in height and blooms in May and June.

Bloomtime: *P. caeruleum*: April to July; *P. foliosissimum*: June to September.

Height: 15 inches to 3 feet (38–90 cm), depending on the species and cultivar.

Spread: 18 inches (45 cm).
Light and soil: Full sun or part shade. Jacob's ladder will grow in average garden soil, but thrives in moist, well-drained soil with much organic matter.
Care and propagation: Easy to grow. Cut faded flower stems at the base when flowering has finished. If mature plants do not flower well, divide and replant the vigorous outer portions, or allow seedlings to take their place. Propagate by seed (except named cultivars) or by division.
Pests and diseases: Generally trouble-free.
Frost hardiness: *P. caeruleum*: to zone 3; *P. foliosissimum*: to zone 4.

Polygonatum biflorum "small Solomon's seal"
Polygonatum commutatum "giant Solomon's seal"
Polygonatum × *hybridum* "Solomon's seal"
Polygonatum odoratum "Solomon's seal" LILIACEAE
(Figure 7-3)

The arching, unbranched stems of Solomon's seal bear handsome leaves and, from April to June, they are hung with lovely white bells. The several species and hybrids in cultivation are so similar that it is difficult to distinguish them. Leaves of all are pointed at each end and have prominent parallel veins; the base of each leaf wraps around the stem. Leaves and stems turn gold in the fall. Each flower is 1/2–1 inch (1.3–2.5 cm) long and the corolla flares into six lobes.

The origin of the name Solomon's seal is unclear; one suggestion is that the markings appearing on a cross-section of root resemble Hebrew letters.

Polygonatum biflorum is the shortest of these species, growing from 1–3 feet (30–90 cm) in height. The yellow green flowers, usually in pairs on short stalks, develop into blue black berries. It is native to eastern North America.

P. commutatum is like a larger version of the previous species. It reaches 3–6 feet (.9–1.8 m) in height and bears its flowers on 1-inch (2.5-cm) stalks in clusters of two to ten. Leaves are to 7 inches (18 cm) long. Flowers are 3/4–1 inch (2–2.5 cm) long, white with a greenish rim. These are followed by large, blue black berries. It is native to the eastern U.S.

P. × hybridum is a name given to a number of hybrids between *P. multiflorum* and *P. odoratum*, both native to Europe and Asia. These

150

hybrids are variable, with leaves 2–6 inches (5–15 cm) long and ¹/₂-inch (1.3-cm) ivory bells, edged with green, in clusters of four to five. Stems are ribbed and reach 3–4 feet (.9–1.2 m). The rare 'Flore-Pleno' has double flowers; 'Variegatum' (*P. multiflorum* var. *striatum*) has creamy striped leaves.

P. ö hybridum is sometimes incorrectly called *P. multiflorum*—a smaller plant whose bells have a "waist." *P. multiflorum* was cultivated in Europe since before the fifteenth century.

P. odoratum has stems that are distinctly angled or ridged. It has 4-inch (10-cm) leaves and solitary or paired 1-inch (2.5-cm) flowers. Growing 1¹/₂–2 feet (45–60 cm) tall, it is native to Europe and Asia. The Japanese variety *P. odoratum* var. *thunbergii* (*P. japonicum*) is taller, to 3 feet (1 m). Its cultivar 'Variegatum' has creamy white leaf edges and tips and 2- to 3-foot (60- to 90-cm), reddish green stems.

Bloomtime: Mid-April to June.

Height: From 1–6 feet (.3–1.8 m) (see above).

Spread: 2 feet (60 cm).

Light and soil: Solomon's seal thrives in shade or part shade, and in moist or damp organic soil. In my experience, however, some will take full sun and surprisingly dry, poor soil. Experiment for sun tolerance by planting one clump in the sun to see how it responds. Leaves will turn yellow in too much sun or too-dry soil; the clump can easily be lifted and moved into the shade.

Care and propagation: Easy to grow. Cut the stems to the ground in late fall; the stems and leaves turn golden in late October, so wait until this show has passed. Propagation by division is easiest, as seed may take over a year to germinate and some hybrids do not set seed.

Pests and diseases: Generally trouble-free.

Frost hardiness: To zone 4; except *P. odoratum*: to zone 5.

Polygonum affine "Himalayan knotweed"
Polygonum bistorta "knotweed" "fleece flower" POLYGONACEAE
(Figure 7-4)

Polygonum affine is remarkable for its long period of bloom. From May until September, it throws up pink pokers above a carpet of bright green leaves. It always looks neat and colorful. The leaves, to 4 inches (10 cm) long, are pointed at both ends, have a smooth margin and a prominent greenish white midrib. They are evergreen, but take on reddish tints, especially in cool weather. Individual flowers are tiny, to ¼ inch (.6 cm), and are borne in dense erect spikes to 8 inches (20 cm) long. The species is native to the Himalayas and is variable; the named cultivars are usually grown. 'Darjeeling Red' is a dark pink and 'Donald Lowndes' is pink. 'Dimity' has pink flowers that change to dark red, giving a two-tone effect. 'Superbum' is a new and outstanding cultivar from Germany.

Polygonum bistorta is native to northern Europe and Asia. Its cultivar 'Superbum' is handsome, with 6-inch (15-cm) pink pokers held well above a 2-foot (60-cm) clump of heart-shaped leaves. The striking flowers—good for flower arranging—and attractive foliage make an interesting contrast in the border.

There are a great many weeds in this genus, so avoid buying other species without doing some research first.

Bloomtime: *P. affine*: May to September; *P. bistorta*: May and June, with a repeat bloom in late summer.

Height: *P. affine*: 6–8 inches (15–20 cm); *P. bistorta*: 2½ feet (75 cm).

Spread: *P. affine*: 12 inches (30 cm); *P. bistorta*: 24 inches (60 cm).

Light and soil: Full sun or part shade in moist soil to which plenty of organic matter has been added.

Care and propagation: Easy to grow. Deadhead after blooming and cut stems down to the ground in late fall if desired. *P. affine* is evergreen, taking on rich autumn tints. Propagate by division. Species can also be grown from seed.

Pests and diseases: Generally trouble-free.

Frost hardiness: To zone 3.

Polystichum munitum "sword fern" POLYPODIACEAE
(Figure 7-5)

Native to the Pacific coastal region, sword fern is one of a number of beautiful ferns well suited to garden culture. Its evergreen, leathery, dark green leaves (fronds) are pinnately compound, to 4 feet (1.2 m) long including the leafstalk. Each leaflet (pinna) is slender and pointed, to 5 inches (13 cm) long, and it has tiny bristles along the leaf margin. An identifying feature is the small tab at the base of each pinna that points to the tip of the frond. The fronds are useful in floral arrangements.

Bloomtime: Like all ferns, sword fern does not bear flowers. It is grown for its excellent foliage.

Height: 2–4 feet (.6–1.2 m).
Spread: 2 feet (60 cm). Over the years and in the right setting, sword ferns can build up into huge clumps, to 5 feet (1.5 m) across, with up to a hundred fronds—a handsome plant for a large shady garden. Sword ferns also make good ground covers and companion plants for rhododendrons and other shade lovers.
Light and soil: Shade or part shade in moist soil enriched with plenty of organic matter.
Care and propagation: Easy to grow and virtually care-free. Propagate by division or, for enthusiasts, from spores.
Pests and diseases: Generally trouble-free.
Frost hardiness: To zone 7.

Primula species "candelabra primulas"
Primula denticulata "drumstick primula"
Primula veris "cowslip"
Primula vulgaris (*P. acaulis*) "primrose" PRIMULACEAE
(Figures 7-6 and 7-7)

The primulas that appear in shops in fall and early spring (*Primula* × *polyantha*) are not truly perennial and have a way of gradually disappearing after a year or two. There are many other species (the genus contains about four hundred) that are suitable to garden cultivation and are longer lived. They are not as readily available in shops, but they are easily grown from seed.

Candelabra primulas. Several species are grouped under this name because their flowers are arranged in tiers. At each tier is a whorl of about a dozen outward-facing blooms; the number of tiers varies from one to eight. The following are the most commonly available.

Species	Height	Flower color	Bloomtime
P. beesiana	2 feet (60 cm)	rose lilac	May–June
P. bulleyana	2¹/₂ feet (75 cm)	gold, yellow, buff	May–June
P. japonica	2¹/₂ feet (75 cm)	rose, purplish, white	May–June
P. pulverulenta	3 feet (90 cm)	magenta	June–July

The leaves are 9–20 inches (22–50 cm) long and most gradually widen to a rounded tip. Some have small teeth along the margin. All are native to China except *P. japonica*, which is native to Japan.

All of the candelabra primulas like moist, rich soil, with as much organic matter as can be provided. *P. japonica* flourishes in wet soil. All do best and remain fresh-looking longer in part shade, but will tolerate sun if the soil does not dry out.

P. japonica has named, single-color seed strains—'Miller's Crimson' and 'Postford White' are two.

P. pulverulenta has a lovely pink form called 'Bartley's Strain'.

P. × bullesiana is a hybrid seed strain of *P. bulleyana* and *P. beesiana*. The range of flower colors includes lilac, mauve, pink and peach. These colors combine well, but should be grown away from other spring-blooming flowers. Try them with ferns or blue hostas. They do well in sun and ordinary garden conditions.

P. denticulata, native to the Himalayas, is called the drumstick primula because the flowers form pompons atop 1-foot (30-cm) stems. They bloom in shades of purple, lilac, purplish pink and white. Butterflies enjoy the nectar they provide early in the spring. Most frequently grown from seed strains, there is also a named cultivar called 'Kerryman' with a yellow leaf margin; it must be propagated vegetatively.

P. veris and **P. vulgaris**, cowslip and primrose respectively, both have yellow flowers and grow to only 9 inches (23 cm). They bloom April to May; in mild winters the primrose may begin blooming as early as February. Cowslip bears a cluster of flowers at the end of each flower stalk; primrose bears solitary blooms on each stalk. Both are delightful woodland or shady border subjects.

If you take an interest in primulas, the Thompson & Morgan seed catalogue lists an excellent selection.

Bloomtime: February to July, depending on the species.

Height: 8–36 inches (20–90 cm), depending on the species.

Spread: 9–12 inches (23–30 cm).

Light and soil: Sun or part shade, in moist soil with abundant organic matter. Mulching soil with compost will conserve moisture. *P. japonica* prefers wet soil. All primulas thrive near a pond or stream.

Care and propagation: Little care is required beyond watering during warm weather. Deadhead after blooming, unless you wish to collect seed or to let the plants self-seed. The dried seed heads can be attractive in winter.

Propagate by division or seed. Sow seed as soon as it is ripe, or as soon as possible from seed companies. Surface sow and cover the seed flats with plastic or glass to maintain high humidity. Keep young plants shaded and well-watered.

Pests and diseases: APHIDS, CATERPILLARS, CUTWORMS, SLUGS, SNAILS, and WEEVILS; the last two can feed undetected below the soil line. Primulas are susceptible to GRAY MOLD, especially in the greenhouse. When growing primulas in the greenhouse in winter, only water plants on sunny days, and then do so early in the morning.

Frost hardiness: To zone 5; *P. denticulata*: to zone 3.

Pulmonaria angustifolia "blue cowslip"
Pulmonaria montana (*P. rubra*)
Pulmonaria officinalis "spotted dog" "Jerusalem cowslip"
Pulmonaria saccharata all also called "lungwort" BORAGINACEAE
(Figure 7-8)

"Musts" for the spring garden, these four species of *Pulmonaria* are native to Europe. They bloom in early spring, when color in the garden is at a premium.

The common name has been used for these plants since the 1400s, because it was believed that the spotted leaves resemble lungs. Robert Turner wrote in 1664 that "God hath imprinted upon the Plants, Herbs and Flowers, as it were Hieroglyphicks, the very signature of their Virtues." (Alice Coats, *Flowers and their Histories*). Since the leaves looked like lungs, they were thought to have medicinal value for lungs. This was not the case, but the name persisted; the generic name continues the same theme.

All four species have pointed, hairy leaves without teeth along the margin. Those of *P. rubra* have an undulating margin. Their rough surface can be irritating to the skin. The leaves are from 4–10 inches (10–25 cm) long; most are evergreen.

Flowers have a tubular corolla that flares out into five rounded lobes. They often open pink, before turning blue. The flowers are held in a prominent five-lobed calyx. The following are some of the most commonly available lungworts.

Species	Height	Flower color	Bloomtime	Leaf color
P. angustifolia	12 inches (30 cm)	sky blue	April	green
P. montana	18 inches (45 cm)	red	March–April	green
P. officinalis	12 inches (30 cm)	purple blue	April–May	white-spotted
P. saccharata	18 inches (45 cm)	blue	March–April	white-spotted

Several cultivars have been named. *P. angustifolia* 'Azurea' is a vivid blue. *P. montana* (usually sold as *P. rubra*) has an excellent new cultivar, 'Redstart'. It has rosy red flowers over several months in the spring and attractive soft green foliage year-round. *P. offincinalis* is the least exciting of the group, having coarse leaves that fade unattractively through the summer.

P. saccharata is a more attractive plant on the whole and has a number of excellent cultivars. 'Bowles Red' has deeper red blooms but is a coarse plant. 'Mrs. Moon' is a popular red, but 'Margery fish' is reported to be even better. 'Argentea' has very silvery leaves and blue flowers. 'Sissinghurst White' has plain green leaves and white flowers.

Bloomtime: March to May, depending on the species and cultivar.

Height: 12–18 inches (30 cm–45).

Spread: 18–24 inches (45–60 cm).

Light and soil: Full sun (as long as the soil is moist), part shade or shade. *P. saccharata* 'Margery Fish' does well in dry shade and 'Mrs. Moon' tolerates damp soil, suggesting there is plenty of latitude in this group. Add plenty of organic matter when preparing the soil.

Care and propagation: Easy to grow. Plants are variable from seed and it is best to get a named cultivar if possible. Propagate by division in the fall.

Pests and diseases: Generally trouble-free.

Frost hardiness: To zone 3.

Pulsatilla vulgaris see *Anemone pulsatilla*

Rudbeckia fulgida "orange coneflower"
Rudbeckia hirta "black-eyed susan" ASTERACEAE
(Figure 7-9)

Bright and bold, the daisy-like inflorescences of these two species of *Rudbeckia* are the epitome of summer. Both are native to North America; the species *R. laciniata*, not widely grown in gardens today, was cultivated by French settlers in Canada—and sent home to their King's herbalist in Paris—as long ago as 1640.

R. fulgida grows to 3 feet (90 cm). It has striking 3- to 4-inch (8- to 10-cm) blooms: golden yellow ray florets surround a black cone-like disk. The pointed, toothed, hairy leaves are to 6 inches (15 cm) long. The variety *R. fulgida* var. *deamii* (also sold as *R. deamii*) has coarser, more toothed foliage and a more erect and bushy habit.

'Goldsturm' is listed as a cultivar of *R. fulgida* var. *speciosa* by its breeder, German nurseryman H. Hagemann, but as a cultivar of *R. fulgida* var. *sulivantii* by other botanists. By either name, it is an outstanding cultivar, more compact than the type, reaching 2–3 feet (60–90 cm), with long-blooming flower heads to 5 inches (13 cm) across. To be true to the original introduction, it should be propagated vegetatively. Seed labeled 'Goldsturm Strain' is often offered for sale but produces variable plants. Seed sold as *R. newmanii* is another variety of *R. fulgida* (var. *newmanii*).

R. hirta and its cultivars and seed strains are short-lived perennials, often grown as annuals. They are easy to grow from seed and bloom the first year. Their daisy-like blooms up to 3 inches (8 cm) across have brown centers and ray florets in shades of orange. The leaves are long and hairy, and taper to a point. Two popular seed strains are 'Marmalade', which grows to 22 inches (55 cm) and has bright gold petals; and 'Rustic Dwarf Mixed', which is the same height but has blooms of yellow, orange, gold, bronze or mahogany, with contrasting rings of color. Both are excellent. 'Goldilocks' won an award for its compact height of 10 inches (25 cm), double blooms that look like golden petticoats and the fact that the masses of new flowers hide the old flowers. For something different, 'Irish Eyes' has 4¹/₂-inch (11-cm) flowers with gold petals and green centers on 30-inch (75-cm) plants. These cultivars are often used as bedding plants.

Black-eyed susans make excellent cut flowers. Sow *R. hirta* seed strains and plant seedlings to fill in for perennials that die down in late summer, such as Oriental poppies.

Note: *Rudbeckia purpurea* has been renamed *Echinacea purpurea*, which see.

Bloomtime: July to October; August to October for *R. hirta* the first year from seed.

Height: 1–3 feet (.9–1.2 m), depending on the species and cultivar.

Spread: 1–2 feet (30–60 cm), depending on the species and cultivar.

Light and soil: Prefers full sun and any well-drained soil to which some organic matter has been added. 'Goldsturm' tolerates damp soil.

Care and propagation: Stake plants, except for dwarf cultivars. Dead-head after blooming and cut stems down to the ground in late fall if desired. Propagate above-mentioned types from seed, except 'Golds-turm', which should be divided.

Pests and diseases: SLUGS and SNAILS.

Frost hardiness: To zone 3.

Salvia × superba (*S. nemorosa*) "perennial salvia" LAMIACEAE
(Figure 7-10)

Carrying rich purple spikes in late summer, perennial salvias make a wonderful contrast with other flower shapes. German hybridizers have produced plants in a range of sizes, so you can pick just the one to complete your picture.

The name *Salvia × superba* is a catch-all for several similar garden hybrids. Many are of uncertain origin, but are thought to be offspring of various species of salvia, most from Europe. (Some catalogues and books list the cultivars under *S. nemorosa*.) All have the square stems and opposite leaves commonly found in members of the mint family. The individual flowers resemble 1/4-inch (.6-cm), purple snapdragons. They are arranged in whorls up the stem, and open from the bottom up. The leaves are dark green, to 3 inches (8 cm) long, squarish at the base and tapering gently to a point. They have tiny scallops along the margin and a prominent midrib.

There are several excellent cultivars available. 'East Friesland' ('Ost-friesland') is the most compact and has the longest season of bloom. It grows to 18–24 inches (45–60 cm) and has 8-inch (20-cm) spikes of violet purple. 'May Night' ('Mainacht') has deep indigo blooms and grows to 18–24 inches (45–60 cm). 'Lubeca' has violet purple flowers that are a bit larger than those of 'May Night' and grows to 30 inches (75 cm). A classic combination is perennial salvia with a dwarf *Achillea* such as 'Moonshine'.

Bloomtime: May to June with repeat bloom in September.

Height: 18–30 inches (45–75 cm), depending on the cultivar.

Spread: 18–24 inches (45–60 cm), depending on the cultivar.

Light and soil: Plant in full sun or light shade in average, well-drained soil. These salvias tolerate dry soil.

Care and propagation: Deadhead after blooming and cut stems down to the ground in late fall if desired. Propagate by division.

Pests and diseases: Generally trouble-free.

Frost hardiness: To zone 5.

Saponaria ocymoides "rock soapwort"
Saponaria officinalis CARYOPHYLLACEAE
(Figure 7-11)

Rock soapwort, a native of Europe, begins to bloom just as aubrietia is finishing and is therefore useful for extending the season of bloom in a rock garden. The evergreen leaves are slightly rough and gray green, to 1 inch (2.5 cm) long, with minute teeth along the margin. They are borne in pairs along the trailing, dark red stems. The five-petaled flowers are rose pink. 'Splendens' has deeper pink flowers. 'Compacta' is more compact, and 'Rubra Compacta' is both redder and more compact.

Note: The name soapwort was originally given to a closely related plant—*Saponaria officinalis*—by William Turner in his book *The Names of Herbes* in 1548. Its leaves and stems were boiled, strained and whipped to form an astringent lather, used to clean woolen fabrics as long ago as the Middle Ages. It is used even today in the Middle East to clean delicate, ancient tapestries and brocades. Its soap-like qualities are due to the presence of chemicals called saponins. Soapwort lather was also used as a hair shampoo; it was last produced commercially in 1930. Like *S. ocymoides*, *S. officinalis* is perennial and is very easy to grow, best for a wild garden. Look for seeds from a specialist seed house.

Bloomtime: May to June or July.

Height: *S. ocymoides*: 3 inches (8 cm); *S. officinalis*: 12–28 inches (30–70 cm).

Spread: 12 inches (30 cm).

Light and soil: Full sun or part shade in any fertile garden soil.

Care and propagation: Easy to grow. Cut back after blooming if necessary to encourage compact growth. Propagate by removing layered pieces of stem or from seed or basal cuttings.

Pests and diseases: Generally trouble-free.

Frost hardiness: *S. ocymoides*: to zone 2; *S. officinalis*: to zone 3.

Saxifraga species "mossy saxifrages"
Saxifraga cotyledon and *Saxifraga paniculata* (*S. aizoon*) "encrusted saxifrages"
Saxifraga umbrosa and *Saxifraga* × *urbium* "London pride"
SAXIFRAGACEAE
(Figures 7-12 and 8-1)

There are about three hundred species of *Saxifraga*—nicknamed "saxes" by some gardeners. They hail from five of the major continents, mostly from rocky or mountainous places. To organize this huge group, they are generally divided into fifteen sections, three of which are discussed here.

Mossy saxifrages. This section (Dactyloides) includes species that give the impression of moss at first glance. Most of the mossy saxifrages in cultivation are selections or hybrids of S. *moschata*, S. *muscoides* (both from Europe), S. *caespitosa* (N. America, Europe and Asia) and their close relatives, and many were made by the German hybridizer Georg Arends. They are listed under any of the three species, and German growers often list them as S. × *arendsii*. They have tiny, bright green leaves that overlap along creeping stems. The stems end in small, 1-inch (2.5-cm) rosettes. Individual leaves are 3/4 inch (2 cm) at the most, often only 1/4 inch (.6 cm) long. They often flare out into three lobes, resembling tiny feet. In April and May, plants are covered with small cup-shaped white, pink or red flowers held above the leaves on delicate stems. 'Peter Pan' and 'Triumph' are both red, 'Pixie' is rosy red and 'Foundling' is white. Plant them in shady parts of a rock garden.

Encrusted saxifrages (Euaizoonia) are recognizable because they have a silver cast and a fine white margin along their leaves. (The leaves actually secrete lime.) The two most common species are S. *cotyledon* (Europe) and S. *paniculata* (Europe and North America). They both form rosettes and produce cup-shaped, 1/2-inch (1.3-cm), white flowers (pink in some forms) on wiry stems in June. S. *cotyledon* is the larger of the two, with leaves up to 3 inches (8 cm) long and flower stems up to 2 feet (60 cm). S. *paniculata* is half those dimensions. Plant them in sunny parts of the rock garden.

S. × *urbium* (and also the much rarer **S. *umbrosa***) are both called London pride. It is a very old name, and it is unclear to which plant the name was originally applied. S. × *urbium* is a sterile hybrid of S. *umbrosa* and S. *spathularis*. The leaves are fleshy and up to 2 1/2 inches (6 cm) long. They have a long leafstalk and scalloped margins and are clustered into rosettes. Like many other saxifrages, the flowers are carried on branching, wiry stems to 8 inches (20 cm) long in May and June. Each tiny flower has five white petals with minute pink and gold spots. 'Variegata' has gold spots on the leaves. These are in the Robertsonia section and are

160

native to Europe. They work well in the rock garden and can also be used for an edging.

Bloomtime: May to June; except mossy saxifrage: April and May.

Height: Mossy saxifrages grow to 1–3 inches (2.5–8 cm) in height; the other species have rosettes of up to 4 inches (10 cm) high, but their slender flower stalks reach 1–2 feet (30–60 cm) high.

Spread: 8–12 inches (20–30 cm).

Light and soil: Mossy saxifrages prefer some shade and a moist soil with plenty of organic matter. Encrusted saxifrages need sweet, well-drained soil (add dolomite lime and organic matter if necessary) and full sun or part shade. London pride does best in part shade or shade in good garden soil.

Care and propagation: Mossy saxifrages grow fairly quickly and need dividing and replanting every two to three years to maintain neatness. The other types only need deadheading. Propagate by division after flowering. Nonflowering rosettes of leaves taken with as long a stalk as possible can also be treated like cuttings. The species can also be grown from seed.

Pests and diseases: In areas with high WEEVIL infestations, the larvae may eat the roots of some saxifrages.

Frost hardiness: To zone 3 or 4.

Scabiosa caucasica "pincushion flower" DIPSACACEAE
(Figure 8-2)

Lovely in the border, wonderful for cutting, the pincushion flower is an excellent middle-of-the-border perennial. Each inflorescence, up to 4 inches (10 cm) across, is made up of a cluster of flowers with prominent stamens—hence the pincushion effect—surrounded by a skirt of ruffled bracts. Inflorescences are borne on wiry stems, making them perfect for picking, and colors include cream, white, lavender or powder blue. If deadheaded, plants will bloom for many months. The seed heads are also very attractive. In fact, the annual *Scabiosa stellata* is grown for its seed heads.

The leaves of pincushion flower are up to 10 inches (25 cm) in length and vary in shape. Some have regular lobes, almost like an oak leaf. Some have lobes at the base and then an entire margin for the rest of the leaf. Some have a few lobes here and there.

'Bressingham White' and 'Miss Wilmott' are white and 'Clive Greaves' is a popular blue. 'Fama' is a seed strain with more intense blue flowers, and a number of seed strains with mixed colors are available. As its specific name suggests, pincushion flower is native to the Caucasus.
Bloomtime: July to September.
Height: 2 feet (60 cm).
Spread: 18 inches (45 cm).
Light and soil: Full sun in well-drained soil to which some dolomite lime has been added. Plants are short-lived on acid or clay soil.
Care and propagation: Insert light twigs into the ground before plants begin to grow to offer extra support. Deadhead after blooming and cut stems down to the ground in late fall. Propagate from seed (except named cultivars that do not come true from seed), or by division of established plants in the spring.
Pests and diseases: SLUGS, SNAILS and POWDERY MILDEW. In heavy, damp soil the plants may get ROOT ROT.
Frost hardiness: To zone 3.

Sedum rockery species
Sedum spectabile both called "stonecrop" "sedum" CRASSULACEAE
(Figures 8-3 and 8-4)

The name *Sedum* comes from the latin for "to sit" because these succulent plants are often found perched on rocks. There are perhaps six hundred species of sedum, and over forty are in cultivation. There are basically two groups from a gardening point of view: the rockery sedums, with dwarf habit and spreading stems, and the upright fall border sedums.

Rockery sedums. Under this heading fall dozens of low-growing or creeping sedums. Their most noticeable characteristic is their thick, succulent leaves. These may be silver, bright green, yellow green or purple in color and range in length from 1/4 inch to 2 inches (.6–5 cm). Small star-like flowers of white, red, pink, yellow or purplish red appear in clusters, mostly in summer (in spring for a few species). Plants root along creeping stems and thrive in very poor, dry soil. Some are evergreen; others die to the ground in winter. The following are some of the most common sedums available in the Pacific coastal region, but there are many more worth trying.

S. acre, golden carpet, creeps rapidly—too rapidly for many rock gardens—and forms a mat. The leaves are triangular in cross-section and overlapping; the flowers are yellow and borne in June and July. It is native to North Africa, Europe and West Asia.

S. cauticola, from Japan, has round, flat, gray green leaves along deciduous, spreading stems. It bears starry reddish pink flowers in August and September.

S. divergens is called "old man's bones" because its leaves are small and round, like ball joints. It is native from northern California to B.C. and has yellow flowers in summer.

S. kamtschaticum has flat leaves up to 2 inches (5 cm) long with notches along their margins. A native of Asia, it has star-like flowers— yellow with red centers—from June to August. These are followed by showy red seed heads. 'Variegatum' is a handsome cultivar with creamy margins.

S. reflexum has cylindrical leaves of blue green and gold flowers in summer. It is native to Europe and is edible.

S. 'Ruby Glow' is a garden hybrid of uncertain parentage. It has sprawling stems and slightly toothed, 1- to 1½-inch (2.5- to 4-cm) leaves, both with a reddish tint. It has loose heads of deep pink to red flowers. A similar hybrid of uncertain parents, 'Vera Jameson' has foliage of a deeper red shade and pink flowers.

S. sexangulare has small cylindrical leaves in six spiral rows. It has yellow flowers in early summer and is native to Europe and Asia.

S. spathulifolium, meaning spatula-shaped leaves, has flat, gray leaves in tight rosettes and bright yellow flowers to ⅝ inch (1.5 cm) wide in May and June. This species is native to the Pacific coastal region. 'Cape Blanco', often wrongly listed as 'Cappa Blanca', has almost white leaves and was found on Cape Blanco on the southern Oregon coast. A purple form, 'Purpureum', is also available.

S. spurium (*S. coccineum*), dragon's blood, has flat, rounded, dark green leaves and rich pink flowers in July and August. It is native to Iran and the Caucasus. 'Album' has white flowers.

Fall border sedums. A must for every garden, the fall border sedums are attractive year-round. Their silvery buds wait through the winter at soil level for spring to arrive, then unfurl to stems about 2½ feet (75 cm) in height, with beautiful, succulent gray green leaves. Round flat clusters of tiny, star-like, pink flowers are borne in August and September, a delight to bees and butterflies. With the chill of fall, they turn russet tones. Left standing in the garden, they look like a dried flower arrangement for months into the autumn. Try fall sedums near other plants with rich fall color, such as bergenia.

S. spectabile is the original species of fall sedum and bears dark pink blooms and opposite leaves, to 2 inches (5 cm) long. 'Brilliant' is a brighter rose, 'Carmen' is bright carmine and 'Meteor' is dark red. There is also a lovely white cultivar, 'Stardust'.

S. **'Autumn Joy'** is a chance hybrid between *S. spectabile* and a similar species of sedum. It has alternate, rather than opposite, leaves and flower-heads of rich coppery red. It is not as attractive to butterflies as *S. spectabile*. All of the fall sedums last indefinitely in water—actually, the stems often form roots in water and can later be planted back into the garden!

Bloomtime: Rockery sedums: May to October, depending on the species; fall border sedums: August to October.

Height: Rockery sedums: under 6 inches (15 cm) or less; except 'Ruby Glow' and 'Vera Jameson': 10–12 inches (25–30 cm); fall border sedums: 2¹/₂ feet (75 cm).

Spread: Rockery sedums: 12 inches (30 cm); fall border sedums: 2 feet (60 cm).

Light and soil: Full sun or light shade and any well-drained soil.

Care and propagation: Before planting the rockery sedums, make sure the ground is totally weed free, as it is difficult to weed later; sedum stems are brittle and their roots are shallow. Divide fall border sedums every few years; they become floppy otherwise.

All sedums are extremely easy to propagate. Stem cuttings inserted into the ground will root if the soil is not too dry. Plants can also be divided. Species can be grown from seed.

Pests and diseases: Generally trouble-free and not usually eaten by deer.

Frost hardiness: To zones 3–4, depending on the species or cultivar.

Sempervivum **species** "hens-and-chicks" "houseleek" "live-forever"
CRASSULACEAE
(Figure 8-5)

This modest succulent plant has an interesting history. In the Dark Ages it was known as Donderblom (Thunderflower) and was commonly believed to protect against lightning, fire, witches and evil spirits.

Indeed, Charlemagne, King of the Franks from A.D. 768 to A.D. 814, required landlords to plant one houseleek on the roof of each of their dwellings to protect from fire and ward off wars, hunger and pestilence to the whole country. Not surprising—considering it will grow on roofs—it is a symbol of vivacity in some cultures.

Sempervivums are easy to recognize because their succulent leaves form neat rosettes. The outer edge of each leaf is curved and comes to a pointed tip. Each rosette is monocarpic, from the Latin "one fruit." Each rosette throws up a flower stalk, which is covered with overlapping leaves, somewhat resembling a leek. At the top of this is a cluster of star-like red, purple, yellow or white flowers. After they set seed, the whole rosette dies. Meanwhile, smaller rosettes are produced around the mother rosette, and they carry on—hence another common name, hens-and-chicks.

There are dozens of species, naturally occurring varieties and hybrids, garden hybrids and named cultivars of sempervivums. Their nomenclature is complex. Most have been developed by breeders in the United States, Great Britain and Germany. Their rosettes vary from 1/2 inch to 6 inches (1.3–15 cm) across, and their leaves may be silver, green or mahogany, often tinted a contrasting color at the tip. Some species have a fine webbing of white hairs, earning them the common name of spiderweb sempervivums. If you have a dry, sunny spot where nothing else will grow, perhaps under the eaves, consider starting a collection of sempervivums. They create a rich tapestry that looks beautiful year-round. Sempervivums are native to Europe, Morocco and west Asia.

Bloomtime: June and July.

Height: 4–12 inches (10–30 cm).

Spread: 8–12 inches (20–30 cm).

Light and soil: Full sun and very well-drained soil. They are drought tolerant.

Care and propagation: Be sure that when you buy sempervivums, there is either one young, nonblooming rosette in the pot, or, if there is a blooming rosette, that it has younger rosettes around it. If a pot has only one blooming rosette, it is likely to die before producing offsets, leaving you with nothing. When planting sempervivums, consider a top-dressing of coarse sand or gravel. It is very attractive and helps to keep the leaves from being splashed with mud and prevents water from accumulating around the crowns. Remove old flower stalks after blooms have faded.

To propagate, remove new rosettes when rooted, during fall or early spring. With the exception of named cultivars, sempervivums can also be grown easily from seed. Thompson & Morgan list a seed mixture from one of the top U.S. hybridizers. Sow seed on the surface and cover flat with a piece of glass or plastic. Germination takes about two weeks. Plant out in the garden in autumn.

Pests and diseases: Birds may uproot young rosettes. RUST may form on the leaves. Deer do not usually eat sempervivums.

Frost hardiness: To zones 3–5, depending on the species.

Silene schafta "rose campion"
Silene vulgaris ssp. *maritima* (*S. maritima*) "sea campion"
CARYOPHYLLACEAE

(Figure 8-6 and 8-7)

Both of these are easily grown species for the rock garden or for a softening effect at the edge of a retaining wall. They can also be used for the front of a border.

Sea campion is a lovely, creeping perennial with evergreen silver leaves and stems. It is always neat and blooms from May to October. While not showy, it is very pretty. The flowers are white, with five two-lobed petals, giving the appearance of ten petals. They are held in an inflated, pale green, balloon-like calyx, which persists and is decorative even after the petals have fallen. The opposite leaves are 1 inch (2.5 cm) long and pointed. This species is native to the coasts of western Europe.

Rose campion is showier, producing its magenta pink blossoms from July to October. It is an excellent addition to the rock garden, because many rockery plants are spring bloomers. It spreads to form a mat of small green leaves. Rose campion also has a noticeable calyx, but it is long and slender rather than round. The calyx is green with red veins and has small hairs. The petals have a notch at the end, rather than two lobes. This species is native to the Caucasus.

Bloomtime: Sea campion: May to October; rose campion: July to October.

Height: 6 inches (15 cm).

Spread: 12 inches (30 cm).

Light and soil: Full sun or part shade in well-drained soil.

Care and propagation: Little care is required. If plants look untidy, they can be cut back lightly after blooming. Propagate by division or seed; Thompson & Morgan lists both species.

Pests and diseases: Generally trouble-free.

Frost hardiness: To zone 4.

Solidago hybrids

× *Solidaster* both called "goldenrod" ASTERACEAE

(Figure 8-8)

While the wild types of goldenrod are weedy, there are numerous dwarf hybrids that add a sunny touch to the border. Goldenrod bears myriads of tiny flowers in fluffy, yellow, arching plumes in August and September. The reputation this striking flower has for causing hay fever is somewhat dubious, but it has dampened goldenrod's popularity in North America. In Britain and Europe, however, they are widely planted.

Solidago. There are many species of goldenrod, native to North America, Europe, Asia, the Azores and South America. The parentage of the dwarf hybrids—superior for garden purposes—is unclear, but it is thought to include *Solidago canadensis* and *S. virgaurea*. The former is native to western North America and the latter to Europe, Asia and North Africa. Some popular cultivars follow.

Cultivar	Height	Flower color	Bloomtime
'Cloth of Gold'	18 inches (45 cm)	deep yellow	August-September
'Crown of Rays'	18 inches (45 cm)	yellow sprays	July-August
'Golden Baby'	26 inches (65 cm)	golden plumes	July-August
'Goldenmosa'	30 inches (75 cm)	golden yellow	August-September

All goldenrods have long leaves, up to 6 inches (15 cm) long, tapering to a point and alternating along the stems. Goldenrods are valuable to birds, butterflies and bees.

× *Solidaster* is a bigeneric hybrid of *Solidago* and *Aster*, thought to have first been made by a French nurseryman, Leonard Lille, in Lyon in 1910. It is represented in cultivation by 'Lemore', which is very similar to a dwarf goldenrod in appearance, except that individual flower heads are more daisy-like than those of *Solidago*. It is a lovely shade of creamy yellow and grows to 2–2$^{1}/_{2}$ feet (60–75 cm) tall. It blooms in August and September.

Bloomtime: July to September, depending on the cultivar.
Height: 1¹/₂–2¹/₂ feet (45–75 cm). The wild species grow up to 8 feet (2.4 m) in height, but are not suitable for the garden.
Spread: 12–15 inches (30–38 cm).
Light and soil: Full sun or light shade in average garden soil.
Care and propagation: Easy to grow. Cut stems to ground in late fall. Propagate by division.
Pests and diseases: CATERPILLARS and POWDERY MILDEW.
Frost hardiness: *Solidago* hybrids: to zone 3; × *Solidaster*: to zone 4.

Stachys byzantina (*S. lanata*) (*S. olympica*) "lamb's ears" "woolly be-tony" LAMIACEAE
(Figure 8-9)

A wonderful front-of-the-border perennial, the leaves of lamb's ears are thick and covered with soft, silver fur. Up to 10 inches (25 cm) long, including a long leafstalk, they are oval in shape. They cluster close together along the ground, and the plant spreads to form a woolly silver mat. In late summer, the plant produces its (somewhat peculiar-looking) inflorescence. A gangly flower stalk reaches up to 30 inches (75 cm) in height, bearing small leaves and small purple flowers. As is typical of most members of the mint family, the stalks are square in cross-section. Because lamb's ears is valued for its neat, silver appearance and is often used to edge beds, setting off taller plants, the awkward-looking flower stalks detract from the effect and are removed by many gardeners. 'Silver Carpet', a cultivar available from specialty nurseries, does not bloom at all. Flower arrangers value the flower stalks of lamb's ears and dry them to use in winter arrangements. The species is native to Turkey and southwest Asia.
Bloomtime: July.
Height: The leaves cluster at ground level to a height of 5 inches (15 cm).
Spread: Plants spread fairly rapidly; plant 12–18 inches (30–45 cm) apart.
Light and soil: Full sun or part shade in well-drained soil. Lamb's ears will grow with only a few hours of sun a day, but will be less compact in habit.
Care and propagation: Young plants are most attractive, so it is worthwhile dividing and replanting the youngest portions every second or

third year. Propagate the species by seed or division, named cultivars by division in fall or spring.

Pests and diseases: Generally trouble-free.

Frost hardiness: To zone 4.

Thalictrum aquilegifolium "columbine meadow rue"
Thalictrum delavayi (commonly sold as *T. dipterocarpum*)
Thalictrum rochebrunianum "lavender mist"
Thalictrum speciosissimum (*T. glaucum*) all called "meadow rue"
RANUNCULACEAE
(Figure 8-10)

Meadow rues add height and gracefulness to the garden border. Their leaves are divided into many dainty, lobed leaflets that resemble a columbine or a maidenhair fern. Individual flowers do not have petals, but have four to five sepals and numerous, often showy, stamens.

Thalictrum aquilegifolium is a native of Europe and Asia. It grows to 2½–3 feet (75–90 cm) and has fluffy inflorescences of lavender, white or rose pink flowers in May and June. The green or white sepals fall soon after the flowers open. Its leaves are blue gray and glossy. 'Thundercloud' has deep purple flowers and reaches 3–4 feet (.9–1.2 m) in height.

T. delavayi (which is usually sold incorrectly under the name *D. dipterocarpum*) and *T. rochebrunianum* have similar flowers, to 1 inch (2.5 cm) across, with persistent reddish or purplish sepals and prominent yellow stamens. Dozens of these blooms are carried on delicate, open, branching stems. *T. delavayi* was discovered in western China by the Abbé Delavay at the end of the nineteenth century. It reaches 4–5 feet (1.2–1.5 m) and blooms from June to August. 'Album' is white-flowered and 'Hewitt's Double' has long-lasting, double purple flowers, but lacks the lovely contrast of sepals and stamens.

T. rochebrunianum is much more vigorous than *T. delavayi* and reaches another foot (30 cm) in height. It starts blooming later and blooms longer. It is native to Japan.

T. speciosissimum has very blue, finely divided foliage, and is very attractive in flower arrangements. It has 2- to 5-foot (.6- to 1.5-m) stems bearing fluffy gold flowers in July and August.

Bloomtime: June to August, depending on the species (see above).

Height: 2–6 feet (.6–1.8 m), depending on the species (see above).

Spread: 12–24 inches (30–60 cm). The branching inflorescences of *T.*

delavayi and *T. rochebrunianum* make excellent cut flowers. If you plan to cut them, space them at least 24 inches (60 cm) apart, so the stems will not intertwine.

Light and soil: Sun or light shade. Plants will grow in ordinary soil, but will thrive (and be taller) in rich moist soil with abundant organic matter.

Care and propagation: Top-dress annually with compost or well-rotted manure. Staking is usually required. Cut stems to ground level in late fall.

Pests and diseases: Generally trouble-free.

Frost hardiness: To zone 5.

Tradescantia × *andersoniana* "spiderwort" COMMELINACEAE
(Figure 8-11)

Related to the popular house plants of the same name, the spiderwort got its peculiar common name because it was first thought to be related to a group of plants said to cure the bite of a particular spider. It is a complex hybrid of at least three species of spiderworts from the eastern and southern United States. One of these species was sent to England by John Tradescant II in 1637, along with the first of the Michaelmas daisies.

Tradescantia × *andersoniana* has flowers 1 inch (2.5 cm) across, with three petals and a central pouf of filaments. The flowers are on long stalks and the flower buds cluster in the leaf joint like baubles. The slender leaves are up to 10 inches (25 cm) long and folded so that they are v-shaped in cross-section. The base of each leaf wraps around the stem. The foliage lasts well in water, but the flowers are not long-lasting when cut. 'Osprey' is white, 'Purple Dome' is dark velvety purple, 'Isis' is deep blue and 'Pauline' is pinkish purple.

Bloomtime: June to September.

Height: 18–24 inches (45–60 cm).

Spread: 18 inches (45 cm).

Light and soil: Sun or part shade in average, well-drained soil that does not dry out.

Care and propagation: Plant with a handful of bonemeal but do not use a fertilizer with nitrogen, as it may encourage too much leafy growth. Stake with small twiggy sticks if plants become floppy.

Pests and diseases: SLUGS and SNAILS.
Frost hardiness: To zone 5.

Trollius × *cultorum* "globeflower" RANUNCULACEAE
(Figure 8-12)

If you can forgive globeflowers for their resemblance to that invasive weed, the buttercup, they make excellent (and noninvasive) border perennials. Their deeply divided dark green leaves look attractive all summer and their yellow cup-shaped flowers brighten the garden from May to July, depending on the cultivar. Globeflowers make excellent cut flowers. The cup of the globeflower is made of sepals; the true petals are usually small.

Most globeflowers are hybrids between *Trollius asiaticus* (native to Asia), *T. europaeus* (Europe and arctic America) and *T. chinensis* (China). For convenience, they are listed under *Trollius* × *cultorum*.

'Brynes Giant' is a late-blooming gold and is a strong grower. 'Earliest of All' is light yellow, 'Etna' is an early orange, and 'Goldquelle' is yellowish orange. 'Lemon Queen' is lemon yellow, 'Moonglow' is soft yellow and long-blooming, and 'Orange Princess' is deep orange. All grow to 2–3 feet (60–90 cm).

'Gold Queen', which is either a cultivar or hybrid of *T. ledebouri* (native to Siberia), blooms from June to August. It has more open cups than the above cultivars and has a striking cluster of narrow, erect petals at the center of each cup. Flowers are orange and up to 4 inches (10 cm) across. Plants can reach 4 feet (1.2 m) in height.

Bloomtime: June to August, depending on the cultivar.
Height: 2–4 feet (.6–1.2 m), depending on the cultivar.
Spread: 12 inches (30 cm).
Light and soil: Full sun or part shade in soil that does not dry out. Globeflowers also thrive in damp soil.
Care and propagation: Easy to grow. Deadhead to keep a succession of bloom coming and cut stems to the ground in late fall. Named cultivars should be propagated by division. Species can be divided or grown from seed.
Pests and diseases: Generally trouble-free.
Frost hardiness: To zone 3.

	Bloomtime	under 1 foot (30 cm)	1–3 feet (30–90 cm)	over 3 feet (90 cm)	full sun	partial shade	shade	tolerates dry soil	tolerates damp soil	good for cutting	woodland garden	rock garden	attracts bees and/or butterflies	attractive foliage	generally pest & disease free

QUICK REFERENCE CHART

	Bloomtime	under 1 ft	1–3 ft	over 3 ft	full sun	partial shade	shade	dry soil	damp soil	cutting	woodland	rock	bees/butterflies	foliage	pest free
Achillea filipendulina fernleaf yarrow	July–Sept.		•	•	•			•		•			•	•	•
Achillea millefolium common yarrow	July–Sept.		•		•			•		•			•		•
Achillea 'Moonshine'	July–Sept.		•		•					•			•	•	
Achillea ptarmica sneezeweed	July–Sept.		•		•				•	•					
Aconitum spp. (summer monkshood)	June–August		*	*	•	•				•	•		•		
Aconitum spp. (fall monkshood)	Sept.–Oct.			•	•	•				•	•		•		
Adiantum pedatum maidenhair fern	doesn't bloom	*	*			•	•				•			•	•
Alchemilla alpina alpine Lady's mantle	June–August	•			•	•						•		•	
Alchemilla mollis Lady's mantle	June–August	•			•	•			•	•	•			•	
Alyssum montanum mountain-gold	April–May	•			•			•				•			
Anemone pulsatilla pasqueflower	April–May	•			•	•						•		•	
Anemone spp. Japanese anemones	August–Sept.		•	•	•	•				•					
Anthemis tinctoria golden marguerite	July–August		•		•					•					
Aquilegia hybrids columbine	May–June		•		•	•				•	•				
Arabis spp. rock cress	March–May	•			•	•						•			•
Armeria maritima thrift	May–July	•	•		•							•			•
Armeria plantaginea & *A. pseudarmeria* thrift	June–August	•			•									•	
Artemisia abrotanum southernwood	July–Sept.	•			•					•				•	•
Artemisia absinthium common wormwood	July–August	•			•			•						•	•

* depending on species or cultivar

QUICK REFERENCE CHART	Bloomtime	Height			Light			Soil		Uses					
		under 1 foot (30 cm)	1–3 feet (30–90 cm)	over 3 feet (90 cm)	full sun	partial shade	shade	tolerates dry soil	tolerates damp soil	good for cutting	woodland garden	rock garden	attracts bees and/or butterflies	attractive foliage	generally pest & disease free
Artemisia lactiflora white mugwort	August–Sept.			•	•	•				•				•	•
Artemisia ludoviciana	August–Sept.			•	•			•		•				•	•
Artemisia 'Powis Castle'	rarely blooms		•		•			•		•				•	•
Artemisia schmidtiana (dwarf cultivars)	September	•			•			•				•		•	
Artemisia stellerana 'Silver Brocade'	August–Sept.	•			•			•				•		•	•
Aster alpinus alpine aster	May–June	•			•					•		•	•		
Aster amellus Italian aster	August–Sept.		•		•	•				•		*			
A. × *frikartii*	July–October		•		•	•				•			•		
Aster novae-angliae & *Aster novi-belgii* Michaelmas daisies	Sept.–Oct.			•	•				•	*		*			
Astilbe × *arendsii* astilbe	June–Sept.*		•		•	•	•		•	•	•		•		•
Astilbe chinensis 'Pumila'	August–Sept.	•			•	•	•		•			•		•	•
Astilbe thunbergii & *A. taquetii* 'Superba'	August–Sept.			•	•	•	•		•	•	•			•	•
Astrantia spp. masterwort	June–July		•		•	•	•		•	•	•			*	
Aubrieta deltoidea aubrietia	April–May	•			•							•	•		
Aurinia saxatilis basket-of-gold	April–May	•			•			•				•			
Bergenia spp. bergenia	April–May	*	*		•	•		•		•	•	*	•	•	
Buphthalum salicifolium sunwheels	May–July		•		•					•					•
Campanula carpatica Carpathian harebell	July–August	•			•	•						•			•
Campanula glomerata clustered bellflower	May–July		•		•	•			•	•			•		•
Campanula persicifolia peach-leaf bellflower	June–August		•		•	•			•	•	•		•		•

* depending on species or cultivar

173

	Bloomtime	under 1 foot (30 cm)	1–3 feet (30–90 cm)	over 3 feet (90 cm)	full sun	partial shade	shade	tolerates dry soil	tolerates damp soil	good for cutting	woodland garden	rock garden	attracts bees and/or butterflies	attractive foliage	generally pest & disease free
		Bloomtime	**Height**		**Light**			**Soil**		**Uses**					
Camp. portenschlagiana bellflower	June–August	•			•	•						•	•		•
Catananche caerulea cupid's dart	June-October		•		•	•		•		•	•				•
Centranthus ruber red valerian	June–July		•		•	•		•		•				•	•
Cerastium tomentosum snow-in-summer	May–June	•			•			•	•			No		•	•
Cheiranthus 'Bowles Mauve' per. wallflower	May–October		•		•			•		•				•	•
Chrysanthemum × morifolium florist's chrysanthemum	Sept.–Nov.	*	*		•					•					
Chrysanthemum × superbum Shasta daisy	June–August		•		•	•				•					
Cimicifuga spp. bugbanes & snakeroots	July–Oct. *			•	•	•				•	•			•	•
Coreopsis spp. coreopsis	July–October	*	*		•			*		•		*			
Delphinium hybrids delphiniums	June–July		•		•	•				•					
Dianthus × allwoodii carnation pink	June–July		•		•					•					
Dianthus deltoides maiden pink	June–August	•			•	•									
D. gratianopolitanus Cheddar pink	May–June	•			•										
Dianthus plumarius cottage pink	June	•	•		•										
Dicentra eximia fringed bleeding heart	May–Sept.		•			•	•			•	•			•	•
Dicentra 'Luxuriant' hybrid bleeding heart	May–October		•			•	•			•		•		•	•
Dicentra spectabilis bleeding heart	April–May		•			•	•			•					•
Dictamnus albus gas plant	June–July		•	•	•			•		•					•

* depending on species or cultivar

174

QUICK REFERENCE CHART

		Height			Light			Soil		Uses					
	Bloomtime	under 1 foot (30 cm)	1–3 feet (30–90 cm)	over 3 feet (90 cm)	full sun	partial shade	shade	tolerates dry soil	tolerates damp soil	good for cutting	woodland garden	rock garden	attracts bees and/or butterflies	attractive foliage	generally pest & disease free
Digitalis ferruginea rusty foxglove	July		•		•	•				•	•				•
Digitalis grandiflora yellow foxglove	July–August		•		•	•				•	•				•
Digitalis × mertonensis	June–Sept.		•		•	•				•	•				•
Digitalis purpurea common foxglove	June–July		•		•	•				•	•				•
Doronicum spp. leopard's bane	April–May	•			•	•				•	*	*	•		•
Echinacea purpurea purple coneflower	July–Sept.		•		•	•				•			•		•
Echinops spp. globe thistle	July–August		*	*	•			•		•			•		•
Eryngium spp. sea hollies	July–August	•			•					•			•	*	•
Eupatorium coelestinum mist flower	Aug.–Sept.	•			•	•				•					•
Eupatorium purpureum joe-pye weed	August–Sept.		•		•	•				•					•
Euphorbia epithymoides cushion spurge	April–May	•			•	•	•	•		•		•		•	•
Euphorbia griffithii spurge	May–June		•		•	•	•	•	•	•					•
Festuca spp. blue fescue	May–Aug.*	*	*		•			•				•			•
Gaillardia × grandiflora blanketflower	June–Oct.	*	*		•	•		•		•					
Geranium spp. hardy geraniums	April–Oct.*	*	*		•	•			*	*	*	*	*	*	•
Gypsophila paniculata baby's breath	June–Sept.		•		•					•					•
Gypsophila repens creeping baby's breath	June–Sept.	•			•							•			•
Helleborus niger Christmas rose	Dec.–March		•			•	•			•	•				
Helleborus orientalis Lenten rose	Feb.–March		•			•	•			•	•		•	•	•

* depending on species or cultivar

175

QUICK REFERENCE CHART	Bloomtime	under 1 foot (30 cm)	1–3 feet (30–90 cm)	over 3 feet (90 cm)	full sun	partial shade	shade	tolerates dry soil	tolerates damp soil	good for cutting	woodland garden	rock garden	attracts bees and/or butterflies	attractive foliage	generally pest & disease free
Hemerocallis lilioasphodelus yellow daylily	May		•		•	•		•	•	•			•		•
Hemerocallis hybrids daylilies	June–Sept.*		•		•	•		•	•	•					
Heuchera × brizoides coralbells	May–July	•			•	•				•	•	•			
Heuchera 'Palace Purple'	July–October	•			•	•				•	•	•		•	
× Heucherella 'Bridget Bloom'	May–July	•			•	•				•	•	•			
Hosta spp. hosta	June–Oct.*	*	*		*	•	•		•	*	•			•	
Iberis sempervirens evergreen candytuft	May–June	•			•			•				•	*	•	•
Incarvillea delavayi hardy gloxinia	May–July		•		•					•				•	
Iris spp. iris, flag	May–June		•		•	*		*	*	*	*				
Liatris spp. gayfeather	July–Sept.		*	*	•			*	*	•					
Lobelia cardinalis cardinal flower	July–August		•		•	•	•		•	•					
Lobelia splendens perennial lobelia	August–Oct.		•		•	•			•	•					
Lupinus hybrids lupines	May–July		•		•	•				•			•	•	
Lysimachia punctata yellow loosestrife	June–July		•		•	•		•	•	•					•
Lythrum spp. purple loosestrife	June–Sept.		*	*	•	•			•	•			•		•
Miscanthus sinensis Japanese silver grass	Oct.–Nov.		•		•	•			•	•				•	•
Monarda spp. bee balm	July–Sept.		•		•	•			*	•			•		
Oenothera fruticosa sundrops	June–Sept.	*	*		•			•				•			
Paeonia spp. herbaceous peonies	April–July*		•		•	•				•					*

* depending on species or cultivar

176

	Bloomtime	under 1 foot (30 cm)	1–3 feet (30–90 cm)	over 3 feet (90 cm)	full sun	partial shade	shade	tolerates dry soil	tolerates damp soil	good for cutting	woodland garden	rock garden	attracts bees and/or butterflies	attractive foliage	generally pest & disease free
QUICK REFERENCE CHART															
Papaver orientale Oriental poppy	May–June		•		•					•			•		•
Pennisetum spp. fountain grass	July–Oct.*		•		•					•				•	•
Penstemon camp. hybrids beard-tongue	June–Sept.		•		•					•					•
Phlox spp. tall border phloxes	July–Sept.			•	•	•				•			•		
Phlox subulata moss phlox	April–May	•			•							•	•		
Phygelius spp. Cape fuchsias	July–Oct.		•		•	•				•					•
Physostegia virginiana obedient plant	July–August	*	*		•	•				•					•
Polemonium spp. Jacob's ladder	April–Sept.*		•		•	•					•				•
Polygonatum spp. Solomon's seal	April–June	*	*		*	•	•	*	•		•			•	•
Polygonum affine Himalayan knotweed	May–Sept.	•			•	•						•			•
Polygonum bistorta knotweed	May–June		•		•	•			•	•				•	•
Polystichum munitum sword fern	doesn't bloom	•	•			•	•			•	•				•
Primula spp. candelabra primulas	May–July*		•		•	•			•	•	•				
Primula denticulata drumstick primula	March–June	•			•	•			•	•	•	•	•		
Primula veris cowslip	April–May	•			•	•			•		•	•			
Primula vulgaris primrose	April–May	•			•	•			•		•	•			
Pulmonaria spp. lungwort	March–May*		•		•	•	•	*	*		•	*	•	*	•
Rudbeckia fulgida orange coneflower	July–Oct.		•		•				*	•			•		
Rudbeckia hirta black-eyed susan	July–Oct.		•		•					•			•		

* depending on species or cultivar

177

	Bloomtime	under 1 foot (30 cm)	1–3 feet (30–90 cm)	over 3 feet (90 cm)	full sun	partial shade	shade	tolerates dry soil	tolerates damp soil	good for cutting	woodland garden	rock garden	attracts bees and/or butterflies	attractive foliage	generally pest & disease free
Salvia × *superba* perennial salvia	May–Jun/Sep.	•			•	•		•		•		*	•		•
Saponaria ocymoides rock soapwort	May–June	•			•	•						•			•
Saxifraga spp. encrusted saxifrages	May–June	•			•	•						•		•	•
Saxifraga spp. London pride	May–June	•				•	•					•		•	•
Saxifraga spp. mossy saxifrages	April–May	•				•						•			
Scabiosa caucasica pincushion flower	July–Sept.		•		•					•			•		
Sedum spp. rockery sedums	May–Sept.*	•			•	•						•	*	•	
Sedum spectabile fall border sedum	August–Oct.		•		•	•				•			•	•	•
Sempervivum spp. houseleek	June–July	•						•				•		•	•
Silene schafta rose campion	July–Oct.	•			•	•						•		•	•
Silene vulgaris ssp. *maritima* sea campion	May–October	•			•	•						•		•	•
Solidago hybrids & × *Solidaster* goldenrod	July–Sept*		•		•	•				•			•		
Stachys byzantina lamb's ears	July	•			•	•				•		•		•	•
Thalictrum spp. meadow rues	June–Aug.*		*	*	•	•			•	•	•			•	•
Tradescantia × *andersoniana* spiderwort	June–Sept.		•			•	•		•	•	•				
Trollius × *cultorum* globeflower	June–Aug.*		•		•	•			•	•					•

* depending on species or cultivar

178

Bibliography
and
Sources

Bibliography

Aden, Paul. *The Hosta Book.* Portland: Timber Press, 1988.

Barton, Barbara J. *Gardening by Mail 2.* Sebastopol: Tusker Press, 1987.

Baumbardt, John Philip. *How to Identify Flowering Plant Families.* Beaverton, Oregon: Timber Press, 1982.

Bloom, Alan. *Alpines for your Garden.* Nottingham: Floraprint, 1980.

Bloom, Alan. *Perennials for your Garden.* Nottingham: Floraprint, 1983.

Clark, Lewis J. *Wild Flowers of British Columbia.* Sidney: Grey's Publishing, 1973.

Clausen, Ruth R.; and Ekstrom, Nicolas H. *Perennials for American Gardens.* New York: Random House, 1989.

Coats, Alice M. *Flowers and Their Histories.* London: Hulton Press, 1956.

Donahue, Roy; Schickluna, John; and Robertson, Lynn. *Soils: An Introduction to Soils and Plant Growth.* New Jersey: Prentice-Hall, 1971.

Edwards, Colin. *Delphiniums, the Complete Guide.* Ramsbury: The Crowood Press, 1989.

The Encyclopedia of Herbs and Herbalism. Edited by Malcolm Stuart. New York: Crescent Books, 1979.

Ferns. Philip Perl and the Editors of Time-Life Books. Alexandria: Time-Life Books, 1977.

A Gardener's Guide to Pest Prevention and Control in the Home and Garden. Victoria: Province of B.C., Ministry of Agriculture and Food, 1986.

Grounds, Roger. *Ornamental Grasses.* London: Pelham Books, 1979.

Harper, Pamela; and McGourty, Frederick. *Perennials: How to Select, Grow & Enjoy.* Los Angeles: HP Books, 1985.

Hessayon, D.G. *The Flower Expert.* Waltham Cross, England: pbi Publications, Brittanica House, 1984.

Hortus Third. Edited by the staff of the Liberty Hyde Bailey Hortorium. New York: Macmillan Publishing Company, 1976.

Hunt, C. *Natural Regions of the U.S. and Canada.* San Francisco: W.H. Freeman, 1974.

The Illustrated Encyclopedia of Plants. Edited by M. Bisacre, R. Carlisle, D. Robertson and J. Ruck. New York: Exeter Books, 1984.

Jeffrey, C. *An introduction to plant taxonomy.* Cambridge: Cambridge University Press, 1982.

Kruckeberg, Arthur R. *Gardening with Native Plants of the Pacific Northwest.* Vancouver: Douglas and McIntyre, 1982.

The Living Webster Encyclopedic Dictionary of the English Language. Chicago: The English Language Institute of America, 1971.

Lyons, C.P. *Trees, Shrubs and Flowers to Know in B.C.* Toronto: J.M. Dent & Sons, 1952.

McGourty, Frederick. *The Perennial Gardener.* Boston: Houghton Mifflin, 1989.

The Ortho Problem Solver Second Edition. Edited by Michael D. Smith. San Francisco: Ortho Information Services, 1984.

Perennials. James Underwood Crockett and the Editors of Time-Life Books. New York: Time-Life Books, 1972.

Perry, Frances. *Collins Guide to Border Plants.* London: Collins, 1957.

Pirone, Pascal. *Diseases and Pests of Ornamental Plants, 5th Ed.* New York: John Wiley and Sons, 1978.

Pizzetti, Ippolito; and Cocker, Henry. *Flowers: A Guide for Your Garden, Volumes I and II.* New York: Harry N. Abrams Inc., 1975.

Readers Digest Encyclopaedia of Garden Plants and Flowers. Edited, designed and published by The Reader's Digest Association. London: 1985.

Schultz, Warren. *The Chemical-Free Lawn.* Emmaus, Pennsylvania: Rodale Press, 1989.

Solomon, Steve. *Growing Organic Vegetables West of the Cascades.* Seattle: Pacific Search Press, 1985.

Thomas, Graham Stuart. *Perennial Garden Plants, or The Modern Florilegium.* London: J. M. Dent & Sons, 1986.

Verey, Rosemary. *The Flower Arranger's Garden.* Boston: Little Brown and Company, 1989.

Alpine Garden Club of B.C. Bulletin. November 1988. "Some deer-proof plants." Jo Bridge.

Alpine Garden Club of B.C. Bulletin. June 1989. "Evening primroses, sundrops and suncups (*Oenothera*)." Dr. Gerald Straley.

Practical Gardening Magazine. EMAP National Publications Ltd. Peterborough, PE2 0UW, England, various issues.

The Garden. The Royal Horticultural Society. Vincent Square, London, England.

Beckett, Kenneth. Letter: "*Sedum spathulifolium.*" August, 1982.

Bloom, Alan. "Achilleas." June, 1979.

Bloom, Alan. "Aconitums." July, 1979.

Bloom, Alan. "Salvias." July, 1980.

Clegg, Frederic. "Talking about plants." November, 1989.

Coombes, Allen. "*Phygelius.*" August, 1988.

Hodgman, Muriel. "In praise of sedums." November, 1980.

Keen, Mary. "Butterflies in the Garden." August, 1982.

Moore, Wayne. "Soap as an Insecticide." October, 1982.

Tait, William. Letter: "*Anthemis* mix up?" February, 1989, page 85.

Commercial growers catalogues

Bressingham Gardens. Autumn catalogue. 1989.

Georg Arends Staudendulturen. Ronsdorf, West Germany.

Hagemann Staudenkulturen. Hannover, West Germany.

Staudengartnerei Gräfin von Zeppelin. Baden, West Germany.

Personal communication:

Bloom, Alan. Bressingham, England. December, 1989.

McGourty, Frederick. Norfolk, Connecticut. November, 1989.

Weber, Susane. Baden, West Germany. June, 1989.

Personal Communications

Bloom, Alan. Bressingham, England. December, 1989.

McGourly, Frederick. Norfolk, Connecticut. November, 1989.

Weber, Susane. Baden, West Germany. June, 1989.

Societies

Alpine Garden Club of B.C. Box 5161 - MPO, Vancouver, B.C., V6B 4B2. $13.00 annual fee includes 40 seed packets from all over the world, tours of members' gardens and quarterly bulletins with articles on many types of plants. Monthly meetings and spring and fall plant sales are open to the public.

Hardy Plant Society of Oregon, 33530 Southeast Bluff Road, Boring, Oregon, 97009. $12.00 U.S. annual fee includes two newsletters per year, which include information on seminars and plant sales.

Northwest Perennial Alliance, P.O. Box 45574, University Station, Seattle, Washington, 98145. $10 U.S. annual fee includes information sheets and announcements of activities and members-only plant sale.

Royal Horticultural Society, P.O. Box 313, 80 Vincent Square, London, SW1P 2PE, England. £18.00 includes a monthly magazine and access to the annual seed exchange (for a shipping charge).

Vancouver Island Rock and Garden Society, P.O. Box 6507, Station "C', Victoria, B.C., V8P 5M4. $8.00 annual fee allows members to receive monthly bulletins, attend monthly meetings and the annual show, join tours of members' gardens and field trips.

Seeds

Alpine Garden Club of B.C. (see above).

Dominion Seed House, Georgetown, Ontario, L7G 4A2, Canada.

Park Seed Company, Cokesbury Road, Greenwood, South Carolina, USA, 29647 (Bulbs are listed also, but these cannot be shipped into Canada.)

Royal Horticultural Society (see above).

Stokes Seed Company
Canadian address: 39 James St., Box 10, St. Catherines, Ontario, L2R 6R6.
U.S. address: P.O. Box 548, Buffalo, New York, 14240.

Thompson & Morgan Seed Catalogue, P.O. Box 1308, Jackson, New Jersey, 08527, U.S.A. (Shipping to Canada.)

Plants by mail order

Canadians wishing to import from the U.S. should obtain an application for a Permit to Import from Agriculture Canada by writing to them at: #103—620 Royal Avenue, P.O. Box 2527, New

Westminster, B.C.; or by faxing them at 604-666-8577; or by contacting your nearest Agriculture Canada office. The completed application can then be mailed to Ottawa, as directed on the form, or you can fax it to Agriculture Canada in Ottawa at 613-995-6833, attention Permits. There is no charge for the Permit to Import, but it does take up to 6 weeks, especially if it is mailed in. When you receive your permit, you can then send the import number and mail stickers with your order. The supplier will then complete a phytosanitary certificate, after the order has been inspected by the U.S. Department of Agriculture. Most suppliers charge for the phytosanitary certificate. Often it is a flat fee, making it worthwhile combining several orders with friends or members of a gardening club.

If you are having the plants sent by mail, you will receive the necessary postal stickers. The drawback of this system is that plants can sit in the post office for several days. You can also bring your shipment across the border yourself; phone your Agriculture Canada office to arrange a convenient inspection time.

For American gardeners to import perennials from Canada, an import permit is generally not required except for certain crops; instead, the Canadian supplier arranges for an inspection by Agriculture Canada and a phytosanitary certificate. Plant inspectors are usually at the border crossings from Monday to Friday, 8 a.m. to 4:30 p.m. If you wish your order to arrive by mail, check with your local U.S.D.A. office before ordering to arrange for inspection.

There are hundreds of mail-order nurseries, particularly in the U.S., for perennials. The following are either Canadian, from Washington or Oregon, or have an exceptional list. Refer to *Gardening by Mail* (see Bibliography) to hunt down more!

C.A. Cruickshank, 1015 Mount Pleasant Road, Toronto, Ontario, M4P 2M1, Canada. (List includes mostly bulbs, but also many kinds of irises, daylilies, Oriental poppies, peonies, Solomon's seal and various woodland perennials.)

Carrol Gardens, 444 East Main Street, P.O. Box 310, Westminster, Maryland, 21157, U.S.A. Catalog US$2.00 (Outstanding selection; shipping to Canada with phytosanitary certificate and with advance arrangements.)

Cricklewood Nursery, 11907 Nevers Road, Snohomish, Washington, 98290, U.S.A. (The nursery is also open by appointment; phone 206-568-2829.)

Delair Gardens, 35120 Delair Road, R.R. 4. Abbotsford, V2S 4N4, Canada. (Formerly Hopestead Gardens, Delair Gardens has an interesting selection of hard-to-get perennials. Catalogue $2.00, refundable on the first order.)

Fancy Fronds 1911 4th Avenue West, Seattle, Washington, 98119, U.S.A.. Telephone 206-284-5332. (Shipping to Canada.)

Ferncliff Gardens, 8394 McTaggart St., S.S.1, Mission, B.C., V2V 5V6, Canada. Telephone 826-2447. (Irises, peonies, gladioli and dahlias; shipping only in Canada at this time. Fields are open for oublic viewing—-it is a beautiful location.)

Gardenimport, P.O. Box 760, Thornhill, Ontario, L3T 4A5, Canada. (Bulbs and a good basic list of perennials, many from Bressingham Gardens.)

Garden Place, 6780 Heisley Road, P.O. Box 388, Mentor, Ohio, 44061-0388, U.S.A. (Shipping to Canada with phytosanitary certificate and approximately 15%-of-order charge.)

Lamb Nurseries, E. 101 Sharp Ave., Spokane, Washington, 99202, U.S.A. (An excellent selection; for Canadian shipments a phytosanitary certificate is required.)

Rainforest Gardens, R.R. #1, Site 2, Box 22, Port Moody, B.C. V3H 3C8, Canada. (Geraniums, hostas, ferns and other shade-loving perennials are featured. Catalogue $2.00, refundable on the first order. Shipping to the U.S.A. by special arrangement.)

Wayside Gardens, Hodges, South Carolina, 29695-0001, U.S.A. (No shipping to Canada.)

White Flower Farm, Litchfield, Connecticut, 06759-0050, U.S.A. (tools and accessories only are shipped to Canada—not plants.)

Plants by personal shopping

In addition to your favorite garden center, the following are good sources of perennials.

Alpenflora Nursery, 17985 - 40th Avenue, Surrey, B.C., Canada. (While mostly wholesale, Alpenflora will also sell retail to the general public.)

Alpine Garden Club of B.C. (This club has a public sale each spring and fall with an excellent selection hard-to-find of perennials. For information see address listed under societies.)

Shop in the Garden, UBC Botanical Garden, has a small but interesting selection of perennials. Phone 228-4804 for details.

VanDusen Botanical Gardens public sale. This annual spring fundraising sale offers many unusual plants. Expect long lineups early in the day. Phone the garden at 266-7194 for dates and times.

Index

Pages given in boldface indicate encyclopedia entries.

Carolyn Jones graduated from Simon Fraser University in 1974 with a bachelor's degree in biological sciences. Since then, she has enjoyed her own garden and worked in several areas of the nursery trades—in a wholesale nursery, in garden centers and as a landscape designer. She managed Massot Nurseries Garden Center, Richmond, for two and a half years and was a regular columnist for *Gardens West*. She holds a B.C. Pesticide Dispenser Certificate and is a member of the Vancouver Rose Society, the Alpine Garden Club of B.C. and the Royal Horticultural Society (Great Britain). *Perennials* is Jones's second book; *Bedding Plants*, the first volume in the Pacific Gardening Series, was published in 1989. It has proved popular with home gardeners and professionals and is being used as a textbook by horticulture students at several B.C. institutions.